BLACK BELT BOOKS

Training for Competition

Brazilian Jiu-Jitsu and Submission Grappling

DAVID MEYER

BLACK BELT BOOKS

Training for Competition

BRAZILIAN JIU-JITSU AND SUBMISSION GRAPPLING

DAVID MEYER

Edited by Sarah Dzida, Raymond Horwitz,
Jeannine Santiago and Jon Sattler

Graphic Design by John Bodine

Photography by Rick Hustead

Demonstration Partner: Adam Treanor

©2008 Black Belt Communications LLC
All Rights Reserved
Printed in the United States of America
Library of Congress Control Number: 2008939541
ISBN-10: 0-89750-167-5
ISBN-13: 978-0-89750-167-5

First Printing 2008

WARNING

This book is presented only as a means of preserving a unique aspect of the heritage of the martial arts. Neither Ohara Publications nor the author makes any representation, warranty or guarantee that the techniques described or illustrated in this book will be safe or effective in any self-defense situation or otherwise. You may be injured if you apply or train in the techniques illustrated in this book and neither Ohara Publications nor the author is responsible for any such injury that may result. It is essential that you consult a physician regarding whether or not to attempt any technique described in this book. Specific self-defense responses illustrated in this book may not be justified in any particular situation in view of all of the circumstances or under applicable federal, state or local law. Neither Ohara Publications nor the author makes any representation or warranty regarding the legality or appropriateness of any technique mentioned in this book.

BLACK BELT BOOKS
A Division of **OHARA PUBLICATIONS, INC.**
World Leader in Martial Arts Publications

Acknowledgments

I would like to sincerely acknowledge the following people who have been crucial in my development as a martial artist and as a competitor.

- John Will, who taught the first Brazilian *jiu-jitsu* class I was in and who instantly became my best friend. He continues to teach me to this day, is the gold standard for coaching, and is one of the best and most knowledgeable overall fighters that I know of in the world. Get on a plane and train with him.
- Rigan Machado, a genius in all things grappling, who shared his world with me and changed my life—his legendary grappling talents are only matched by the size of his good heart.
- Jean Jacques Machado, an absolute magician on the mat who continues to blow my mind with what is possible—and he does it all with a smile without even breaking a sweat.
- Carlos Machado, who is a fighter, a scholar, a consummate champion and a gentleman.
- John Machado, a master warrior and friend who is an inspiration to all his students.
- Roger Machado, a great fighter whose balance both on the mat and in life is an inspiration.
- Richard Treanor, my loyal student, life coach and friend.
- My many excellent training partners whom include Bob Bass, Joe Bass, Casey Olsen, Ica Medina, Ricco Rodriguez, Rick Williams, Chris Haueter, Andy Wang, Travis Gambino, Todd Nathanson, Eddie Bravo, Paulo Guillobel, Cesar Gracie, Ryan Gregg, Jake Shields, Gilbert Melendez, Eduardo Rocha, Mike Valentine, Josh Rosenthal and many others. I mention them because each one of these guys is a tough fighter who taught me, even if they sometimes beat the crap out of me in the process. They are my team, and even if I don't know a single person at a tournament, I never feel alone because they are all present with me in spirit.
- Carlos and Helio Gracie, who changed the modern world of martial arts, and also Carlos Gracie Jr. for his friendship and skill in guiding the growth of his family's sport.
- *Sensei* Jack Seki, my first *jujutsu* instructor who inspires me even today, long after his passing.
- Professor Wally Jay for taking me under his wing and teaching me that curiosity and thinking outside the box is a never-ending journey.
- The late sensei Steve Copping, who was my training partner and great friend.
- Daniela Dutra for opening the door to the Brazilian jiu-jitsu world for me and for taking more interest in my well-being than I have often taken myself.
- My parents, Donald and Dena Meyer, and my brother Bill, who may have thought I was crazy but always supported me and are a blessing in my life.

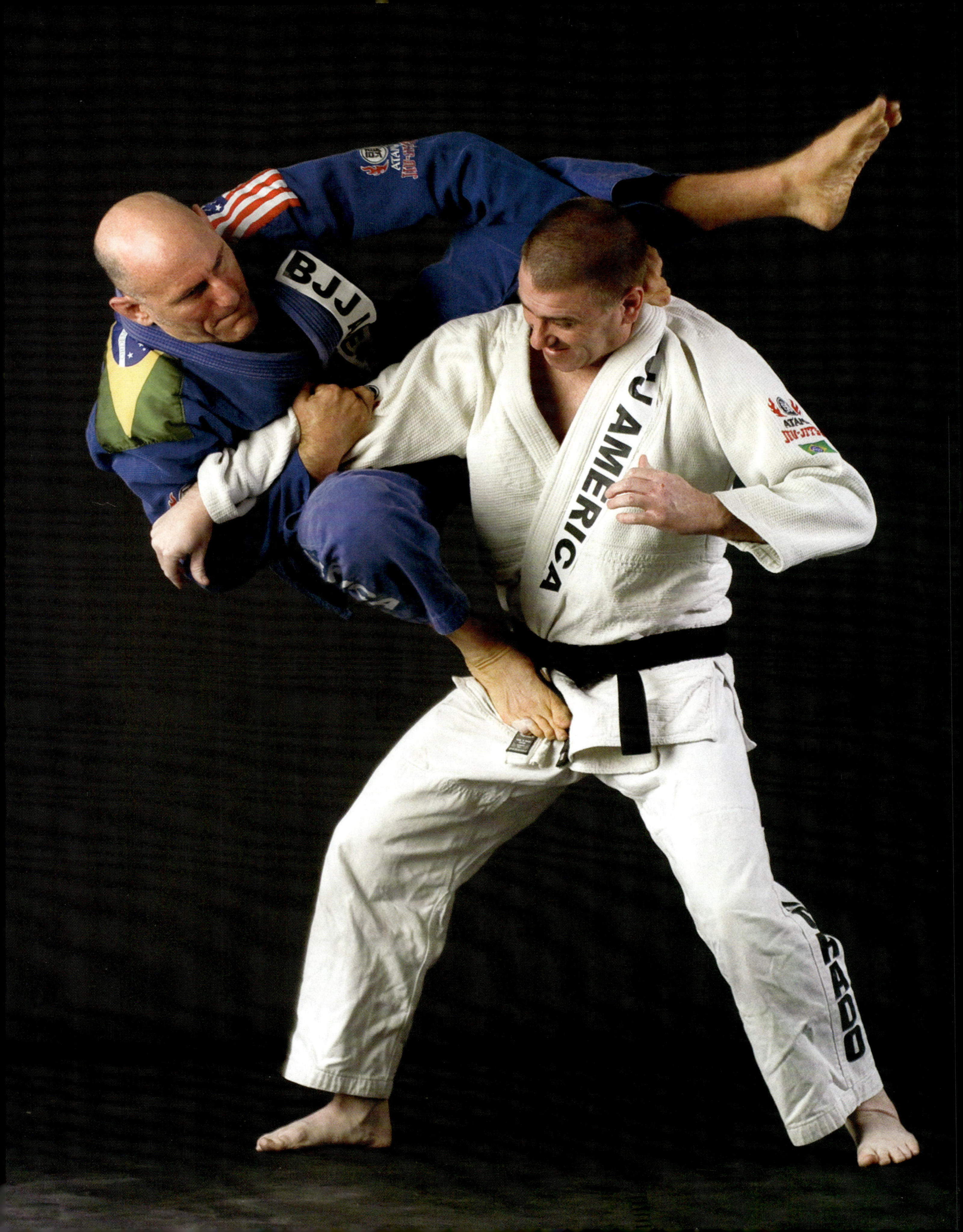
BJJ
J AMÉRICA

Table of Contents

Acknowledgments 5

Introduction 11

Section I: KNOWING YOUR COMPETITION
Brazilian Jiu-Jitsu and Submission-Grappling Formats

Chapter 1: Brazilian Jiu-Jitsu 16
    History Overview 16
    Competition Overview 17
    Winning or Losing Overview 21
    Points Overview 30

Chapter 2: Submission Grappling 41
    History Overview 41
    Competition Overview 41
    Points Overview 43

Chapter 3: Choosing Your Competition 46
    Choosing Your Format 46
    Choosing a Division 48
    Sign Up Now! 49

Section II: BEING THE BEST OVERALL FIGHTER YOU CAN BE
Things You Should Always Do and Know

Chapter 4: Improving Your Overall Performance 54
    Injury Is the Enemy 56
    Come to Class No Matter What 56
    Experiment With New Moves 57
    Don't Stop When You Are Tired 58
    Be a Copycat 59
    Find the Crux 59
    Do Your Homework 62
    Seek Out the Best Coaches 62
    Seek Out the Best Partners 64
    Leave the Comfort Zone Behind 64

Chapter 5: Improving Your Grappling Conditioning 67
    Improving Your Grappling Strength 67
    Explcsive vs. Tenacious Strength 69
    Building Your Upper Body 70
    Strengthening Your Core 73

Table of Contents

    Building Your Lower Body 78
    Improving Your Grappling Flexibility.. 82
    Improving Your Grappling Endurance 96
    Athletic Performance and Your Grappling Diet 98
    Coping With Injury.. 100

Section III: FOCUSING ON THE GOAL
Competition-Specific Training and Strategies

Chapter 6: Game Plans 104
    Blocking Your Opponent's Plan 104
    Your Starting Game Plan 115
    How to Restart the Match After the Clock Stops 123
    Your Overall Game Plan 127

Chapter 7: Learning to Use the Points and Clock 128
    How to Play the Points 128
    Point-Deficit Practice... 135
    Playing the Clock by Stalling 138
    How to Stall While Standing 147
    How to Break a Stall on the Ground... 150
    Baiting Your Opponent to Escape a Stall or Bad Position 154
    How to Use Aggressive Mat Control... 164

Chapter 8: Taking Risks and Going Against the Norm 167
    Developing a Specialty 167
    Surprise Finishes... 168

Chapter 9: Good Match Coaching, "The Eye in the Sky" 180
    What You Need From Your Corner Coach 180
    If You Are a Corner Coach 182
    What Not to Do as a Corner Coach 183

Section IV: THE PAYOFF
Final Preparation and Competition Day

Chapter 10: Tying It All Together 188
    Practice vs. Competition 188
    Practice Competition Matches 188
    Train Your Weak Spots 189

Table of Contents

Chapter 11: The Final Week 195
    Don't Overtrain 195
    Cutting Weight 196
    Stressing Out 196

Chapter 12: Competition Day 200
    Uniform 200
    Eat Breakfast and Lunch 200
    Bring a Friend 201
    Pre-Competition Jitters 201
    How to Warm Up 203
    Own the Mat With Attitude 207
    Psych Your Opponent Out 207
    Start One Point Down 208
    Win Fresh, Lose Spent 208

Chapter 13: Sportsmanship—Win Like a Champion, Lose Like a Warrior 209
    Honor Your Opponent 209
    Excuses Are Pathetic 210
    Dissect Your Win 210
    Dissect Your Loss 211

Conclusion 215

Appendices 217
    Competition Listings 218
    Recommended Off-the-Mat Homework Materials 219

About the Author 220

To reach a goal, you must know exactly what your goal is and why you have it. To win the fight, you must first master the fight within yourself.

—D. M.

Introduction

This book contains instructions, tips and experiences that you can use to transform yourself into a champion. However, there are no shortcuts on the journey to becoming a champion, and the path you are taking will be long and at times difficult.

Before I share with you the most important secrets and techniques in Brazilian *jiu-jitsu* and submission grappling, allow me to introduce myself.

My name is David Meyer, and I have been training in the martial arts since I was a child. I was one of the first Americans to earn a black belt in Brazilian jiu-jitsu and have competed in many world-championship formats, ranging from striking to pure grappling, Brazilian jiu-jitsu to submission grappling, and *gi* to no gi.

By luck I discovered Brazilian jiu-jitsu in Los Angeles in 1991, two years before the first Ultimate Fighting Championship took place. At the time, I was 30 years old and "past my prime" by the average measure, but I was in great physical shape and had already earned several black belts in other styles of *jujutsu*.

A new student arrived at the jujutsu class I taught and introduced me to the sport by challenging me to a grappling match. Even though he was larger and stronger than me, I still thought I could tap him out because I possessed a lifetime of jujutsu experience.

We grappled for a long time. Finally, after a great deal of effort, I submitted him with a choke hold. When I asked him how long he had been training, he admitted that he had started studying jiu-jitsu only a few months earlier. Clearly, he was a good athlete, but I found it hard to believe that someone so talented was just a novice. He explained that he had been training with Rickson Gracie. It was the first time I had ever heard of the Gracie family.

Several months later, one of my former students returned to my class and told me that he had been training with Rigan Machado, who was Rickson's first cousin and the current BJJ world champion. Like before, I had a very hard time beating my former student, so I decided to go down to Rigan and his brothers' school to meet them.

John Will—a purple belt who would later become the first Australian black belt in Brazilian jiu-jitsu—taught my first class at the school. He beat me so easily that I shuddered to think what the black belts were like. The next night, I found out: Rigan submitted me so effortlessly that I thought I was dreaming. I was so impressed that I closed down my own class, told my students to go train with Rigan, and set for myself the goal of becoming the best American in the art. I willingly took off my jujutsu black belt and started training again as a white belt.

At the time, Brazilian jiu-jitsu was new to the United States, so martial artists like myself only had one option: the rock-hard training offered at the BJJ school run by the Gracies or at the BJJ school run by their cousins, the Machados. As I studied with the Machados, I realized that there was a direct relationship between hard work and winning, and jiu-jitsu grapplers like Will and the Machados embodied this training ethic. This helped shape my belief that I had to be the "first on and last off the mat" because I knew I had a lot of catching up to do.

Another important aspect that shaped my growth in the sport is that, during the era, many people believed Americans did not stand a chance against BJJ fighters from Brazil. Even I believed this claim because the only Brazilians I knew were the Machado brothers, who really seemed invincible—they were even legends in Brazil! So when I would tap out a visiting grappler from Brazil, I often assumed that the grappler either wasn't that skilled or trying very hard. Even during my first BJJ competition, which I believe was the first official BJJ event held in the United States, I thought I only won because I didn't have to face any Brazilian opponents.

It wasn't until the first Pan-American Games in 1995 that I realized that the Machados' training system was among the best in the world. A brown belt from our school, Bob Bass, beat a previously undefeated brown belt from Brazil. Because of his victory, I knew that my team was a force to be reckoned with.

Over the years, the skillful coaching and the relentless workouts of the Machado brothers gave me the tools necessary to match and beat BJJ black belts, regardless of experience or nationality. I lost my first match as a black belt by a single sweep in the final seconds and then won my next match, taking the silver medal at the 1998 Pan-American Brazilian Jiu-Jitsu games in Hawaii. Then, I won the Korean Air Black Belt Challenge, which took me to Brazil for the International Brazilian Jiu-Jitsu Federation World Championship in 1998. I won the bronze medal in the black belt open weight class division, making me the first American to win a medal in a BJJ world championship at the black-belt level.

In addition to my success in competition, instructors of other martial arts began to approach me, asking me to teach them the sport and help them bring the curriculum to their own grappling schools. I eventually partnered up with Will in 2002 to create BJJ America in order to pass on the excellent instruction we received from the Machados. The curriculum we wrote is now used in more than 500 schools and benefits both instructors and students. In fact, many of these students have gone on to win competitions around the world, and the competitors I personally train are virtually undefeated.

From these experiences, I have learned what attitudes, mind-sets and disciplines improve and destroy performances under pressure. I also learned what experiences and training methods help and hinder the growth of a grappler's skill level. But perhaps most importantly, I've discovered the true benefits of competition and how to best obtain the desired results.

It is these insights that I will share with you in this book, and there is no doubt in my mind that the book will make you both a better grappler and competitor, regardless of your grappling background. But in order for me to fulfill such a promise, you need to bring two things to your training, as well: honesty and courage.

Honestly look at your real motivations. Ask yourself: Why do I want to excel in competition?

Also, have the courage to put yourself on the line in a public arena and face defeat if it comes. Courage is not a lack of fear but the ability to act in the face of fear. Anyone can train for a competition when they feel great, and anyone can compete when they are likely to win, but a champion trains when he does not feel motivated and still competes against the odds. The preparation and the path are where champions are made. The victory, when it comes, is just the icing on the cake.

In addition, I need you to understand the single most important secret to winning a competition and unleashing your true potential. That secret is:

You can't control who wins.

For the most part, you can control how hard you train, how often you train and whom you train with. You can control your attitude and many other variables. But you can't control who wins.

Why not? While this may sound obvious, the most basic reason is that your opponent has also put in the time and effort to win. Because a grappling match is a story with two authors, you can't control the entire outcome of that story.

If you give your best effort and lose, there's no reason to be upset. When competing against a person who is significantly better than you, barring some fluke, you are going to lose. Likewise, if you are better than your opponent, then you are going to win. No matter how much you train and prepare for a competition, there is always at least one element that you cannot control: your opponent and his skill level. Remembering this will prevent you from beating yourself up if you lose and getting a swelled head if you win.

When I earned my BJJ black belt in 1997, I was one of the first Americans to accomplish this and my BJJ team was filled with up-and-coming fighters. I felt like an awesome responsibility was wrapped around my waist, and for the first time, I found myself unable to train properly. I was stiff, defensive and unwilling to take any risks during training that might give someone the opportunity to "tap out a black belt."

When I told Rigan my problem, he laughed and said, "My friend, I give you permission to be a black belt and tap. Everybody taps." I took Rigan's words to heart, and in that magical moment, my ego was pushed aside, my game opened up and my training returned to normal.

I stress this issue of control to my students because it helps them let go of the stress of losing and permits them to have fun, which helps them win. It's a paradox, but trust me: Letting go of an irrational attachment to winning allows you to take the rational steps to win. Of course, a competitor's goal is to win, but part of becoming a champion is learning the lessons that can only be taught from losing.

So what should you do if you find yourself on the mat with a better opponent? Competition against good opponents exposes your weaknesses, and improving your flaws is an integral part of winning. Consider the phrase "losing is learning." Of course you can learn from a win, but you rarely learn as much. The average grappler rarely analyzes and learns from his performance after a victory. They will certainly relive the experience, but it will be a celebration of victory rather than a serious dissection of the match.

Losing, on the other hand, forces the intelligent grappler to seriously reflect on what went wrong. The worse the loss, the more the grappler learns. In fact, I've learned some of my favorite techniques from competitors who I lost to. There's nothing like being caught by a technique in front of a big crowd of spectators to ingrain the experience into your mind. It causes you to master the move so you can defend against it, and the lesson is doubly beneficial because you can use that technique against others in future matches.

So if losing is not the enemy, what is? Cheating yourself of the opportunity to learn, grow and challenge your game because you are too scared, proud or egotistical to put yourself on the line and compete. The fear of failure is the main barrier that keeps people from entering a competition. You must remove these hurdles to achieve your best results and true potential, no matter what path it takes to get there. You can't control who wins, and accepting that is a huge first step.

There is a medal out there waiting for you, but earning it is going to take a lot of work. Are you up for the challenge? Stepping into an arena full of people for a hand-to-hand fight against someone who you have never met is a true challenge, but I'm here to help. So let's get busy.

Interviews and Extras

To help you determine your grappling goals, I've included several interviews and informational sidebars in this book. For the interviews, I talked with several grappling experts to see what their thoughts are on competition, training, grappling formats, etc. You'll find answers from the following professionals throughout the book:

- Professor Wally Jay *(See Page 51.)*
- Nick Diaz *(See Page 66.)*
- Bas Rutten *(See Page 166.)*
- Cesar Gracie *(See Page 185.)*
- Frank Shamrock *(See Page 199.)*
- Gene LeBell *(See Page 214.)*

I hope you'll take a moment to consider what these experts have to say. You may discover something about yourself and the two formats that you never knew before.

Section I

KNOWING YOUR COMPETITION
Brazilian Jiu-Jitsu and Submission-Grappling Formats

Chapter 1
Brazilian Jiu-Jitsu

Before we talk about all the ways you can train to become a champion, let's take a look at the sport of Brazilian *jiu-jitsu* and how it developed over the years. We'll also closely examine the standard rules of this format because they can strip a competitor of a victory just as easily as an opponent. Think of the rules as the third fighter on the mat who, if you don't know him, becomes another wild card that you can't control. This is why you must know the rules.

History Overview

In Japanese, *jujutsu* means the "gentle art" because it fundamentally does not rely on striking an opponent like in karate. Instead, a jujutsu practitioner uses leverage to obtain a joint lock or choke hold in order to overcome an opponent and force him into submission. Because of this, the martial art encompasses a wide variety of throwing techniques known as *tachi waza*, which are designed to put an opponent to the floor, and ground techniques known as *ne waza*, which are designed to hold down and further incapacitate an opponent once he is on the ground.

Around 1900, Jiguro Kano codified a new style of jujutsu, which he called "judo" (the gentle way). However, it was a top-level disciple who would eventually bring this grappling art to Brazil in 1914.

In 1917, Kano's disciple Esai Maeda began teaching judo to a 14-year-old Brazilian boy named Carlos Gracie, who in turn taught the art to his brothers—Osvaldo, Gastão, Jorge and Helio. Even though Carlos Gracie learned tachi waza and ne waza techniques from Maeda, the Gracie brothers concentrated their training efforts on ground moves rather than takedown techniques. They found that most confrontations tended to devolve into a clinch, which meant that they could easily trip or throw down their opponent, bringing the fight to the ground.

By concentrating on these ground techniques and practicing against each other and other fighters of different styles, the Gracie brothers developed their own form of jujutsu, which focused on grappling and fighting on the ground. They proved their new system through *vale tudo* (no-rules) fights in Brazil in which the winner was declared by forcing his opponent to submit or by knocking his opponent out. These fights often occurred as public contests, which the Gracies advertised in local newspapers, or in spontaneous street challenges. The Gracies even fought in other martial arts schools before the disbelieving eyes of classical-style instructors.

As time passed, the Gracie brothers' family of fighters grew as they taught their art—then called "Gracie jiu-jitsu"—to their large, extended family. Others outside the family began to study the art, as well. Rules were eventually developed for a standard competition format with no striking, and sport competitions began to take place in Brazil. Fighters generally wore a traditional Japanese martial arts uniform known as a *gi* or kimono during daily practice and nothing but swimming trunks during vale tudo fights.

In the 1970s, the art continued to evolve in Brazil as a sport, and it became evident that two good fighters could compete for many minutes before either tapped out. Therefore, the Gracies introduced a time limit and point system to decide the victor, even if the match ended without either fighter forcing the other to submit. The points were designed to reward advances in a position that would most likely achieve victory in a real street fight. However, the incorporation of this point system fundamentally changed the practice of Gracie jiu-jitsu from a competitor's standpoint because it now became possible to win simply by fighting in a way that amassed points.

The sport became known by it's more generic name of Brazilian jiu-jitsu in the 1980s, when the Gracie family and their Machado cousins brought the fighting format to the United States and taught it to the public. When Royce Gracie won the first Ultimate Fighting Championship in a televised airing in 1993, Brazilian jiu-jitsu grabbed the spotlight. The UFC at that time used the vale tudo format and had no weight categories or time limits, making Royce Gracie's victories all the more impressive. Since that event, the vale tudo format has been reorganized with rules for safety and weight categories and is now called a mixed martial art. Because of Royce Gracie's victory at the UFC, virtually all great MMA champions today strive to have a strong background in grappling skills, and it is on these skills that they have built their MMA career.

Competition Overview

As mentioned earlier, Brazilian jiu-jitsu is closely related to the classical martial art of judo because of Maeda's ties to Kano. Like judo, Brazilian jiu-jitsu is practiced in a gi and is a one-on-one grappling system that does not allow striking. Competitors are matched against each other by belt rank, weight, gender and age, and both sports' matches end if an opponent submits to or taps out from a joint lock or choke hold.

In contrast, judo allows a fighter an immediate victory if he throws the opponent cleanly and decisively to the ground, or if the fighter pins his opponent's back to the ground for 25 seconds. This relates back to ancient times when armor-clad, sword-wielding soldiers in Japan fought in battles. If a soldier was knocked off his feet or held to the ground, he was left vulnerable in a position in which his adversary could pierce him with a blade. This made the fallen soldier the decisive loser in the battle. In Brazilian jiu-jitsu, however, the match does not automatically end with a clean throw or a clean pin. Instead, the goal in Brazilian jiu-jitsu is to make the defender tap out because it more closely mimics the realities of a modern street fight in which the battle does not end until an opponent is beaten unconscious.

For the most part, all BJJ competitions follow a standard format and set of rules, even though rules can vary from tournament to tournament and their enforcement can vary from referee to referee. The best way to be prepared is to get a copy of the rules and read them closely before any event you compete in. Rules are usually posted on the same Web site where you register for the tournament. If they are not, you should contact the tournament organizer (also on the Web site) and request them. Rule clinics often take place in the morning on the day of the tournament, but ideally you would have gone over them long before the event.

In regards to a tournament's standardized aspects, competitions generally group fighters into certain divisions based on belt level, weight, age and gender. There are five belt levels in Brazilian jiu-jitsu (white, blue, purple, brown and black), and most competitions have a division for each. Men and women almost never compete against each other and have separate matches, and belt color and weight divisions usually encompass weight ranges of 14 pounds (167-181 pounds, 181-195 pounds, etc.). There is generally an "open" or "absolute" division for each belt in which fighters of all weights can enter. Winning in this division is the most prestigious because it indicates that the victor can

WEIGHT	JUVENILE	ADULT, MASTER AND SENIOR	FEMALE
ROOSTER	118 lbs.	126.5 lbs.	
SUPER FEATHER	129 lbs.	141 lbs.	118 lbs.
FEATHER	141 lbs.	154 lbs.	129 lbs.
LIGHT	152 lbs.	167.5 lbs.	141 lbs.
MIDDLE	163 lbs.	181 lbs.	152 lbs.
MEDIUM HEAVY	174.5 lbs.	194.5 lbs.	Over 152 lbs.
HEAVY	185.5 lbs.	207.5 lbs.	
SUPER HEAVY	196.5 lbs.	221 lbs.	
SUPER SUPER HEAVY	Over 196.5 lbs.	Over 221 lbs.	
OPEN CLASS	Over Middle Weight	FREE	FREE

Figure 1—International Brazilian Jiu-Jitsu Federation Weight Divisions

beat all competitors in their belt rank regardless of weight. (The official International Brazilian Jiu-Jitsu Federation weight divisions appear in Figure 1.)

Some tournaments offer separate divisions for older fighters to be grouped into. The same belt and weight divisions usually apply, but these divisions are usually limited to fighters older than 30 and are referred to as Masters Divisions. Official IBJJF tournaments usually include the following divisions for men only: Masters (ages 30 to 35), Seniors 1 (ages 36 to 40), Seniors 2 (ages 41 to 45) and Seniors 3 (over 46). Generally, there are not enough older female fighters to constitute a separate division.

No matter the division, a match lasts up to five, six, seven, eight or 10 minutes, respectively, but many tournaments are shortening the match times to keep up with the growing number of competitors. It prevents the tournaments from running late into the night. Despite the change, most tournaments will always guarantee at least a five-minute rest period to all fighters between matches, which in actual practice, is usually more than five minutes between fights.

Tournament organizers usually arrange who will fight whom in what division before the day of the competition. By preparing brackets, or listings, they match up fighters within each division, trying to prevent people from the same school from competing against each other. However, if people from the same school win in the same division, then a meeting between teammates is inevitable. Also note that because all competitors will most likely have registered in advance, which is normal, the organizers will have all the information they need to group fighters accurately.

Brackets are usually single-elimination brackets, as shown in Figure 2, which means that the fighter who wins each match moves on to the next fight and the defeated fighter is out. However, if you signed up for your weight division and the open weight division, you would be listed on two separate brackets. This guarantees you at least two fights for the tournament.

If there are an odd number of fighters, one fighter will not compete in the first round and will advance to the next, like Eriksson in Figure 2. This is called a "bye" and means that a grappler who is fresh will have his first fight against someone who has already fought (and won) his first match. Tournament organizers are supposed to choose that competitor randomly, but no matter the choice, it still gives a distinct advantage to the person who is given the "bye." From my point of view as a coach, you don't want your competitor to have the "bye" because it means he is deprived of a match that could be a good learning experience.

While most tournaments take place at a high-school or university gymnasium, all fights occur on a mat. The size of the mat area varies from tournament to tournament, but most mats are generally 20-by-20 feet, and boundaries are often indicated by a row of different-colored mats surrounding

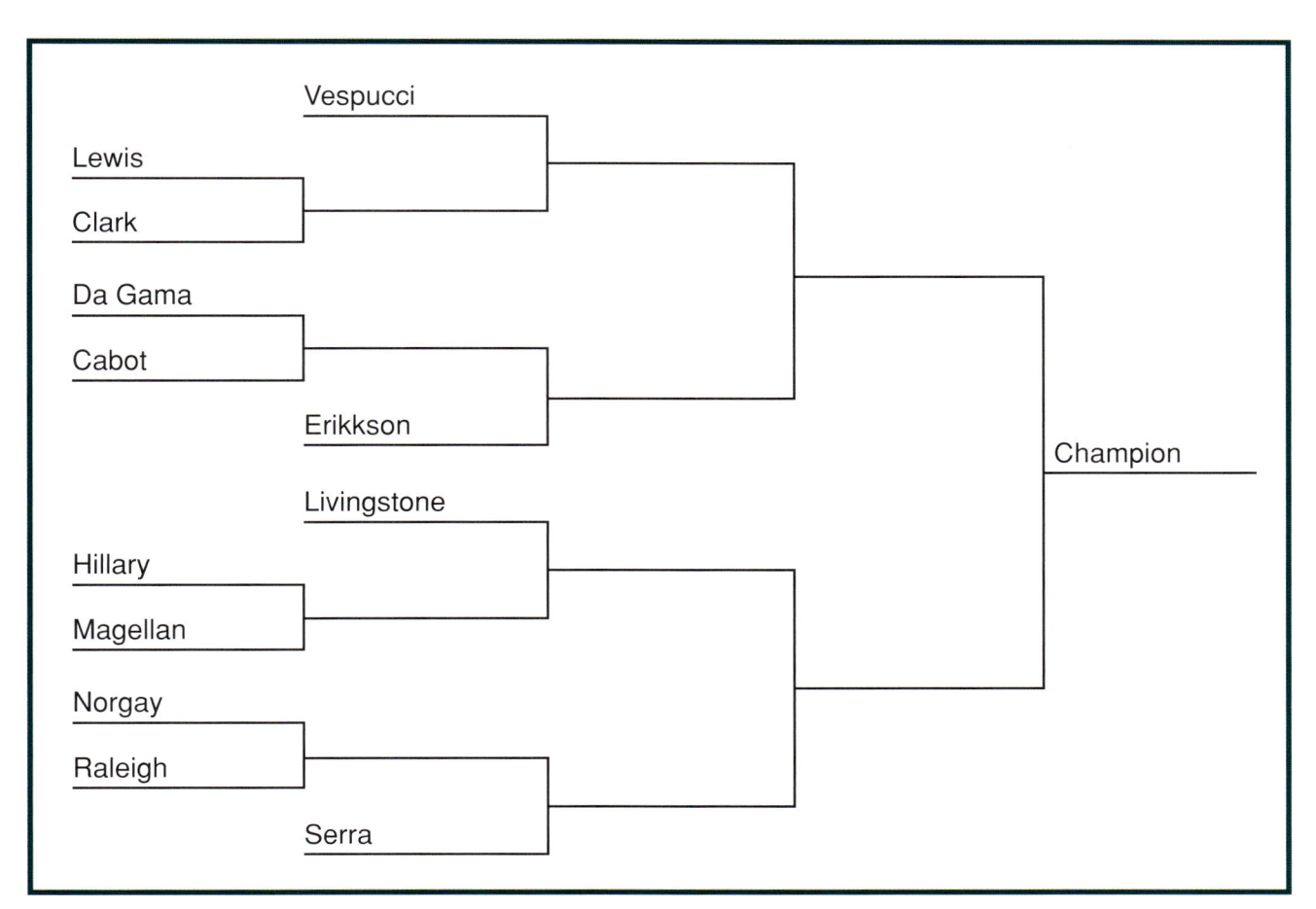

Figure 2—Single-Elimination Bracket

the competition space. Most tournaments have four to eight competition areas that function simultaneously.

Each competition mat has a single referee whose role is to officially start and stop the match, ensure the safety of the fighters, enforce the rules, award points as they are achieved, and decide the winner if no submission occurs or if the points are tied. Coaches are not allowed on the tournament mat and are increasingly not allowed to even sit on the corner just off the mat. Generally, coaches must sit or stand in the walking space that surrounds the competition mats and coach from there.

Each fighting area usually has a scorekeeping table. At the table sits the person in charge of watching the referee and keeping score. He often uses flip cards to show the current score to the audience and the fighters. A timekeeper also sits at the table. He starts the match, stops the clock for timeouts per the referee's instructions, and ends the match when time runs out. The timekeeper usually indicates the end of the match by tossing a brightly colored beanbag, or other object, into the center of the mat to catch the referee's attention.

Fighters are required to wear a traditional judo uniform top, pants and belt. (See Figure 3.) Most tournaments only allow competitors to wear a gi that is solid white or blue in order to avoid a breakdown of decorum if people decided to wear oddly colored uniforms. However, all tournaments generally allow fighters to display school and sponsor patches on their uniforms.

Figure 3—David Meyer wears a standard Brazilian jiu-jitsu uniform.

The cut of the uniform has limitations to ensure that it is not unfairly tapered, prohibiting the opponent from getting a good grip. In general, there must be a four-finger width space from the wrist to the edge of the cuff, both in terms of the sleeve's length and the space inside the sleeve. (See Figure 4.) There are no particular rules enforced on the length or tapered aspects of the pants—as long as they do not appear to be out of the ordinary.

The uniform can be a factor in a match by giving you a slight edge or even a disadvantage. For example, if your gi top fits too snugly, especially in the shoulders and back, it can restrict the movement of your arms. This is a huge disadvantage, especially if you are defending yourself on your back, because your uniform will bunch uncomfortably under you. In contrast, a slightly thicker or stiffer collar makes it more difficult for your opponent to choke you, which is good because it makes it harder for him to make you tap out in a match. In addition, shorter pants that are slightly stiff are preferable to those that aren't because they are harder for your opponent to hold and control when passing your guard.

This doesn't mean that there is a "black" and "white" when it comes to uniforms. For example, it can be detrimental to your game if the ends of your sleeves are too long and wide because it's easier for your opponent to hold and control your hands. Conversely, a grappler who is a fan of "sleeve tip" chokes may prefer looser sleeves. A sleeve-tip choke requires that a grappler encircles his opponent's neck and applies pressure by grabbing onto his own sleeves. This is why, for this particular fighter, longer and looser sleeves on the uniform can be a benefit.

For almost every tournament, you should register in advance because it helps organizers prepare the brackets. At that time, you also need to decide the weight division you want to compete in. Remember, the number you include on your form will be verified at an official weigh-in at the tournament. While some weigh-ins occur a day or two before the match, usually at a local martial arts school, most weigh-ins take place the day of the tournament at the venue. The reason officials do this is to ensure that you are not heavier than the heaviest weight allowed in your division. If you do weigh more, then you will most likely be disqualified and unable to simply move up to the appropriate weight division. Also, you will probably be wearing your uniform during the weigh-in, so take this into consideration when selecting your weight category on the registration form.

Figure 4—Meyer measures the sleeve's width with four fingers.

Winning or Losing Overview

A submission always ends the match, unless time runs out first, and is usually indicated by the opponent himself through a verbal cue or a visible tapout. Usually, the opponent verbally gives up or clearly taps the opponent with his hand or foot as a sign of submission. When a submission is admitted, the referee steps in and ends the match. Occasionally, the referee can signal the submission if he believes that injury is imminent, regardless of whether the defeated fighter has given up. In some tournaments, a coach is also allowed to submit on behalf of his fighter if the coach thinks the fighter is in danger but has not given up. Another de facto submission is unconsciousness, which if it occurs, is usually the result of a choke in which the defeated fighter did not submit before passing out.

We'll now discuss common submissions. (See Pages 22 to 28.)

Armbar Submission

An armbar traps your opponent's extended arm between your legs. When you lift your hips, it hyperextends your opponent's elbow so he must tap out.

Armbar From the Guard Submission

An armbar from the guard hyperextends your opponent's elbow while you are underneath him.

Arm Lock (Americana) Submission

An arm lock bends and twists your opponent's arm so that the ligaments in the elbow are stressed, causing the opponent to submit.

Shoulder Lock (Kimura) Submission

A shoulder lock twists your opponent's wrist behind his back, which stresses the ligaments of his shoulder and causes him to submit. When done by the hands, the shoulder lock is known as the kimura submission, but if it is done with the legs, it is known as an omo plata.

Shoulder Lock From the Guard Submission

A shoulder lock from the guard puts stress on your opponent's shoulder, even though you are underneath him.

Leg-Driven Shoulder Lock (Omo Plata) Submission

An "omo plata" uses the power of your legs to stress your opponent's shoulder, forcing him to tap out.

Cross Choke From the Mount Submission

When in the mount, you are in a good position to grab your opponent's collar to anchor your forearms and choke him for the tapout.

Cross Choke From the Guard Submission

You can grab your opponent's collar from the guard and choke him out from there, as well.

Front Choke (Guillotine) From the Guard Submission

This front choke does not rely on the material of the gi, but instead, it traps your opponent's head while cutting off his ability to breathe.

Front Choke (Guillotine) From a Standing Submission

The guillotine, which is a front choke, can also be applied from a standing position.

Half-Nelson Choke From the Mount Submission

When your opponent tries to escape from the mount, he moves into a vulnerable position in which you can wrap the material of his own gi around his neck for a half-nelson choke.

Back Choke (Figure-4 or Rear-Naked) Submission

This is a very common choke that can be done from behind the opponent without the use of a gi. It cuts off the blood supply to your opponent's head, causing him to either tap or pass out.

Foot Lock Submission

By isolating the movement of your opponent's leg, you can force his foot to flex and stress the top ligaments of the ankle for a tapout.

Legbar Submission

Isolating your opponent's leg allows you to pull back on his foot while you press forward with your hips, causing his knee to hyperextend and force the submission.

A match also ends as a result of a disqualification, which happens when a fighter fails to follow the instructions of the referee or if the referee determines any egregious behavior that warrants it. Such behavior might pertain to unsportsmanlike words or conduct directed at the opponent or the referee. A disqualification can also occur because of an injury or excessive bleeding from a cut, or because a competitor doesn't appear on the mat on time, doesn't make the proper weight or doesn't conform to the uniform rules.

Certain holds may be barred in a match depending on the belt ranking of the grapplers. White belts, for example, are usually barred from doing all foot or leg attacks as well as neck cranks or twists. This is because there is a chance of causing injury with these techniques, and the injury caused, whether to the knee or neck, can be severe and long-lasting. Experienced fighters of the higher belt ranks are assumed to have more control in their application of these techniques. They also generally have a greater skill in escaping from them or in knowing when to wisely tap out in time before they are injured.

Neck Crank

David Meyer (top) performs a neck crank called a "can opener" on Adam Treanor. The crank can strain the ligaments and vertebrae in the neck.

Blue belts are usually only allowed to do straight foot locks that do not twist the heel and straight legbars that do not twist the knee. No other foot or knee attacks are allowed because a straight foot lock is less dangerous than a heel hook, especially if an injury does occur. Foot locks tend to hyperextend the ligaments at the top of the foot, which can sprain the ankle. Even more damage can occur if the defender of the straight foot lock escapes by rolling sideways. This is because the competitor holds the opponent's foot in a fixed position, and the rolling action can cause damage to the

Heel Hook

A heel hook twists the opponent's foot in a way that can cause injury to the ligaments of the knee.

defender's knee ligaments. Generally, people assume that blue belts know this danger and will not roll out of a straight foot lock.

Heel hooks are usually not allowed even at the blue-belt level because they immediately create a twist on the knee that can cause ligament damage. Heel hooks are also dangerous because no warning pain is felt in the knee until the injury occurs. This is not the case with straight foot locks, which cause pain during the stretch before an injury occurs and alert the less-experienced fighter that it is time to submit.

For all belt levels, picking up an opponent when he is trying to execute a triangle or other attack from the guard and then slamming the person down on the head is strictly prohibited because of the high risk of neck and head injuries. And of course, no strikes are permitted at any belt level. Incidental contact may occur in the normal course of grappling and is allowed, but any intentional attempt to hit or strike an opponent will be met with an immediate disqualification.

Points Overview

Assuming there is no disqualification and if no submission occurs during the match's allotted time, the fighter with the most points wins. If the competitors are tied, the fighter with the most "advantage" points wins. A single advantage point is awarded to a competitor for nearly completing a point-scoring move or finishing hold. If there is a tie on the advantage points, then the referee will make a judgment on who was more aggressive, and that person will be ruled the victor.

We'll now take a moment to discuss techniques for which points are regularly awarded. (See Pages 31 to 36.)

Takedown That Causes the Opponent to Fall to the Ground (Two Points)

A takedown is any move that begins with both fighters standing, and one fighter initiates a move that causes the other fighter to end up on the ground. David Meyer (right) executes a basic takedown by tripping his opponent backward and down to the ground (1-3).

Passing the Guard and Establishing Control (Three Points)

A guard pass is any move in which the opponent is already on his back while the competitor is facing his legs (1). The competitor then succeeds in getting past the opponent's legs (the guard) to establish a control position (2-3).

Sweep From the Guard, No. 1 (Two Points)

A sweep is any move in which the competitor begins on his back with his legs facing his opponent. The competitor will use the sweep to reverse his position on the bottom with that of his opponent on top. In this scenario, David Meyer is on the bottom (1). He uses a sweep to reverse positions so that his opponent, Adam Treanor, is on his back and Meyer is either above him in the guard or in a control position (2-4).

Training for Competition: Brazilian Jiu-Jitsu and Submission Grappling

Sweep From the Guard, No. 2 (Two Points)

Sweeps occur in all kinds of positions, and they take fighters in all kinds of directions (1-4). Note: Points are not awarded for what is sometimes called a "reversal," which is when a competitor escapes from a pinned position and rolls the top fighter over to reverse the position. It's a great escape, but it will not earn you points. BJJ moves are not designed to reward a grappler for escaping a bad situation that he never should have been in.

34

Knee on the Stomach (Two Points)

Knee-on-stomach points are only awarded to competitors that have one knee on the opponent's stomach and the other knee off the ground. The position is so exact because, in a real street fight, the competitor (fighter on top) would be able to strike at his opponent and still easily disengage into a standing position to deal with other threats. That's why this particular position is rewarded in a BJJ competition.

Mount Position (Four Points)

A competitor achieves the mount by straddling his opponent, who is on his back. The technique is similar to mounting a horse. The top competitor must have both feet free on the outside of the opponent's legs or around the opponent's thighs.

Controlling the Back With Both Heels Around the Opponent's Hips, No. 1 (Four Points)

Control of the back is achieved when the competitor faces the opponent's back and has both feet wrapped in front of the opponent's hips.

Controlling the Back With Both Heels Around the Opponent's Hips, No. 2 (Four Points)

Back-control points are awarded regardless of whether David Meyer is on top while both competitors face the mat or whether he is on bottom while both competitors face the ceiling.

Competitors receive points when they demonstrate control by maintaining a position for three seconds. For example, two points are awarded for a takedown if one competitor shoots in for a double-leg takedown, catches his opponent's legs, and drops the opponent to the ground in such a way that the opponent is held on the ground for several seconds and is unable to instantly recover to a standing position. Another example would be when a competitor is awarded three points for a guard pass and holds his opponent for several seconds, even if the opponent struggles to recover the guard or escape onto his hands and knees. The referee awards points if he sees that the opponent has been held down for at least three seconds before a change in position.

Referees award advantage points if a competitor initiates a move that causes a near submission or near-point situation, such as almost passing the guard or sweeping someone. An advantage point is also awarded to a competitor who, while passing the guard, goes from a full-guard to a half-guard position, or a competitor who forces the defender to escape onto his knees rather than be pinned.

Advantage Point: Advancing to the Half-Guard Position

Advancing to half-guard means partially passing your opponent's guard but still ending up with one of your legs trapped in between his legs (1-4). You are awarded an advantage point for this partial passing of the guard.

Advantage Point: Escaping to the Knees

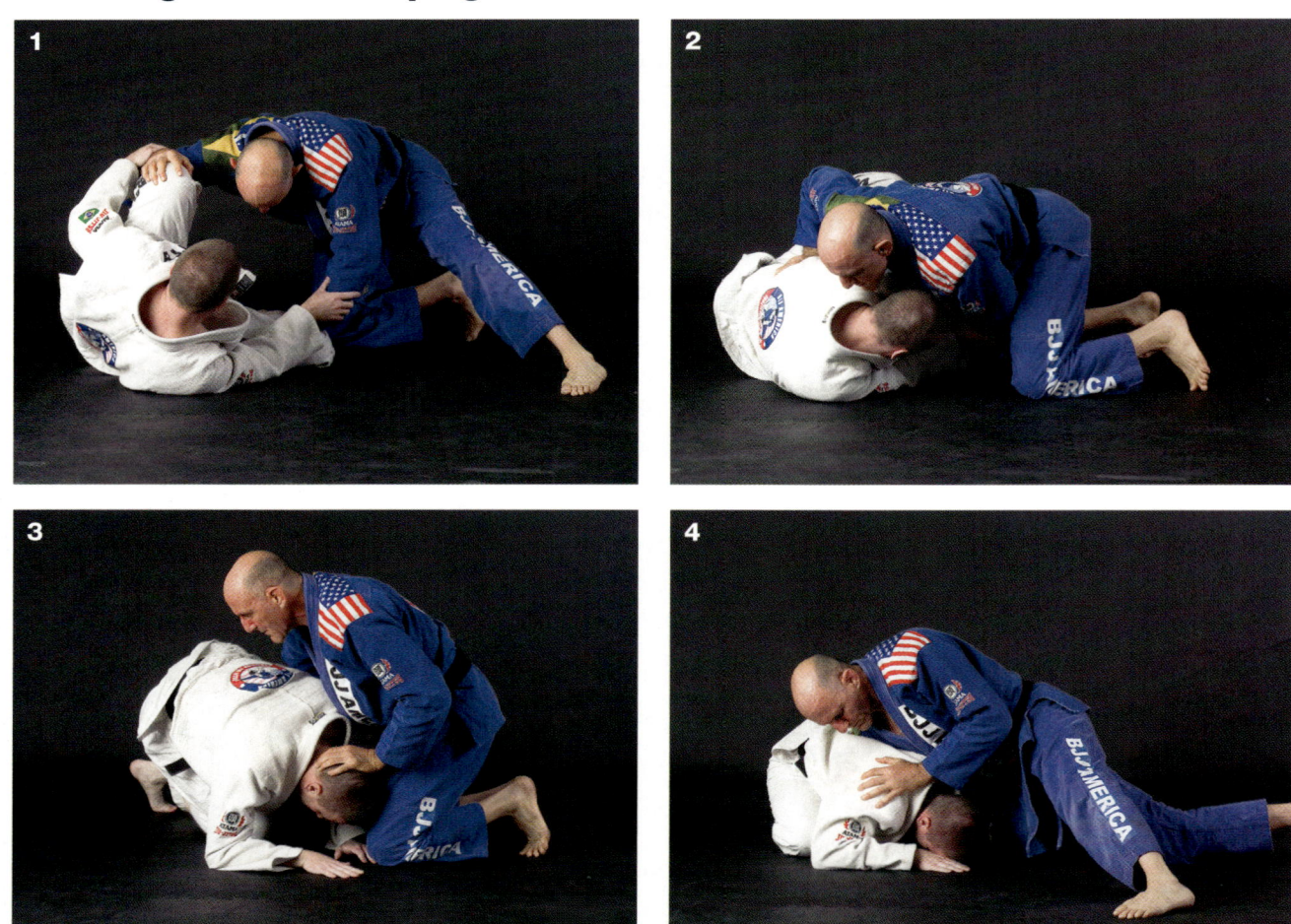

If the defender avoids having his guard passed by having to escape onto his knees, the attacker is awarded an advantage point (1-4).

Referees are required to keep the action going in order to provide a more exciting sport for spectators to watch. Also, one fighter stalling can prohibit the other fighter from executing techniques, so referees generally want to keep the fight moving. If they think the fight is stalling, they may break the fighters apart and stand them up, or even remove points from competitors who are consistently not being active.

As a competitor, you must decide whether you want to remain more true to the fighting roots of the art, i.e., attempt finishing holds, even though it may result in a loss or reversal of position. Or you must decide whether you want to "play it safe" and focus your efforts on winning with points.

For example, I remember two high-profile matches I had against the great Rickson Gracie Team fighter Fabio Santos, who is a real warrior. The first match was at the 1998 Korean Air Black Belt Challenge. It was a night of "superfights" in which selected, well-known black belts were pitted against each other for individual matches on a raised boxing ring in the large stadium at the University of California, Irvine. The winner of each match would receive a free airline ticket to the Brazilian Jiu-Jitsu World Championships in Rio de Janeiro, Brazil, that year, and this acted as an incentive for black belts to participate.

I remember feeling pressure because I was one of the only American black belts in the sport. I also wanted to make my coaches, Carlos and Jean Jacques Machado, and my teammate, Renato Magno, proud because they were present and also fighting that night. In the end, Carlos Machado and Magno lost their fights in extremely close and well-fought matches. Because of their losses, I really wanted to make Santos tap out when I entered the ring. I wanted to demonstrate the power of our Machado team.

Santos and I fought 10 minutes with nonstop action. We both tried to finish each other with attacks and force the other into submission at every chance we got. We scored many points during the match and the action never stopped. My memory of the match's end is simply of the referee separating Santos and myself. Barely able to breathe, I looked at the crowd and asked my teammate Fernando Vasconcelos, "How much time is left?" He responded, "No time. It's over." I asked, "Who won?" He replied, "You did!" I had won with points even though neither Santos nor myself had counted points; we only wanted the tapout.

A year or two later, I fought Santos again in a rematch, but I fought it very carefully, trying to pay close attention to the points. Santos almost took me down with a foot sweep, but I recovered with a transition into a double-leg takedown and landed on top of him in side control. I then held Santos as long as I could, even when he recovered the guard, and held him for the rest of the fight while he struggled to sweep me off-balance and choke me.

I won the second match, 2-0, but I fought very cautiously because I wanted to win without making mistakes. However, the first match in Irvine, California, in which I took chances and was fighting for the tapout, is the proudest fight of my career. People who were present often tell me that that fight with Santos was the most exciting match they have ever seen. Even though I took chances and Santos scored many points, I showed my heart. That gave me a sense of accomplishment that I would never feel in a cautious fight.

If you haven't guessed, I prefer to win by submission, even if such an attempt might cost me the match. This is because my personal competition goal is not simply to win but to perfect my fighting skills as they would apply in the real world. But as a coach, I take the approach that winning either by points or a submission is equally good. The fact of the matter is that good fighters can only be made to tap

Using the Rules to Your Advantage *(Example)*

David Meyer (right) faces Adam Treanor in a match (1). Because he is capable of executing takedowns, Meyer does a standard double-leg takedown. He penetrates forward with a deep step, catching his opponent off-balance before Treanor sprawls (2-4). Then Meyer lifts and twists him down to the ground, earning two points (5). Because he executed the move with ease, Meyer realizes that he might be able to take advantage of the rules.

continued on next page >>

Training for Competition: Brazilian Jiu-Jitsu and Submission Grappling

Using the Rules to Your Advantage (Continued)

To do that, Meyer allows Treanor to regain his feet (6-8). If he weren't skilled at takedowns, Meyer would want to maintain the advantage of his first takedown. However, because he is skilled in this technique, Meyer knows that he'll not only be able to take down Treanor again but also amass more points with it. Meyer shoots in immediately for a second takedown, earning two more points in conjunction with the initial two (9-10).

out infrequently, especially in the limited time allowed during a match. So almost always, the true strategy and test of skill in a competition will determine how grapplers score points.

Now you know the standard rules in Brazilian jiu-jitsu, and it is crucial to know them because they will allow you to develop strategies on how to string moves together, when to stall for time and when to explode. The possibilities are endless, and by being familiar with them, you ensure that you are seizing every opportunity available to you.

Chapter 2
Submission Grappling

Submission grappling is similar to Brazilian jiu-jitsu but without the gi and with some modifications to the rules regarding points and permissible techniques. It draws its roots and techniques from Brazilian jiu-jitsu, Western wrestling, Russian *sambo* and other grappling systems. With that in mind, let's take a look at the history of submission grappling and then learn the rules.

History Overview

In 1993, national TV audiences saw the first Ultimate Fighting Championship and watched Royce Gracie take on and defeat all competitors, no matter their fighting style or size. Brazilian jiu-jitsu had been growing in popularity, but that TV airing showed martial artists everywhere the power of grappling.

Another important consequence was that Gracie chose to wear a gi in his early UFC fights against opponents who did not necessarily wear one in turn. Because competitors can use their opponent's gi as a weapon in Brazilian jiu-jitsu, mixed-martial art competitors began to realize that if they instead wore tighter clothing, then they could avoid this danger. Eventually, all MMA tournaments standardized the uniform and protective-gear requirements so that most matches are now conducted by fighters who do not wear a traditional gi but instead wear shorts and no top at all.

At the time of the UFC's debut in the 1990s, the more widely practiced martial arts, like karate and *taekwondo*, did not emphasize grappling, but the showcase on television naturally led people who had no experience with grappling and/or who had no experience wearing a gi to learn it. As a result, BJJ tournament organizers began to offer "no gi" competitions based on the standard BJJ rules. By allowing a "new" grappling format that did not involve a uniform, tournament organizers opened the matches to people skilled in other styles of wrestling (freestyle, Russian sambo, western wrestling, Greco-Roman, etc.). This gave tournament organizers a chance to alter the rules of standard BJJ competitions and allow certain grappling holds that are typical in mixed martial arts today but that are not allowed in Brazilian jiu-jitsu. These previously barred techniques include ankle and knee attacks as well as leg locks, foot locks and heel hooks.

Today, submission-grappling competitions are growing in size and frequency because interest in the sport has increased. Submission grappling also continues to serve as a steppingstone for many competitors who wish to participate in MMA competitions but don't have a background in grappling.

Competition Overview

Submission-grappling tournaments are similar to BJJ tournaments in many ways. They do not allow striking, a submission always wins the match, and a point system is used to resolve matches when no submission has occurred. They have the same general physical setup as BJJ competitions in regards to mat size, scorekeeper tables and the role of the referee. Tournaments usually use single-elimination brackets along with the same disqualification criteria as in Brazilian jiu-jitsu for unsportsmanlike conduct, etc.

However, submission-grappling rules, unlike BJJ rules, vary from tournament to tournament, mostly in details on how points are awarded, what moves are allowed and the match's length. Again, you should request a copy of the rules of your tournament when you register. That should give you at least several weeks to adjust your game as needed, and then you can train for various point situations outlined in this book and edit them to reflect the point system you will be competing in.

Submission grappling also allows more holds at all levels that would disqualify a BJJ fighter in a tournament. These holds include heel hooks, knee attacks, neck cranks, and in some cases, body slams (such as picking up an opponent from his guard and smashing him down again), all of which can cause more serious injuries. The reason these techniques are allowed is because of the MMA nature of submission grappling. There is simply a greater diversity in the background of competitors than in Brazilian jiu-jitsu.

In regards to divisions based on experience, there are no belt-rank divisions in submission grappling. In almost all cases, competitors can enter a tournament in a beginner, intermediate or advanced division. A beginner division generally covers grapplers with less than one year of training in any grappling format. The intermediate division usually pertains to competitors with one to four years of training in any grappling format. The advanced division usually groups together fighters with more than four years of experience.

Figure 5—Standard Submission-Grappling Attire.

Weight categories also vary from tournament to tournament, and like in Brazilian jiu-jitsu, you need to report your weight at the time of registration, which is almost always done in advance. This weight will be verified at an official weigh-in. Sometimes the weigh-in occurs a day or two before the tournament, but most weigh-ins take place the day of the tournament at the venue.

Most submission-grapping tournaments require competitors to wear either a T-shirt, a skintight rash guard or no shirt. As for pants, most fighters wear shorts, but some wear skintight full-length bicycle pants. Specific limitations on clothing can vary from tournament to tournament, but if you wear tight-fitting shorts or a long-sleeve shirt with shorts, you should be fine. Many submission-grappling tournaments also allow competitors to wear wrestling shoes, which are tight-fitting shoes with rubber soles that have traction on the mat. But the standard attire for most fighters is a short- or long-sleeve rash guard, board shorts and no shoes. (See Figure 5.)

In submission grappling, you are never allowed to grab your opponent's clothing like you may in a BJJ tournament with a gi. There is frequently very little clothing to grab in any case, but if a competitor were to grab an opponent's clothing, it could easily result in tearing.

It pays to think about what clothes you feel most comfortable in and what fits your game, especially if the particular tournament gives you latitude as to whether you can wear a tight-fitting rash guard versus a regular T-shirt. If you are a smaller person or you find yourself fighting from the bottom and needing to escape a lot, you may prefer to wear slipperier Lycra shorts with no shirt or a short-sleeve Lycra rash guard. If you tend to be on top or like to have more friction to hold onto an opponent, you should wear cotton shorts and a cotton shirt. If allowed, a long-sleeve cotton shirt is best. If you are particularly good at armbars and/or triangles, you might want to find long board shorts made of cotton. They will give you more friction between your legs, helping you keep your opponent in tight when you apply a move.

I personally prefer the friction I get with cotton because my game relies a lot on tight crushing, which I learned from my coach, Rigan Machado. I also have a good triangle, so I want grip between my thighs. This is why I also wear a long-sleeve cotton shirt and longer board shorts.

As for wrestling shoes, they can give you more traction, but that very same traction can cause your own foot to get caught on the mat, resulting in a knee injury. I have seen this happen enough times that I never wear shoes on the mat. I'd rather slip during a takedown on some sweat or otherwise lose traction and points than risk a knee injury, which might require surgery and a year's recovery. Wearing shoes also makes you more vulnerable to foot locks and heel hooks because they give your opponent a better grip to hold onto your foot with.

Points Overview

Many submission-grappling tournaments use the standard BJJ point system, but there are some competitions that follow the rules of the Abu Dhabi Combat Club. These rules are specifically used in the ADCC Submission Wrestling World Championship, which was created by Sheik Tahnoon Bin Zayed Al Nahyan after his introduction to Brazilian jiu-jitsu and grappling. The championship now has qualifying tournaments around the world and offers significant prize money to the winners.

The ADCC rules award points for the following:

- a clean takedown that ends in full control and not in the guard (four points)
- a takedown that ends in the guard or half-guard (two points)
- passing the guard (three points)
- a clean sweep that lands the fighter on top in a control position (four points)
- a sweep that lands the fighter in the opponent's guard or half-guard (two points)
- a reversal, which occurs when the competitor is trapped on the bottom and escapes from it by rolling the opponent over and finishing the move from on top. This is considered a sweep in ADCC rules but not in BJJ rules. (two points)
- knee on the stomach (two points)
- mount position (two points)
- back mount that controls the opponent's back with two heels or "hooks" around the hips (three points)

Another notable feature of the ADCC rules is that there are point deductions. If a competitor voluntarily pulls the opponent into his guard or goes from standing to a ground position and stays down for three seconds or more, he is penalized by a loss of one point. Also, if a competitor backs up or avoids engaging in the fight, he will first be warned, and if the behavior continues, he will lose a point. These rules are designed to reward aggressiveness and discourage sitting down defensively into the guard position or otherwise running from the action. Generally, a point is deducted, but even though there is a standard, these rules can vary from competition to competition. So remember to check the rules.

Pulling an Opponent Into the Guard (Deduct One Point)

David Meyer pulls Adam Treanor to the closed guard (1-4). Some submission-grappling formats penalize fighters for doing this.

Avoiding the Fight (Deduct One Point)

Circling at the mat's boundary can appear to the referee that you are avoiding action or running from the fight (1-3). This behavior is often penalized in ADCC submission-grappling matches.

Many of my coaches, training partners and students have competed in the ADCC Submission Wrestling World Championship, and I have coached fighters to victory, as well. My coaches, Rigan and Jean Jacques Machado, have done very well in that format. Jean Jacques Machado won his division in 1999 and was awarded the Most Technical Fighter Award for the tournament. That being said, I personally prefer submission-grappling tournaments that do not use ADCC rules. The ADCC rules discourage fighters from pulling the opponent into their guard, which I think disregards a very important and legitimate part of grappling.

If you prefer to fight from your guard, you will need to know whether you will lose points for pulling an opponent directly into it, like in ADCC competitions. If that is the case, a smart grappler would practice takedown attempts as a method to land safely in your guard. Otherwise, the competitor might choose to accept the lost point, pull the opponent into his guard and have faith that he will recover the point.

Now you know the general outline of the rules for submission grappling. Remember, there is nothing more frustrating than making the effort to enter a competition only to lose because you didn't realize how the point system worked or because you executed a move that got you disqualified. Therefore, knowing the rules in advance of your submission-grappling competition is crucial and will allow you to practice specific scenarios and strategies to maximize your chances of winning.

Chapter 3
Choosing Your Competition

To find a tournament in your area, ask your coach, friends or search the Internet. (See Appendix A.) Many organizations affiliated with grappling also have e-mail lists that notify members about upcoming competitions; you just need to find them. Before you register for an event, however, you will have to make some important decisions—the first of which is to choose whether you want to compete in submission grappling or Brazilian jiu-jitsu. And if there are no competitions in your area, speak to your coach or other coaches about the possibility of hosting one.

Choosing Your Format

Some grapplers claim that it's better to train in submission grappling because it is more realistic. This means that they believe a submission-grappling tournament more closely reflects an actual self-defense situation than a Brazilian jiu-jitsu match. There are many reasons this can be true, but mainly it is because submission grapplers do not wear a jacket with a thick lapel on which to perform grabs and chokes. The gi is not similar to average "streetwear," and some people believe this makes BJJ training more "unrealistic."

Conversely, some grapplers tend to get caught up in the mystique behind Brazilian jiu-jitsu, the success of BJJ fighters in arenas like the UFC and the belief that submission grappling is based less on technique and more on brute strength. Basically, a strong athletic fighter without a gi and covered in sweat can sometimes slip out of submission holds only using brute strength and explosive power. BJJ proponents might also be inclined to believe that their BJJ skills alone will carry the day in an actual street fight.

The truth is that both formats have real-world applications. For instance, from a BJJ point of view, people almost always wear shirts and jackets, and BJJ fighters could perform gi techniques using these articles of clothing. In a similar vein, several minutes of submission grappling makes both fighters slippery with sweat in a way that bears no similarity to what would happen in a short street fight. If we go by hard facts, more technical skill is actually required to control an opponent without the aid of a garment to hold on to, and that skill is valuable on the street.

But the objective truth is that both submission grappling and BJJ fights are not real at all; rather, they are sports formats. They both occur in a controlled environment with a competitor who faces a single, often barefoot, opponent on a soft, wide-open surface that is free of obstacles. Both formats prohibit striking, and they assume that a fight begins when both fighters are prepared to start and in the ready stance. None of this relates to a real street fight, and the only major difference between the two sports is that one provides a lapel to grab for throws, control and chokes and the other does not.

It's important to recognize that the sports of submission grappling and Brazilian jiu-jitsu are just that—sports, and they both have a great importance in the overall arsenal of a good fighter. It is worth noting that grapplers who first learn to fight with a gi and then graduate to no-gi competitions tend to have better overall control and a finer repertoire of sweeps, reversals and finishing holds. Many of the world's top submission grapplers—including Marcelo Garcia, Roger Gracie,

Jean Jacques Machado and others—all learned Brazilian jiu-jitsu with a gi first, and they continue to practice primarily in a gi. This is precisely because the uniform slows the fight down and provides friction between the two fighters, allowing them to learn and perfect certain techniques. It is then an easy matter to train without a gi and modify your holds to adapt to a newer and slipperier situation. In fact, the only holds not possible to do without a gi are certain pins, sweeps and chokes that require the uniform to execute.

But these slight differences also are what characterize and distinguish the two formats from each other. Because BJJ fighters have the ability to grab and hold onto a uniform, BJJ matches can be slower, sometimes with less action and more holding or stalling, if one fighter chooses to stall. This tends to make Brazilian jiu-jitsu more accessible to fighters who are older or, for whatever reason, not in as good cardio shape. In contrast, submission grappling tends to move faster and favor fighters who are in better shape, mainly because the fighters get sweatier, making it harder to hold a position or execute a finish. Brazilian jiu-jitsu also lends itself to judo players who rely on gi grips for throws and pins, while submission grappling lends itself to people with a background in Western wrestling, which is sometimes practiced in a singlet—a skintight, sleeveless jumpsuit.

In the final analysis, both styles of grappling are closely related, great for exercise and have obvious street-fighting applications. The final decision of which format you prefer to compete in may be determined simply by what the school you train at offers and what tournaments are available to you locally. I recommend that you train both with and without a gi during the course of your normal practice. Then you can choose which you prefer for competition, and I encourage you to participate in both kinds. This gives you the best chance to learn, and any competition will only improve your overall skills.

If you train at a school that only practices submission grappling, competing in a BJJ tournament with a gi and using all the related grips and controls may seem unfamiliar. It will of course also require that you purchase or borrow a gi. Because you may be unranked in Brazilian jiu-jitsu, you will probably want to enter as a white belt, unless you are a more experienced grappler. If you are experienced, I recommend you purchase or borrow a blue belt and enter in the blue-belt division. Wearing a higher belt color than blue starts to seem disingenuous even if you have advanced judo or wrestling skills that may allow you to do well at higher belt ranks. If you primarily train with a gi in your school, then entering a submission-grappling tournament will be an easy transition. Without the gi, however, you will not have the use of many of your chokes as well as some of your sweeps and throws, but otherwise, the format will be familiar. And you can choose if you are a beginner-, intermediate- or advanced-level grappler.

Whichever form you compete in, you must know the rules. This will only help you have a better chance of winning and reduce the frustration you will feel if a move you are attempting is ruled illegal, or worse, if you are disqualified as a result. The ideal situation is to know the rules of a tournament so well that you could be the referee. You should attend a tournament or two before you compete because it will help you see what you will experience and because it will give you an opportunity to pretend you are the referee and see whether your assessment of the matches mirrors the calls you see the official making.

Choosing a Division

When registering for a tournament, you must choose a division in which to compete. In Brazilian jiu-jitsu, you must compete with people of your own gender and in your belt level. While you can never fight in a weight category lighter than your weight allows, you do have the option to compete in a higher/heavier category. It is very unusual for someone to elect to compete in a higher weight category because, in general, it is more difficult to beat people heavier and, as is probably the case, stronger than you. But if you want a challenge, you can do it. Also, some people who are hoping to get a medal for fewer fights might wait to register to see whether the next heaviest weight category has fewer competitors. If so, they may choose to enter into the heavier division for a better chance of winning, but I would not recommend that as a reason to fight in a higher weight class.

You also need to decide in what weight division you will compete on the registration form. Remember, this is a number that will be verified at an official weigh-in at the tournament. While some weigh-ins occur a day or two before the match—usually at a local martial arts school—most weigh-ins are increasingly held the day of the tournament at the venue. The reason officials do this is to ensure that you are not heavier than the heaviest weight allowed in your division. If you do weigh more, then you will most likely be disqualified and unable to simply move to the appropriate weight division. Also, remember that you will probably be wearing your uniform during the weigh-in, so take this into consideration when selecting your weight category on the registration form.

Note that most tournaments also have an "open" weight class in which you can fight all the fighters of your age and belt rank regardless of weight. This gives you a chance to win two medals—one for your weight class and one for the "open" class if you enter.

Some tournaments also allow grapplers 30 years or older to compete with opponents from their age group only. They can choose to compete in their appropriate age category, generally known as the Masters/Adult/Senior divisions, or they can choose to compete in regular divisions, which are based only on belt rank and weight. In other words, a 38-year old BJJ blue belt who weighs 168 pounds can decide to fight in the Masters 167 pound to 181 pound blue-belt category, or he can fight in the regular 167 pound to 181 pound blue-belt category in which he may face opponents who are much younger.

Submission grappling is similar, with the exception that there are no belt divisions, and you must select a division based on whether you consider yourself a beginner, intermediate or advanced grappler, depending on your years of experience.

For many people, there are few decisions to make in terms of what divisions to enter. Those people are a particular weight and skill level. But often, you do have a choice. You may be old enough to compete in the Masters or Senior divisions, or you can lose some weight to drop into a lighter division.

If you are pursuing a BJJ and submission-grappling competition to enhance your skill level, then it stands to reason that your goal should be to enter into whatever division you are qualified for where there are potentially the most competitors so you have more matches.

Note that entering into a division with more fighters is the opposite of what you should do if all you want is the chance at a gold medal. If you just want to win a gold medal, then you should seek out the easiest and smallest competition venues and hope to fight against poor opponents. But if you aim to improve yourself and want that gold medal to mean something if you can achieve it, then you should enter a bracket that will give you the most competition and the most matches.

This might mean going up one bracket in weight. Don't confuse this with what I mentioned earlier in that competitors who are overweight in their division get disqualified. Moving up a bracket is acceptable even if you are lighter than the fighters in that division. With that in mind, you should enter a competition with the intention to register for the open weight division, your own weight division, and if you are inclined to the challenge, a weight division that is above your own, ensuring that you will get at least two fights—one for each division. Competing in the open weight division means that you might face heavier fighters, but this may not be a problem if you are already in one of the heavier weight divisions yourself (in which case you may fight lighter fighters than yourself). You also never know who will be in this division until you step onto the mat. If your opponent is so large that you fear for your safety, you can always forfeit the match.

If you see you are in a division with many fighters, don't get stressed out about how many matches you will have to win in your division. Just remember that your opponent will likely have had the same amount of fights as you, so they will be tired, too.

Unless you are very close to the bottom of your weight bracket, I strongly discourage you from dropping or "cutting weight." Cutting weight is not the healthy long-term loss of extra fat because of proper diet and exercise. It is an unnatural attempt to deprive your body of water in order to artificially become lighter by the competition weigh-in. The assumption is that you will regain the weight over a day of rehydration.

It is possible to drop quite a few pounds in the days before a competition, largely by depriving yourself of water, and that weight can be quickly regained after the weigh-in. But this practice is fundamentally unhealthy for your body and can severely degrade your competition-day performance, especially if you are not fully rehydrated. This is because sweating out weight in the days and hours before a competition leaves you depleted of vital minerals that you have to quickly replenish. Your body cannot function well when it doesn't have enough electrolytes and hydration. I have seen fighters who have cut weight on the day before a fight and have lost because, even after a day of rehydration, they still felt weak and off their game.

Also, cutting weight in this manner assumes that you will have at least one day after weigh-ins to regain the water you lost. But increasingly, tournaments are conducting the weigh-in on the day of the event, so there is no time to rehydrate and heal before your fight.

Sign Up Now!

If you are not committed to entering the next competition in your area, let me encourage you to do so. A well-trained fighter is like a race car. What's the point of owning it if you don't take it out for a spin? This book will help you win in competition, but I can't help you win if you don't sign up and get some experience.

When I got my blue belt in Brazilian jiu-jitsu, there were not enough competitors in the United States to warrant any official BJJ competitions. However, Rigan Machado encouraged me to compete wherever and whenever possible, whether the tournament was a sambo, judo or wrestling competition. Even though I was a BJJ blue belt, Machado told me to put on a black belt and enter judo competitions with him, which I did. My confidence soared because I learned that I was able to tap out experienced judo black belts with my new BJJ skills, but I never would have learned that if Machado had allowed me to stay in my comfort zone.

I also remember a time when I was a black belt and competed in a BJJ tournament. It was a BJJ "superfight," but my scheduled opponent did not show up. Instead, the tournament organizers put me against a significantly larger and stronger BJJ black belt from Brazil. Remember, it was the late '90s, and as an American, I still felt uncertain about how I stood against Brazilians. I fought well, lost by two points and was exhausted. However, minutes after I lost, I was told to be ready to face another opponent in 15 minutes—if I wanted to fight again.

I was tired. My ego was bruised, and these factors made me decline the chance to compete. I'll never forget the disappointment in Machado's face when he learned of my decision. He said, "You've come all the way to the beach, and you don't even want to swim?" From that day on, I vowed to never pass up another chance at a match, and I have kept that promise. In fact, I often fight extra matches, even in weight categories far above my own.

It is very tempting to delay entering a competition because you are not in the shape you want to be in, you don't feel confident enough, you want to wait until your game improves a little more, etc. But there is a warrior within you. Don't suffocate him—let him out. If a warrior were faced with a challenge in the present moment, would he respond to it by saying, "I'm not ready?" Would you tell an attacker on the street to come back in two weeks after you get into better shape or come back in an hour after you warm up? The mental attitude that carries you to victory in a competition is the same attitude you need in life when the chips are down. Would you tell a person trapped in a crashed car that you'll be back later once you are better prepared?

A warrior acts. You do not dictate when life sends you challenges. Instead, you rise to the occasion and kick ass. And if you can't kick ass, you can go down fighting—like a warrior.

During a seminar I attended by professor Don Jacobs of Trinidad, he said, "You are a tiger, and I am just a pussycat. And if you fight me, I know I'm going to end up a dead pussycat. But you sure as hell are going to end up a one-eyed tiger."

So if you are injured or ill with the flu, then, fine—don't compete. You don't want to worsen your injury or your health, and you don't want to make others sick. But if you are tired, out of shape or otherwise unprepared—great! Now is your chance to test yourself as you are—today—in the moment—just as you will be if life throws a challenge at you.

A competition is a challenge. Take the challenge because you have nothing to lose and everything to gain. You should compete anytime, anywhere. Competing is learning, and you were born ready to learn. So sign up now for a competition!

Interview with **Professor Wally Jay**
Small-Circle Jujitsu Founder

Q: Do you prefer to fight in *gi* or no-gi competitions?

A: I like the gi because you can use the cloth to perform chokes and other different techniques.

Q: In your opinion, what's the most important thing about competition conditioning?

A: I think that the most important thing [for a grappler to do] is to get into shape. It's very important that you have the stamina to last.

Q: What advice do you have for coaches? (See Page 180.)

A: A lot of times, the fighter is thinking [too hard], and it's hard for them to follow the coach's instructions even though the coach can see [what's going on] better than the student. When I coached, I'd check everybody after the match when they returned to the gym. I'd write it all down, like what should have been done, and I became a better and better coach after that. In the end, I helped coach a lot of national champions.

Q: What do you recommend grapplers look for in a coach? (See Page 62.)

A: You have to look at the teacher to see how he expresses himself. I know some teachers get angry if their students don't catch on. But [a good coach] has to have patience.

Q: Why do some grapplers perform so poorly in competition?

A: A lot of times, a guy has stage fright. When they are on the [home] mat, it's different than in competition. In the end, it's experience that matters, and that's all. When grapplers get more experience, they're more confident.

Q: What do you think about open weight divisions?

A: Most times, a big guy will win—most of the time. But sometimes, a good little guy can beat a bad heavy guy.

Section II

BEING THE BEST OVERALL FIGHTER YOU CAN BE

Things You Should Always Do and Know

Chapter 4
Improving Your Overall Performance

Why does every martial art or sport seem to have competitors whose abilities defy all logic? The answer is not just genetics. Instead, the answer begins with the fact that these masters train more days a week, spend more time on the mat each class and pay more attention in training than other fighters.

But it's not simply a matter of just training longer and harder. These competitors also train smarter than their opponents. Too often, people believe that if they train twice as hard and twice as long as others, they will improve exponentially and be better in competition. Training smarter includes being more efficient with your time, getting better coaching and doing exercises more relevant to your sport.

The truth of the matter is that during a competition, you are not just watching a grappler's performance at that moment as an athlete; instead, you are seeing the sum of all his preparation, expressing itself in the heat of battle. Consider that a match is won or lost before you even step on the mat. Such a perspective isn't supposed to be fatalistic; instead, it's supposed to open your eyes to the fact that the competition is just the proof of who trained better.

Your training includes what you do inside and outside class, and you want to maximize the effectiveness of your efforts so that you can perform at your highest potential on competition day. These factors are numerous and include increasing your strength, endurance, flexibility, training ethic, quality of your coaching, quality of your training partners and even your diet. Think of these factors distilled down to a simple equation:

Technique x Strength x Endurance = Performance

Like any mathematical formula, you need to attend to all three factors on the left to achieve the solution on the right. However, here's the good news—unlike the performance of your opponent on competition day, which is not under your control, all these variables to some extent are under your control.

Most people think that because they are attending as many classes as they can afford or have time to go to, the only extra thing they can easily do to gain a competitive edge is to focus on increasing their strength and endurance. But think about it: What would it take for you to lift five times as much weight or have five times the endurance that you have now? The answer is that it would take a lot of work. I began my BJJ training 16 years ago, and while I am probably 100 times better today than I was in the past, I am not 100 times stronger. What I mean is that even though I've done grappling for 16 years and won competitions around the world, I can't lift 100 times the weight I was able to lift when I started. Instead, I know 100 times more about techniques than I did when I began as a white belt so long ago.

So when you consider the formula (Technique x Strength x Endurance = Performance), remember that it is through the technique variable in which you will always have the most room for improvement. By focusing on that one variable, it will also multiply the value of your strength and endurance many times over. With that in mind, this chapter will focus on steps that you should always do to improve your technical grappling skills whether you are training for competition or not.

Train Smarter

Consider Ron and Jim who are two friends of equal technical skill and competition potential. Jim attends a 90-minute class once a week, while Ron attends a 90-minute class three times a week. Jim always comes to class 10 minutes late, takes time getting into his uniform and always takes a break when the instructors allow. Jim only does the minimum number of reps during warm-up and often leans against the wall to talk to his friends. In a 90-minute class, this may mean that Jim's actual mat time is about 30 minutes.

In contrast, Ron arrives early to all three of his classes. He immediately changes into his uniform to get out on the mat. After a good warm-up, Ron practices techniques with a partner for about 20 minutes before class begins. During class, he always tries to do more reps than what the instructor asks. He also never stops moving or practicing, unless the teacher says, "Stop." Ron tries to remain on the mat to ask questions and get in extra training if the instructor allows. In a 90-minute class, this may mean that Ron's actual mat time is about 60 minutes.

So what does this story tell us?

If Jim comes to one lesson a week and gets 30 minutes of mat time a lesson, then:

1 x 30 = 30 minutes a week

If Ron comes to three lessons a week and gets 60 minutes of mat time a lesson, then:

3 x 60 = 180 minutes a week

Ron gets six times as much mat time as Jim each week.

In addition, Ron always pays close attention in class, asks relevant questions to the instructor, seeks to understand what went wrong in a sparring match if he loses, and always asks for pointers from the best students in the class. Basically, while Jim is just there to have some fun, socialize and exercise, Ron is getting and retaining instruction that is twice as useful.

6 x 2 = 12

Ron gets six times as much mat time as Jim, and that time is twice as useful.

Through numbers, you learn that by training three times a week, arriving early, staying late, paying close attention, asking the right people good questions, watching and training, Ron is making the best use of limited mat time and maximizes his training by a factor of 12 compared to Jim. So Ron could, in theory, achieve gains in his technical skills in a single month that would take Jim 12 months to achieve. This is the essence of training "smarter," so discipline yourself to never stop until the instructor says you must get off the mat because remember that you will never have this training day back again—ever. Use your limited time wisely.

Injury Is the Enemy

Before we talk about what you should do to make your technique better, let's talk about what you should not do. In most cases, the absolute worst offender in impairing any part of the performance equation is injury. If you can't train, you can't improve, so the No. 1 rule of training smarter is that you must train in a manner that does not cause injury to you or your partners. Note: If your partners are injured, it not only stops their learning but also affects your learning because you have fewer people to train with.

So how do you train effectively without experiencing or causing injury? Here's a simple list of rules to follow:

- warm up thoroughly
- practice on a safe, good-size mat and padded area with no corners or sharp objects
- make sure you have enough room between partners during sparring practice
- don't grapple in an overly aggressive manner with your partners
- don't resist tapping out

These rules may seem obvious, but they are difficult for competitors to learn, whether they compete in Brazilian jiu-jitsu or submission grappling. I have seen people pull muscles because they were more eager to start training than warm up. I have seen partners collide with other people on the mat during practice. And I've certainly seen people be too aggressive on the mat during training and resist tapping out, which will cause injuries.

For example, when I was a BJJ white belt, I was paired with another white belt who was not only heavier but also fresher than me. I had just faced several opponents in practice matches, and while I was tired, this white belt was just out of the Marines, packed with muscles, aggressive and determined to win. We grappled for several minutes before I caught him in an armbar. He resisted tapping out. I slowly increased the pressure on his elbow, but he still didn't submit. Then I felt a "pop" in his arm, and the white belt began to scream. I felt terrible about being overly aggressive, and the white belt was very apologetic for being overly competitive. Of course, he had to go to the hospital because he had torn his biceps. The injury not only kept him out of training for a year but also deprived his classmates and myself of his assistance in our grappling growth.

So remember: Injury is the enemy. Avoid it.

Come to Class No Matter What

To train more efficiently, you need discipline. In this case, discipline means taking action even when you don't feel motivated. Anyone can come to class and train when they feel great, but a champion becomes a champion by training even when he does not feel up to it.

For example, I once faced a difficult time in my life when I was a BJJ blue belt. I was very upset and depressed, and it would have been easy for me to slack off in my training. But each day, I dragged myself to class with no expectation of performing well. In fact, I would just give myself applause for driving to class and stepping onto the mat. During those many months, I really disciplined myself and continued to improve, albeit slowly. I even won my first BJJ competition. In the end, that sad epoch was a pivotal time in my life, which showed me that even though I could easily have slacked off or stopped training altogether, I had the strength to keep going.

Pushing yourself to train when you don't feel up to it will also help condition you as a fighter, teaching you to take action even when you are not motivated. Of course, you definitely should not train if you are injured or ill because it is not only bad for you but also unfair to your partners who might get sick or fail to improve as quickly as they should.

Experiment With New Moves

Think of how often you try to execute your favorite moves in training. Now consider how often you try to execute a new move you recently learned. If you're like most people, the chances are that you've learned a new move, tried it several times in sparring (if at all) and then stopped trying it, especially if it didn't work. Now, how likely is it that a move you have just learned will work in sparring the first or second time you try it? It is not likely to work until you have tried it many, many times and really begun to understand the setup, timing and execution of a move.

If you don't add new moves to your arsenal, your game will never improve. By far, the greatest tendency most people have in training is to practice what works and avoid what does not work at all costs. While it certainly makes sense to refine what works, the fact of the matter is that people spend years repeating their favorite moves. They are unwilling to try new techniques that might fail or that they can't use immediately.

One way to make sure that you are learning new moves is to review your entire game every three months. In short, become conscious about what techniques you are constantly practicing. Make note of your favorite moves and then stop doing them. Because you do them well, they will still be available if you need them. Instead, it's more important to take note of the moves that you execute poorly and/or develop new moves by seeing what other students are doing well. Ask your instructor about areas of grappling in which you feel inadequate, then learn from whatever instructional materials you can find. You should also pick a specific new move or position and then spend several weeks focusing on it.

For example, let's say that you want to practice a new move for escaping the mount. Start each sparring match with your partner in the mount position. By intentionally handicapping yourself, you are forced to operate in a certain area that demands that you develop, incorporate or strategize new moves and skills. It's also possible to start all sparring matches on top in a side-mount position or pinned under the opponent in a side-mount position. The key is that you pick a starting position in which your favorite, predictable or usual moves are unavailable, so you must defend and win through unfamiliar means.

Often, it is a minor injury that forces you to learn new moves or will prevent you from using your favorite ones. If an injury does not stop you from training but inhibits a certain motion needed for your favorite move, it can be a blessing in disguise. But rather then let chance force you into learning new moves, do it consciously now.

During my movement up in the BJJ ranks, I was always known for my guard. But when I got my black belt, I decided I wanted to dominate my opponent even more in competition, so I intentionally stopped pulling my opponents to my guard. When I found myself in my guard as a result of being swept or taken down, I stopped all submission attempts and made my goal to sweep or otherwise escape to the top or to my feet. People who train with me now talk about how powerful I am on top. What they don't know is that this is a result of a decision I made to focus on my top game and abandon an entire area of my game that had worked well for many years.

I believe Carlos Machado is also a great example of a BJJ competitor who is always willing to experiment and learn. I always would see him immersed in a learning process that caused him to thoughtfully and calmly study moves and angles as well as experiment with new ideas in each sparring match. If his experiment failed, Machado was never bothered. Instead, he would note his mistake and handle the consequences as they arose. Adopting this attitude will require that you slow down your pace of training, become a bit less competitive, and be more experimental and willing to tolerate failure, but it is well worth the payoff.

Remember that training is your chance to experiment and try new things, while competition is the time to excel at what you know. If you train as if you are in a competition all the time, you only increase you and your partners' chances of injury as well as deprive yourself of a crucial aspect of practice. That aspect is the learning that comes from slowing down and seeing mistakes you and others make.

Don't Stop When You Are Tired

To train for a winning spirit, you must discipline yourself to not give up just because you are tired. This is not to be confused with a tapout, which you must and should always do in training to avoid an injury. However, giving up in training because you are tired should never occur.

Often in training, students practice hard on the mat until they are breathless. Then, they go and lean up against a wall to recover, but this can turn into a bad habit for competitions. In a match, the clock is always ticking, and there is no wall to rest on, even if you can't fight anymore.

To teach his students how to fight their fatigue and still maintain their technique, Rigan Machado has his students play a game called "King of the Hill." The game follows the simple idea that two students would spar in the middle of the mat. The winner would immediately face another fresh student. The idea is that the winner, or "king," must continue to face new opponents, without rest, until he is tired and replaced by a new champion, who must then undergo the same training.

Once when I was a blue belt, Rigan Machado gave each of us a piece of paper with a number on it that corresponded to another piece of paper he had in a hat. He then told us that he would select a number from the hat. Whoever had his number called would have to remain in the center of the mat as the king of the hill, regardless of whether he won or lost. This meant that one person would have to fight every single grappler in the 18-student class without rest, win or lose, in what could stretch into an hour of unbroken training with everyone watching.

Many students quickly whispered their hope that they were not chosen. However, I remember thinking that the challenge would actually be a good learning opportunity, even if I lost to guys I normally would beat. Fortunately, it was my lucky day because my number was chosen.

I look back on that day as the most difficult training session that I can remember. Machado took no pity on me. He immediately started the game by sending the toughest students against me, meaning that I first had to face classmates who could beat me on a normal day anyway. They were merciless.

Next, Machado matched me up against classmates I could usually beat, but by that time, I felt totally drained. Suddenly, it was very difficult to make these "easier" opponents submit. But there was no way I could stop the challenge because all eyes were on me, and Machado kept egging on my opponents to punish me.

After 45 minutes into the ordeal, I felt a surge of energy flow through me. I began tapping out the last of my opponents, who were white belts. In his infinite wisdom, Machado began setting up the final matches in positions that favored my opponent, such as in the mount or back control. This, of course, made the last moments of the challenge even more difficult to fight through. I felt like I was going to die, but instead, I made a serious leap forward in my skills that day, which I have never forgotten. In fact, I kept that scrap of paper with my number "15" on it in my wallet for years because it reminded me that some things that seem bad are actually blessings in disguise.

The Machado brothers have a saying: "When the body says, 'No,' the mind says, 'Go.'" Despite my absolute exhaustion during that challenge, I learned that I still had the strength to press forward. In fact, those moments of absolute exhaustion are exactly the moments that I believe a fighter should seek because they give you the opportunity to show the world that even when you feel you can't go on, you will push on and not give up. Not giving up when you are tired is both a skill and a habit that must be practiced. So remember, you can always rest when you go home, but if you have taken the time to drive to class, get dressed and get out on the mat, then you owe it to yourself to spend every second you can training, win or lose.

Be a Copycat

When people watch great grapplers like Marcelo Garcia or Rigan and Jean Jacques Machado, they often sit back in awe and say, "Wow! That guy is great!" Or, they think, "He's a natural."

However, it's important to remember that these magnificent competitors are not using magic. They have bodies made of flesh and bone just like us. It's just that there is something or some set of things that their bodies are doing that yields great results. I learned this from John Will, and it has helped him become Australia's top BJJ coach as well as the country's first BJJ black belt. That's why if you watch great fighters and do the exact same body movements they do, then you too would probably do some amazing stuff.

It is true that some people have exceptional strength, flexibility, or just a great sense of timing, but don't use that fact as a cop-out. When you see a person do something great, analyze exactly what he is doing with every part of his body and do it yourself. If you are watching a DVD, view it frame by frame. If you do exactly what a great fighter does, you will be a great fighter yourself. So watch great fighters, and copy them.

Find the Crux

The crux is the most crucial aspect of a move. For every technique that you learn, discipline yourself to analyze and understand why a move works and, by extension, what might cause it not to work. This is also a strategy that I learned from John Will and it has served me well.

Each time you learn a new technique—whether from a DVD or from your instructor or training partners—ask yourself: "What is the crux of the move?" With that information, you can make your own corrections in the move as you train and discover how to counter moves when your opponents apply them.

Consider a basic double-leg takedown as an example (See next page.):

Basic Double-Leg Takedown

David Meyer (right) and Adam Treanor face each other in the ready stance.

Meyer lowers his level by bending his knees.

He takes a deep penetrative step forward with his front foot toward Treanor.

Meyer collapses his front knee and prepares to bring his rear leg around and forward.

As he "turns the corner," Meyer lifts his head high to force Treanor off-balance and defend against a possible guillotine attempt.

Meyer continues the turn to his right, taking Treanor off his feet and onto the ground, avoiding landing in Treanor's guard.

Meyer then consolidates his position on side control.

The above example shows that there are many important details to remember about the double-leg takedown. Lowering your level, using a strong, penetrative step and turning the corner are just a few of them, but they are not the crux of the technique. Instead, the crux of the move is to bring your hips as quickly and as close as possible into your opponent so you can take control of his balance before he can sprawl his legs back and away from you. This is the goal of everything you are doing in the move. By lowering your level, you create leverage to push forward off your back leg and bring your hips in closely and quickly. By taking a deep penetrative step, you bring your hips right up against your opponent. By turning the corner, you make it difficult for your opponent to sprawl, which keeps your hips in close. By understanding the crux, you'll understand how interrelated all aspects of a technique are, and you'll even learn how to modify the move for your unique body type, so long as you achieve the crux.

Another important way to break down a technique is to ask: What role does each of your limbs play during a move? This is another important lesson I learned from John Will that continues to serve me well in competition.

To understand this idea better, let's look at a basic scissor sweep:

Basic Scissor Sweep

David Meyer begins with Adam Treanor in the closed guard.

While Meyer's left hand grips Treanor's left collar, his right hand maintains his control on Treanor's left hand and arm. This prohibits Treanor from placing his left hand on the ground to "post" and stop the motion of the sweep.

Meyer then unlocks his legs and presses off his left thigh to swing his hips far out and to the left, making ample space for his left shin across Treanor's belt line.

Meyer drops his right foot to the ground as he pulls Treanor with both hands, bringing Treanor's weight forward and off Treanor's knees to make him easier to sweep.

Meyer then pulls hard to the left with his right leg at Treanor's knee and kicks hard to the right with his left shin across Treanor's waist, thereby creating a "scissorlike" action.

Meyer follows through while his left leg is across Treanor's belt line and his right hand is gripping Treanor's left arm. Meyer's right leg is free and ready to move him into a position of control on the mount.

Meyer then finishes on the mount.

For the scissor sweep, your right hand controls your opponent's left hand and stops him from posting. Your left hand pulls his collar, bringing his weight forward and off his knees. Your right leg blocks your opponent's left knee from posting, and your left leg kicks your opponent over, forcing him to fall. No matter how basic the move, your limbs are somewhere doing something, and if you consciously try to understand what they are doing, then they are more likely doing something useful. Also note, that even though this critical dissection doesn't help you find the crux of a move, it is something you can do just as easily off the mat by going through your techniques, mentally. Consider it as homework that preps you for the ultimate exam.

Do Your Homework

As I mentioned in the previous section, finding the crux of a move or analyzing the roles of your limbs is homework in that it is a type of learning, preparation and training that takes place off the mat. In training for competition, there are many different kinds of "homework" for you to take advantage of, and here are just a few:

- Your physical homework pertains to exercises that increase your strength, endurance and flexibility. By going to the gym, running and watching your diet, you physically affect your chances of success on the mat.

- Your mental homework includes any time spent thinking about and visualizing yourself executing the techniques. It also includes any time spent thinking about how a technique works, whether you focus on the crux, the roles of your limbs or something else.

- Your supplemental homework refers to any instructional DVDs, videos and books (like this one) you can use to add to your training off the mat. There are a number of products available that teach grappling and Brazilian jiu-jitsu in a systematic way, and by using one of those tools, you may be able to fill in gaps in your understanding of the sports and their moves. (See Appendix B.)

Supplemental research also allows you to familiarize yourself with major competitions. In fact, I recommend that you watch as many competition videos as possible, especially those that highlight matches at the Brazilian Jiu-Jitsu World Championship, Grapplers Quest or the ADCC Submission Wrestling World Championship. When you see something work, watch it in slow motion, make a note of it and try it on the mat. Even though you're only a spectator, you should still find the crux of the move.

Seek Out the Best Coaches

Finding a great coach may not be totally under your control—depending on where you live, how much time and money you are willing to spend, etc.—but it can be a worthwhile investment because a great coach can, in a matter of months, move you along a path that it took them years to travel. Sports tend to evolve over time through the trial and error of former and current competitors, and a good coach is a repository of accumulated wisdom who should help you train on the cutting edge of your grappling format. A good coach will also push you beyond your limits. Your workout will always be tougher if someone else gets to decide when you can stop.

I was fortunate to train with the Machado brothers, especially at a time when they were new to

America and all five of them trained on the same mat. Their training methods were relentless, and their workouts were the hardest ones I have ever done. For instance, Rigan Machado would collect his 20 best fighters, including me, for training several days a week at 6 a.m. to run the infamous Manhattan Beach Sand Dune Park in Los Angeles. We would race up and down a long, steep hill of sand as many as 10 times until our legs were completely drained of strength. Then we would return to the school and grapple for hours. It is that mixture of pressure to work hard and technical guidance on the mat that is so difficult to find and so valuable when you find it.

The ideal coach is someone who can teach you the skills you need in a systematic and organized way while providing a controlled and safe environment. Remember that good fighters are not necessarily good coaches and that good coaches are not necessarily good fighters. Competing and coaching require different skill sets. For example: You don't need Dale Earnhardt Jr. to teach you how to drive; instead, you just need someone who knows how to drive better than you and who knows what you need to learn.

Finding a good coach may mean driving extra distance or paying extra money. It may mean taking a monthly trip to another state. You can search the Internet for recommendations or scout around to see who is coaching the best fighters in your area. Perhaps by seeing who is winning local competitions, you'll find a worthwhile person to train you.

If you can't find a great instructor, try to find the best grappler with whom you can train with and who has a similar body type to yours. This helps ensure that whatever moves he is successful with will also work for you.

In some areas, it might be easier to find a judo or wrestling coach to train with, which is fine because they will still help you develop certain aspects of your game like throws or takedowns. In fact, you may even wish to train in several grappling styles at once in order to develop a well-rounded game. But in the end, do whatever you need to do to find the best coach. Each day you spend without great coaching is a day you never get back.

If you have to evaluate a coach or teacher without any prior knowledge of his methods, try to take a few classes to see whether you enjoy the instructor and whether the instructor teaches in a clear, methodical manner that helps you learn and assimilate the material quickly. All too often, schools teach techniques as random moves. Beginners are tossed in to grapple with experienced fighters on day one. The idea behind this method is that students will learn more from the actual sparring as they go along, but successful learning is best done through a step-by-step approach in which each new skill builds on the last one. Fortunately, more and more schools are organizing what they teach and offering it in a logical order for students to learn. This method tends to work better for most fighters because it ensures that you will have the prior knowledge you need each time you are presented with a new move.

As a final note, once you do find a coach, take personal control of your training. Ask your coach questions. Frequently, a coach doesn't have the time to give attention to every grappler equally, which is why you need to become a squeaky wheel. This might mean simply asking your coach what general area to work on and then taking it upon yourself to practice it for several weeks. Many coaches appreciate when a student takes ownership of his education, and they generally will respond well to your desire for direction as well as independent action.

Seek Out the Best Partners

I cannot overstate the importance of having good training partners. By good, I mean friends who are open-minded, eager to help, not overly competitive, and are good, competent grapplers. You preferably want to train with a mix of people, some who you can beat (so you can experiment with new attacks) and others who can beat you (so you can hone your defenses and have people to model yourself after). A good rule to follow is that you should find people who can beat you without hurting you. Usually, this means they are beating you with technique, not with brute force.

It's also important that you be a good partner in that you share all your knowledge. Don't keep any secret techniques to yourself because, in the end, you not only are hurting yourself but also are hurting your partners. Your skills will augment the skills of your partners and vice versa. By training together, you want your partners to boost your techniques from their current level to a higher level, which means that you want to tell them everything and that your partners should reciprocate. Basically, the better each grappler becomes individually, the more everyone in the group will improve.

Ideally, you want to train in what becomes a laboratory of fighters with different body types and skill sets because it gives you the greatest exposure to new ideas and because it provides you with a constant challenge. If you can't find that environment, try to create it in your own backyard by inviting others to come and train with you.

Leave the Comfort Zone Behind

One of the biggest challenges in competition is that you will have to fight opponents that you have never met. Generally, you become very familiar and comfortable with your regular training partners, and often, you end up unintentionally repeating the same fighting sequences with them. However, in competition, the biggest variable you will face is your opponent's strengths and weaknesses. What are they? Who knows. The chances are very high that he will execute moves that you've never seen before.

Rigan Machado taught me that the best way to prepare for the unknown is to leave the comfort of your school and training partners and train in new venues with new people. I would watch Machado and his brothers enter wrestling, judo and sambo competitions and win because they were genuinely interested in other fighting styles and in learning new moves. In fact, Machado even won a silver medal in the sambo world championships without even knowing the rules. It wasn't only Machado's BJJ talent that helped him win, but it was also his well-rounded knowledge of grappling in all its forms.

In regards to his students, Machado regularly took us to wrestling, judo and sambo gyms as well as anywhere else we could find good grapplers who would execute techniques we didn't know. He is not just a genius as a fighter but also as a thinker. His is a walking encyclopedia of grappling moves, and his goal was and is to ensure that unfamiliar moves surprise his students in training rather than during a competition. He strove to incorporate a very well-rounded curriculum into our training, and the door to the Machado school was always open to any grappler no matter his style.

In my own training, I stick to the following motto: "There is nothing that I haven't seen." I continually try to maximize and diversify my training with new techniques, venues and partners. When the Machados began to spread out and open their individual schools, I used to drive 90 minutes between their individual schools to train with the maximum number of partners each week. Whenever my coaches asked who wanted to volunteer and train with someone new, I always jumped at the chance.

Having the exposure to different and unfamiliar styles will give you the confidence that your game will stand up to any opponent, no matter his grappling background. Also, the knowledge of how trained fighters from different styles react will prove very useful when you fight in competition.

So remember that whenever someone new visits your school, train with them. When you travel somewhere on vacation or for work, find a local grappling school. If there is another grappling school in your local area, especially if it is a different style from yours, call the school, get the instructor's permission and drop in for a workout. This will shake you out of your comfort zone and prepare you for anything someone throws your way in competition.

Interview with Nick Diaz
Mixed-Martial Arts Fighter

Q: Why compete?
A: I like to have something to train toward, and the thing about competition is that there is a [physical] goal to meet. [The feeling to me] is kind of like when someone gets out of jail. For a while, he's all locked up and having a horrible time, but once he gets out, it's like freedom, and it's great. Nowadays, everything seems so convenient and easy, and some people just become stagnant and get bored. Competition gives me a chance to put myself through the type of self-discipline and training where, when it's all over, I feel like I'm free. I feel alive.

Q: Do you prefer training with a *gi* or without a gi?
A: I prefer training with a gi because the workout, to me, is more interesting. Of course, I have to train gi-less because my job [as an MMA fighter] is to fight. But I still train with a gi when I can. In fact, right after an MMA fight, I'll sometimes train with a gi on for a month.

Q: Why are training partners so important?
A: You are only as good as the level of competition you are training with. How else are you going to know what level you [compete] at without some sort of stick to measure how you are doing? In other [types of] competition, athletes often try to beat their personal best, i.e., beat a best time. For example, I do triathlons because they record my [personal] progress throughout the years. But it's hard to [gauge your progress] like that in Brazilian *jiu-jitsu*, which is why you have other competitors that are at the level of competition that you are now. By training with these people, you are going to have an idea of the level you are on. Say your buddy just won the championship of some organization. Now you are doing really well with this guy. It is going to give you the confidence level that you need. It is going to help make your training be that much more positive.

Q: What conditioning do you recommend? How do you condition?
A: I think endurance workouts are good because you end up getting hurt less, and it's not as hard to do as a warm-up. They also consist of more training in that you get to go over more techniques by being in the gym longer. For my [general] conditioning, I like to swim, which I developed as a conditioning foundation when I was really young. I like to swim once or twice a week.

Q: What advice would you give to nervous grapplers?
A: The only way to win a competition is if you're not afraid to lose. Always keep that in mind. A trick that I use [to do this] is to go over the worst-case scenario in my mind, which is that you lose in the worst way possible. What is worse than that? Whatever is worse, I think of them all and then start to cancel them all out. At the same time, I try to deal with the situation as if it's already happened. I say, "I can deal with this." I imagine it as if it's already happened and this is what life is going to be like from now on as a result of that worst-case scenario. Then I decide where I stand, whether I can handle it and then I go into competition. In the end, you're only going to be able to tone [the fear] down a little bit, but that little bit is going to seriously count.

Chapter 5
Improving Your Grappling Conditioning

There are 24 hours in a day, but people only spend a few of those hours training on the mat. What you do off the mat with the rest of your hours will certainly make a difference in how you perform during a competition, especially in regards to how your strength and endurance affect your technique. Different from the mental homework discussed earlier, your physical homework is the training you do off the mat. Think of your body like a race car—your techniques are akin to the skills of the driver, but you still need an able car (your body), with a powerful engine (your strength and stamina) and a good suspension system (your flexibility) to bring to the racetrack in order to execute your techniques.

When it comes to conditioning, many grapplers generally just stretch and exercise. They do groin and hip stretches to stay loose, bench presses and squats to stay strong, and they assume that any general gains in flexibility or strength will help them with the specific requirements of a grappling competition. This logic should make as much sense to you as an Olympic sprinter who assumes that by developing the muscles used for swimming, he will become a better runner. OK, it may help a little, but wouldn't it make more sense to use very specific stretches and strength-building exercises that are 100 percent relevant to your submission-grappling and BJJ game?

The term "relevant" is important here. Marathon runners have awesome endurance, but they tire as quickly as anyone else during a grappling match. This is because their endurance is relevant to the motion of repetitive running and not the muscular twists, turns and crushes you experience as a grappler. Likewise, a champion weightlifter can lift immense weight, but if that ability were relevant to grappling, all BJJ and submission-grappling world champions would be huge powerlifters, which they are not. Of course, super strength or super flexibility is useful on the mat, but building muscles that have power in irrelevant ways to the movements you use in grappling is a waste of training time, meaning it's not relevant and it's definitely not smart.

Improving Your Grappling Strength

People often talk about using technique over strength when grappling. That's a good rule to follow, but if you were to use no strength at all, you'd be lying on the floor unable to sit up. What "not using strength" really means is that you should not rely on brute strength to compensate for lapses in technique. Proper body strength is necessary to support proper technique and can exponentially multiply your effectiveness on the mat.

This section discusses strength-building exercises to improve your grappling skills. These exercises tend to:

- strengthen specific muscles that you need for grappling,
- strengthen your overall body without building too much muscle,
- teach the body to coordinate movement between muscle groups and
- correct any strength imbalances.

The last category is mentioned because focusing on any single sport will create physical imbalances. For example, grappling helps fighters develop a strong upper body but sometimes at the expense of developing the lower body. Of course, veteran grapplers know that strong legs and thighs are very useful in grappling, but the act of grappling itself will not develop those muscles. Instead, this must be done in off-the-mat conditioning exercises.

An imbalance can also occur if a competitor only focuses on a specific body part because he might be in danger of overly developing certain muscles. Realistically, fighters with big muscles usually can't tuck their limbs in and away from an opposing grappler nor can they defend themselves against joint attacks. For example, if a competitor has overly developed chest muscles, he won't be able to keep his arms and elbows tight against his body. This makes him susceptible to setups for armbars.

This conditioning imbalance also leads to another danger that occurs when grapplers go to the gym and artificially isolate a specific muscle, i.e., triceps, biceps, etc, to build it up. Instead of strengthening the arm, this actually teaches the body to use those muscles individually rather than train the body to use the entire muscle group in a coordinated action. These muscular guys are very common on the mat, but from my experience, I see them tire quickly because they do something like bench-press an opponent off their chest instead of bridging and moving their body in a coordinated effort. Remember, your conditioning goal is to develop strength relevant to grappling by not creating physical imbalances that will throw off your game.

So what exercises build strength, are relevant to your grappling skills and balance out your conditioning? Basically, any exercise is good that allows your body to move with its own natural bodyweight as well as increase balance, muscle and tendon strength. Plyometric exercises, like jumping up on and off a box or catching and tossing a medicine ball, strengthen muscles' stretch and explosion reflex. Real-world strength enhancers such as rock climbing also are ideal for grappling because it combines grip, flexibility and balance.

Note that for weightlifting, ideally you should find a trainer who is either familiar with grappling or willing to watch you grapple in order to understand your strength needs and provide you with relevant conditioning.

To Warm Up or Stretch?

Most people confuse warming up and stretching, thinking they are similar when they aren't.

A warm-up is a set of exercises that gets your heart pumping, your temperature rising and creates a good flow of blood through the joints, muscles and tendons. This helps avoid injury during the exercise.

In contrast, stretching is designed to loosen and extend the muscles for the purpose of creating more permanent flexibility. Stretching is best done when the body is already warm. It can also be used as a good cool-down. By making sure that the muscles you have just worked are reset to their elongated and relaxed position, stretching prevents the buildup of lactic acid that usually causes the tight and sore feeling the following day.

In the end, a good rule of thumb is that before you do strength training, always do a good warm-up. Then finish your workout with light stretching.

Explosive vs. Tenacious Strength

Most successful grapplers do a combination of exercises, building both explosive muscle strength for quick bursts of power and building tenacious tendon strength for maintaining long and persistent pressure. However, as mentioned earlier, be careful not to favor one type of strength training over the other. For instance, while explosive movements are useful and help grapplers break out of dangerous positions, they can also fatigue a competitor, especially if done many times in a match.

For explosive-strength conditioning, work with heavier weights and fewer repetitions. On any weightlifting exercise, do a warm-up set of 10 repetitions with light weights, and then work at least five sets with higher weights. The first and second higher-weight sets should be 10 reps long at a weight that makes it fairly hard to complete the 10th repetition. The third and fourth set should last about three reps and be done with the assistance of a spotter. You should use the maximum weight you can lift when your last rep is near "failure," meaning you can barely complete it without assistance. On the fifth set, do 10 reps again, and decrease the weight just enough so that you can still complete your 10 reps, with the final rep again being close to failure.

BJJ and submission-grappling fighters whose personal styles are geared more toward tenacity and endurance, such as smaller or lighter fighters who are always fighting opponents stronger than themselves, tend to work lighter weights at a higher number of repetitions. Building up this strength in which the grappler remains strong, even after making the same movement for many minutes, is useful because it allows him to hold onto an object tightly even after a long time. It also helps the grappler build up stamina.

To develop tenacious tendon strength, do your exercises in "supersets" during which you do a small circuit by moving between two to three exercises in a loop. Rather than wait for a full recovery to begin your second set of repetitions on the first exercise, begin your second set on a related exercise, which keeps your body moving. It also allows your muscles to recover even as they continue to work in different ways. For example, you can alternate between squats and seated leg extensions because they both work your quads but in different ways. You could also superset bench presses and triceps pull-downs. Basically, the idea is to move between two or three related exercises, doing a set of reps on each, and never spending a lot of time recovering in between while you make the loop to the next exercise.

You also can develop tenacious tendon strength by modifying the exercise for explosive strength. Like the other exercise, you will do at least five sets, but instead of doing 10 reps during the first two sets, you'll increase them by a factor of three and do 30. For your third and fourth set, you'll increase the reps by a factor of three and do 15, and for your last set, you'll do 30 again. Another difference is that you'll also do all reps using a lighter weight because you want to build up your tendon strength instead of your explosive-muscle strength. The weight depends on each grappler's individual abilities and preference. However, remember that you still want to push each rep through to failure.

Another versatile conditioning exercise is from Jean Jacques Machado. You can easily adapt it to either train for explosive or tenacious tendon strength by doing a high number of reps at a low weight for tenacious strength and a low number of reps at a high weight for explosive strength. The exercise is as follows: Run on a treadmill at full stride for 10 minutes until you have a very high heart rate and are significantly out of breath. Then move quickly to muscular exercises like biceps curls or squats, doing them quickly to maintain your high heart rate. Eventually your heart rate will slow because you can't maintain the same pace. When this happens, change exercises. In the case of Machado, he would jump onto a treadmill and run for another four minutes at top speed. By quickly changing exercises and doing all sets to the extreme, you ensure that all your conditioning is done when in a state of oxygen debt. This, according to Machado, trains the muscles in a way that most closely mimics a grappling match. I've also found the technique useful in building strength and endurance.

Whether you are improving your explosive or your tenacious tendon strength, be sure to move with control in all directions. For example, when doing a bench press, there is the "positive" motion of pushing the bar or dumbbells away from your chest but also the "negative" motion of lowering them back down again. Both the positive pressure of pushing away and the negative pressure of collapsing back in must be executed with control.

Building Your Upper Body

The act of grappling itself builds up upper-body strength. But you can only grapple for so many hours on the mat during your limited class times. You can, however, increase your upper-body strength outside of class, either at home or in the gym, and you can do so around your own schedule. Any increases in upper-body strength that are relevant to grappling can be very useful in BJJ or submission-grappling competition.

It's very important that you have the strength necessary to hold someone off, push an opponent away or slide away from a grappler who has you pinned. These movements specifically work the triceps and pectoral muscles, which is why it's a good idea to do off-the-mat conditioning. There are many exercises you can do that include, but are not limited to, triceps pull-downs, dips, close-grip push-ups and close-grip bench presses.

Triceps Pull-Downs

Whether you use a bungee, weight or other tool, pull-downs help develop your ability to push an opponent away. To start, grip the handle palm down with your shoulder directly above your elbow.

Engage your triceps and your shoulder by pressing down with your hand. Note: You are not trying to overly isolate the triceps muscle because you want your muscles to work together as a group.

Continue pressing down with your hand until the arm is fully extended, completing the "positive" pressure of the motion. Then slowly bring your hand up with control for the "negative" or retracting pressure.

Push-Ups

Push-ups and bench presses develop your ability to create space between you and your opponent. To start, place your hands on the ground shoulder-width apart, keeping your body straight and your head looking forward.

Lower your body to the ground and keep your elbows in tight to your body, just as you would do when grappling to protect against arm and shoulder attacks.

Suspend yourself just above the ground before slowly pushing back up, always keeping your elbows close to your sides.

Pulling an opponent in during a grappling match is just as important as pushing him away. To pull a fellow competitor in tight to you, apply a choke hold or resist armbars, you need to work on biceps strength. For conditioning, biceps curls are an excellent staple exercise because they strengthen a competitor's ability to pull his arm back toward his body, which is especially useful when trying to resist an armbar. Equally useful are seated rows, which allow you to increase your "pulling" strength by developing your deltoid muscles. (See sequences on next page.)

Biceps Curls

Grip the handle palm-up. Of course weights are also appropriate and preferred.

Engage your biceps by pulling up on the handle. You can do complete movements or stop at small intervals to build up tendon resistance strength.

Pull your hand all the way up before releasing and slowly changing direction, controlling the buildup of the negative as well as positive movement.

Seated Rows

Seated rows help you pull an opponent in close, especially when you are standing in a clinch. It also helps you pull your arm back and away from an opponent who wishes to execute an armbar in his guard. To start the exercise, reach forward and grip the handle on the machine or bungee cord with one hand.

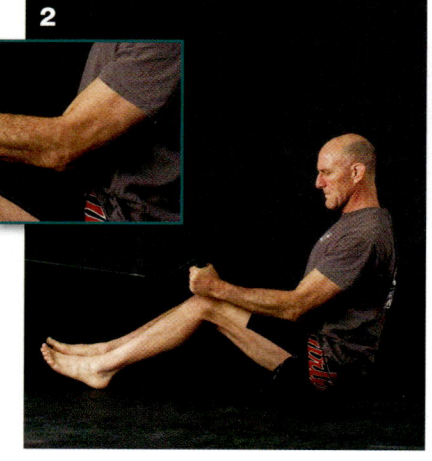

Sit with your back at a 90-degree angle.

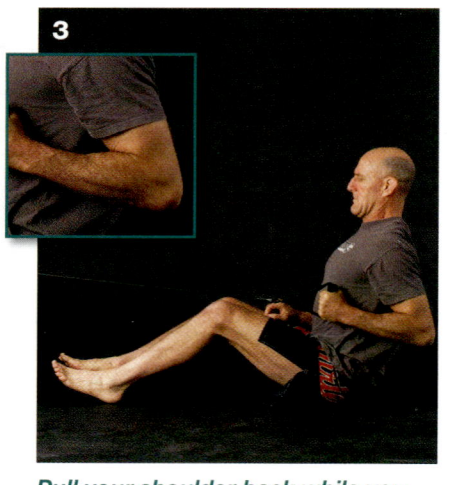

Pull your shoulder back while you retract your hand and maintain your straight posture. Then release your hand slowly, feeling the negative pressure of the movement. Remember to vary the way you execute seated rows. Mimic the "pulling" your arms would do to escape an armbar as well as the "pulling" both your hands would do if you were to hug an opponent closely.

Other important parts of the upper body to focus on are the shoulders and back. In fact, the shoulder and back muscles are extremely important in takedowns like the double-leg takedown. Because you need to hold your opponent's legs as he tries to sprawl his legs away, you need the power of those muscle groups to help your arms execute the move. Wide grip pull-ups and pull-downs are excellent exercises that target these areas. However, because these exercises are meant to develop your strength for holding onto an opponent's leg while he sprawls, you should vary the distance of your hands in each set. This is because your opponent's legs will be at a variable distance, too. In addition, vary the direction of your palms, meaning that they should sometimes face away from your body and sometimes face inward to mimic changes in positions and muscles that you need to engage for certain takedown positions. As a final variation, do the pull-ups and pull-downs both in front of your chest and behind your neck to maximize your strength in all potential takedown situations.

Pull-Ups

Grab the bar with both hands.

Pull yourself up, using your core muscles to stabilize yourself so you do not swing forward and backward.

Pull yourself as far up as you can go before slowly lowering yourself down, limiting any forward or backward swing.

These upper-body exercises can be modified for other equipment like weights or bungee cords, as well as done while standing on a ball or other unstable surface. In addition, even though these exercises focus on strengthening the upper body, they also engage the lower stabilizing muscles in the legs and stomach, which allow your conditioning to more closely reflect a grappling environment.

Strengthening Your Core

Core strength refers to your stomach and lower back. It is the "core," or central strength of your body, and is especially important in the twists and turns needed in grappling. Stomach and lower-back strength are crucial, especially when it comes to having a strong sprawl to defend against takedowns or in defending yourself when a defender is in your guard. Don't forget that spine flexibility is equally important in core conditioning because you cannot strengthen the muscles that allow you to curl forward or backward if your spine is stiff.

Bridges and backbends develop the power and flexibility of your lower back, and they are the movements you will need to lift your opponent and create space when trying to escape from a bottom position. Arching your back in these exercises also helps you execute a good sprawl because of how the move arches the back when you sprawl your legs away from the opponent.

Bridges

To start, begin on your back with your head off the ground. Bring your hands to your chest and pull your feet in close to your rear end.

Press up onto your toes and lift your hips as high into the air as you can. Notice how this creates space.

Keeping your hips as high as possible, turn as far onto your left shoulder as you can while keeping both feet on the ground and reaching out toward your upper left with your right arm. Slowly lower yourself back to the ground and alternate with the other side. This mimics how a grappler twists to unbalance a "top" opponent.

Abdominal exercises are key when it comes to increasing your core's physical power, which is important when you need to keep your guard closed around an opponent, pull an opponent toward you or sit up toward an opponent. Remember that any abdominal exercise should be done in a way that does not cause pain to your lower back. If you ever feel your back overly straining or cramping, stop the exercise.

If, however, your back is strong and healthy, then doing stomach exercises at odd angles with the twists that mimic the extreme movements used in Brazilian jiu-jitsu and submission grappling are a must. Again, remember that these exercises should not cause you pain beyond the strain of normal exercise. If they do, stop and modify them into a simpler format.

Side Sit-Ups

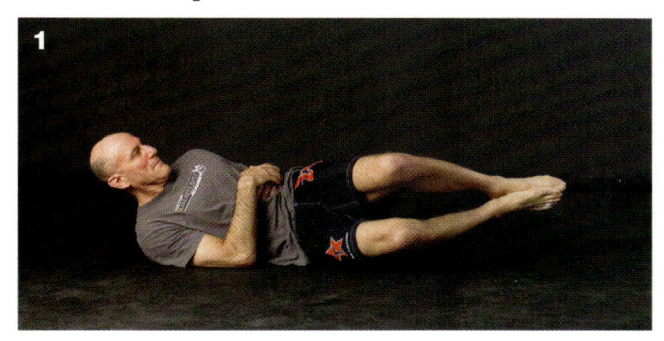

This exercise will help you develop the side abdominals. Begin on your right side with your knees slightly bent and your head, knees and feet off the ground.

Pull your upper body and your legs toward each other simultaneously.

Hold yourself as high off the ground as you can before lowering yourself back down to your start position. Repeat. Notice how the side sit-up mimics the twist you may experience when you are rolling on the ground grappling.

Side Leg Lifts

Side leg lifts develop stomach muscles that give you the power for twisting. This is useful in almost every technique in grappling. To start, lie with your back on the ground. Lift both legs off the ground and to the left, keeping them together and straight.

Circle your legs to the center. Keep your hands on your stomach to make sure your abdominals are tight and working.

Circle your legs to the right until they nearly touch the ground, then lift them again in the other direction.

Training for Competition: Brazilian Jiu-Jitsu and Submission Grappling

The guard sit-up is a useful variation to develop strength for the most extreme kind of angles in grappling because your feet will be high above your head. Situations in which this kind of conditioning is useful include when you are on your back and must sit up powerfully, when you lift and twist your opponent for a takedown, and lastly when your opponent stands up inside your guard. Guard sit-ups not only work the total grip power of your core but also work your legs and allow your partners to simultaneously condition by developing their leg strength and stability to keep you steady.

Guard Sit-Ups

With your partner in a stable stance—feet spread slightly wider than his shoulders and his head arched back—place your hands on the back of his shoulders, jump up and cross your legs around his hips.

Once your partner stabilizes himself, lower your upper body to the ground.

While you lower your body, your partner must lean back to counterbalance your weight and avoid being pulled forward.

Slowly rise back up so as not to unbalance your partner. If needed, hold onto your partner's arms to help pull yourself up.

Finish with your upper body high and ready for another sit-up. Or you can grab your partner's arms and release your legs while jumping back to a standing position. (Note: To make the exercise easier, your partner can stand with both of his knees together, which takes the pressure off his lower back and puts it on his shins. This also makes it easier for you because it provides your lower back with support.)

Another variation of this sit-up is the side guard sit-up. Like the other exercises, it will also help condition your body for the twists and turns of a grappling competition. However, it more specifically can lend itself to certain competitions that allow or do not allow certain moves. For example, some competitions prohibit a competitor from slamming an opponent down in his guard. Because of this, you may want to hold onto an opponent who tries to stand in your guard, then execute an armbar or sweep. This movement relies on the core muscles because, otherwise, you won't have the strength to maintain your grip or maneuver. Side sit-ups, more so than other sit-ups, help strengthen the core muscles for the extreme angles of this action. Remember to do the exercise carefully so you avoid muscle strain.

Side Guard Sit-Ups

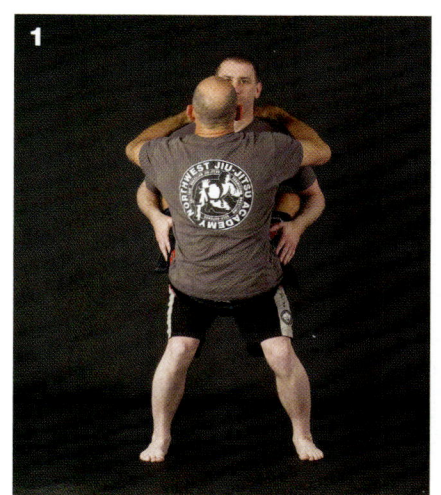

1. With your partner in a stable stance—feet spread slightly wider than shoulder width and head arched back—place your hands on the back of his neck and jump into your guard, locking your legs around his hips.

2. As your partner leans away to counter your motion and maintain balance, lower yourself down and to the left in a half circle.

3. While doing the half-circle movement, maintain smooth control with your abdominals.

4. Bring your body up and around on the right side in that same, smooth circular movement.

5. When you've returned to your start position, you can continue with another rep, or switch directions.

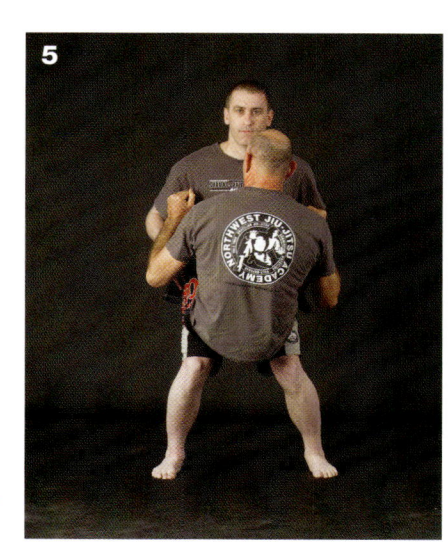

Building Your Lower Body

Oftentimes, grapplers are relatively weak in the legs because grappling favors the upper body. However, your lower body is still very important, especially during the later minutes of a match.

Think about it: After struggling to force an opponent to submit, the referee stops the match and separates you and your opponent. Suddenly, you're back on your feet, facing your opponent in a standing position. In scenarios like this, explosive leg strength is imperative because it helps you shoot toward your opponent's feet for a takedown, which means you need to lunge.

The most basic way to develop a powerful and deep penetrative step for takedowns is a basic lunge. Also note that you can do lunges with or without weights. They help develop the ability to penetrate deeply for takedown setups.

Basic Lunge

Start with your feet parallel to each other and at shoulder-width apart. They should line up with your hands, which are held in front of your chest. Look straight forward.

Take a moderate step forward with your left foot. You shouldn't be able to bend more than 90 degrees on the front leg because bending farther will injure your knee over time.

Dip your right knee to just above the ground, but keep your head and posture up.

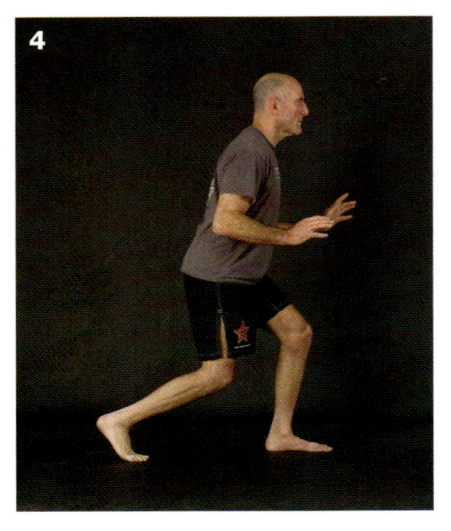

Push off your left foot to rise back up.

Step back into your neutral stance. You can continue your reps with the same leg or alternate legs.

Side Lunges

Side lunges develop good lateral movement needed to adjust angles for takedowns. To start, begin with both feet parallel to each other and shoulder-width apart. Keep your hands held in front of your chest and look straight forward.

Take a moderate step forward and to the right with your right foot. You shouldn't be able to bend more than 90 degrees on your front leg because bending farther will injure your knees over time.

Dip your left knee to just above the ground, keeping your head and posture up. Then push off with your right foot to rise back up to a neutral stance.

Another way to work lunging strength (as well as do cardio) is to run sets of stairs. Experiment by running one, two or even three stairs in a single stride. This develops a range of lunging strength and also helps involve your calf in explosive action.

Another exercise for takedown entries, which helps you develop fast acceleration from a static starting position, is to stand in your ready stance and apply pressure on both legs. This means that your rear leg is pushing you forward but that your front leg is pushing you backward. By doing this, you create an arc of tension between your legs so that when you lift up your front leg to step, you are launched forward like a slingshot. Practice circling the mat while creating this arc of tension, then lift your front leg to lunge forward toward an imaginary opponent.

Leg strength not only is important for penetrating forward to execute takedowns but also is important for lifting your opponent during a takedown or in pushing him away when you are on your back. Leg strength is also important so you can stand up in someone's guard with his legs wrapped around you and use gravity to help break your opponent's legs open.

To develop the strength to stand up in someone's guard (or even just stand balanced when you are fatigued) you should practice squats, with or without weights. Also note that you do not need to use extremely heavy weights on your shoulders for your squats because the weight of your opponent will almost never be centered there. You just don't need the massive strength that serious weightlifters develop when doing the exercise. Instead, you just need a good amount of stable leg strength that you can depend on even if you are tired.

Be sure to maintain proper posture and form to protect your knees and lower back from strain. Always have a small arch in your lower back and look to the ceiling when you do your squats. Never bend forward and never allow your knees to bend more than 90 degrees.

Squats

Start with both feet parallel and your hands held up in front of your chest. Look forward.

Bend both knees at the same time, lowering them the same distance so they are always parallel. Keep your head and chest up, and do not bend forward.

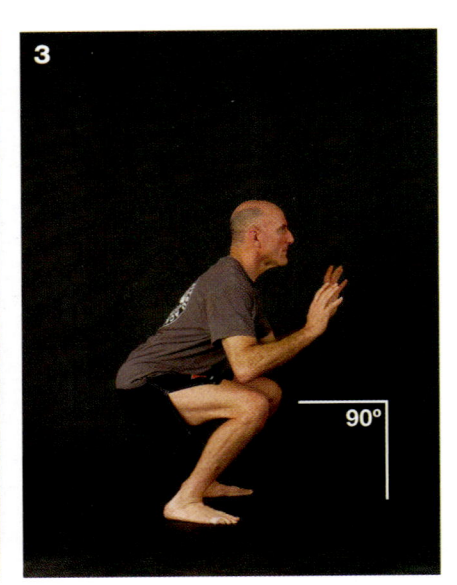

Stop when your knees are bent at 90 degrees.

Rise back up with your head and chest up. Do not bend forward.

Finish in a neutral stance with your legs slightly bent.

Another great exercise for building up the strength necessary for standing up in an opponent's guard is to practice the motion using "guard squats," in which your partner holds his legs around you while you stand up. This is a great exercise because it warms up your legs and lower back, and it also warms up your partner's legs and stomach as he practices staying attached. Your partner should hold your elbows as you stand up, helping you to safely lift his body weight off the ground. Make sure to maintain proper body posture to avoid lower-back strain while gently lowering your partner to the ground with control.

Guard Squats

1. Start in your partner's closed guard with your chest and head up. Maintain the posture throughout the exercise because it will prevent you from straining your lower back when standing up.

2. Rise onto your knees. Then lift up your left leg and put your left foot on the ground.

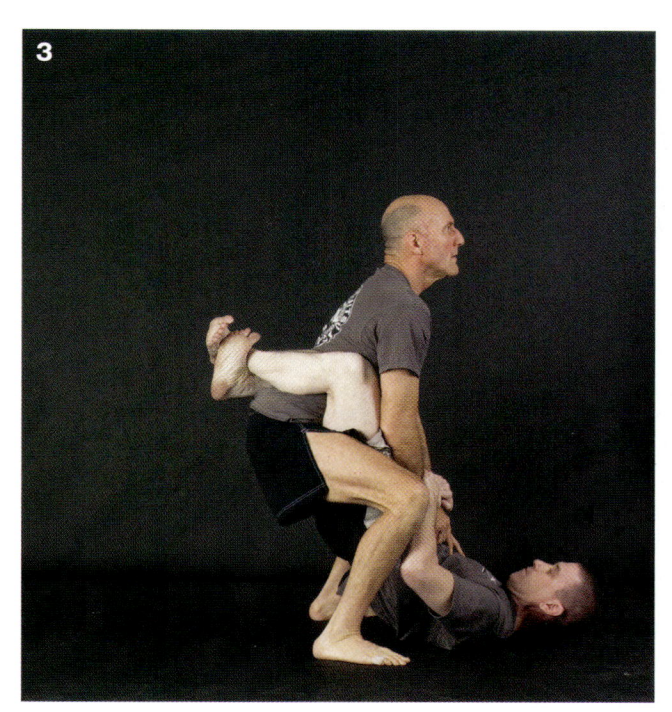

3. Press off your left foot to rise up onto your right foot. Keep your head and chest up.

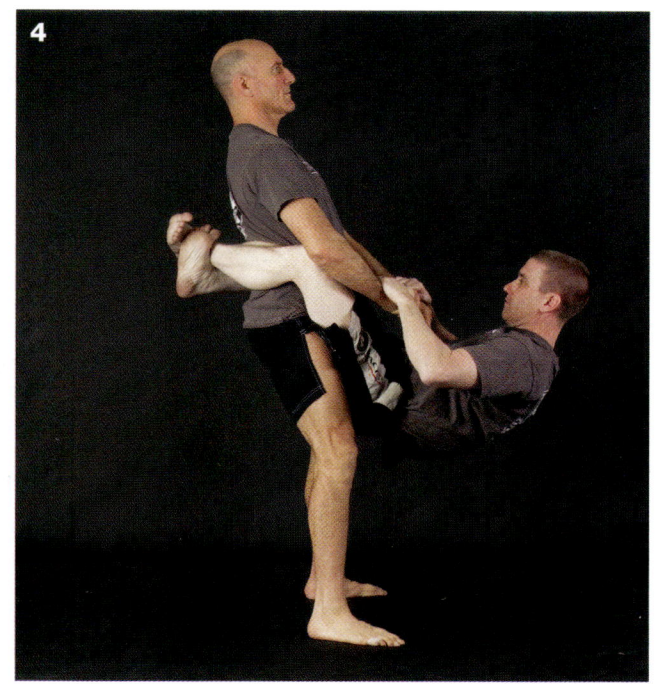

4. Stand up, picking your partner up as he holds your hands or elbows. Then slowly lower your partner and yourself back to the ground, lowering your knees one at a time, until you have returned to your original position.

Squats engage the quads by pressing the feet away from your hips while lifting. This is important because your quads are also needed in grappling to lift and sweep an opponent who is sitting on your feet.

To develop the lifting action necessary for many sweeps, you should practice quad extensions. Quad extensions are done on a machine in which you sit on a chair, and the machine provides resistance as you straighten your legs out in front of you. Perform the exercise one leg at a time because that more accurately mimics grappling in which you are almost always lifting an opponent with one leg as you turn to the side. Be sure that when you do the exercise, you don't use too much weight that will cause stress or discomfort on your knees.

You should also work hamstring curls to develop the strength used to hold someone in your guard, to bend your legs in tight for an armbar, and to defend your own leg against a legbar. Hamstring curls are usually done on a machine in which you either sit on a chair or lie on your stomach. The machine provides resistance as you pull your heels in to your rear end. Like quad extensions, do this exercise one leg at a time because this ensures that you are not covering for weakness in one leg by having the other leg do most of the work.

Improving Your Grappling Flexibility

Flexibility is useful for grapplers. It prevents muscles, tendons and ligaments from tearing and bones from snapping when they're forced into odd positions. Flexibility allows you to execute and defend against a wider variety of techniques. For example, while shoulder flexibility makes it easier for the defender to survive a shoulder lock, hip flexibility makes it easier for the attacker to apply it. It also can help a defender escape a joint lock without tapping out, and for this reason, flexibility can be your "get out of jail free" card.

Flexibility also increases the effectiveness of your muscles, enabling them to contract more. This is especially important because muscle contraction makes locomotion possible. Whenever you move, a relaxed muscle group contracts, springing the body into motion. For example, when you bend your arm, the biceps contracts. Conversely, when you straighten your arm, the biceps relaxes and the triceps contracts. Whenever you are tense, your muscles are partially contracted, which means part of your potential explosive power and range is lost. Keeping your muscles in a relaxed state achieves maximum strength and explosive power because this ensures that more of your muscles move in unison from a relaxed to a contracted position. This not only enables you to execute more moves but also helps you to resist them.

To become more limber, stretch properly. Proper stretching increases how far your limbs can bend and returns the tissue to a relaxed and elongated state. Many great BJJ and submission-grappling fighters like Rickson Gracie and Roger Machado use yoga as a way to increase limberness. For the most part, any stretching you do will increase your grappling game, but focus a bit more on areas that general exercises tend to overlook, such as the spine, hips, neck, shoulders and groin.

This section contains stretches that target areas that are important to grapplers with some basic, effective flexibility exercises. Some of these stretches are borrowed directly from yoga and retain their yoga names, while others are modified for grappling. When performing the stretches, try to hold each one for 30 seconds to one minute. Between stretches, loosen the muscles by relaxing. Then perform the stretch again, but push yourself slightly harder. Like all stretches, do it slowly and, if possible, only after your muscles are warm. Never stretch so hard that it causes sharp pain.

The butterfly stretch develops the kind of groin and hip flexibility that's useful when defending in the butterfly guard because it mimics how an opponent presses down on your knees. A flexible groin will prevent the opponent from getting around your guard.

The Butterfly

1

Sit on the ground. Pull your feet close to your groin, with the soles touching.

2

Use your elbows to push your knees as close to the ground as they will naturally go.

3

Tilt your hips forward, rolling your hips and belly to the ground.

4

Drop your head to the ground and relax into the position. This causes your muscles to lengthen and lets gravity pull you down. You can also gently press down on your knees with both hands to add to the stretch.

Training for Competition: Brazilian Jiu-Jitsu and Submission Grappling

In contrast to the butterfly stretch, the pigeon stretch provides an intense and deep stretch for one hip at a time. To avoid injuring lateral ligaments in the knee, perform this move slowly, placing your weight on your hands and putting as much pressure on your leg as you can comfortably bear.

The Pigeon

Face the ground with your right leg pulled forward and bent 90 degrees at the knee. Apply your weight gently to the bent leg and do not over-stress your knee ligaments. If this feels uncomfortable, bend your right knee more and bring your right heel closer to your rear end.

Relax your right hip and place both your hips on the ground, carefully balancing your weight on your hands and legs.

Exhale and relax as you lower your head and chest to the ground. Do not apply more pressure onto your right knee than is comfortable.

84

The cross-leg pull is another hip flexibility exercise that brings your feet closer to your head. This stretch is important for two reasons. First, it protects you from injury when an opponent who is trying to pass your guard presses on your feet and pushes them toward your head. Second, this stretch will improve your guard because it means your legs can defend a larger area. The cross-leg pull is easy to incorporate into your training, specifically when you are finished on the mat and cooling down.

Cross-Leg Pull

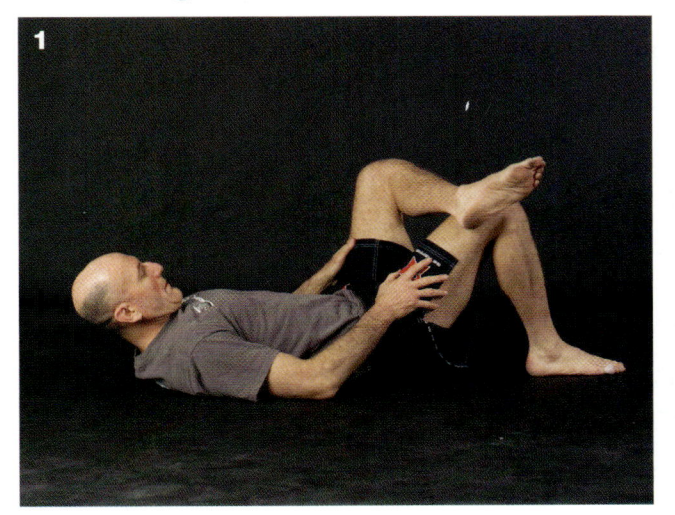

Lie on the ground and pull your right foot in. Rest your left ankle across your right knee.

Twist your left knee to the left while joining both hands together around your right knee.

Pull your right knee down to your chest, allowing gravity to assist you as you relax. Try not to lift your shoulders up too much to meet your knee because this will cheat you of the full effect of the stretch, which requires you to pull your leg down and relax your left hip.

The twisting lunge works the front and side of the hip and abdominal muscles. The improved flexibility will help you lunge farther when stepping in for a takedown and prevent muscle tears in the abdominal muscles that occur while grappling.

Twisting Lunge

Like with regular lunges, step forward with your right foot, leaving your left knee on the ground. Because you are relaxing into a stretch and will not be pressing off your left leg as you would when executing an actual lunge for a takedown, you can step out far with your right foot and allow your right knee to bend more than 90 degrees.

Lower your left hip as close to the ground as it will comfortably go. This will stretch the front of your left hip.

Place your left hand on the ground in front and to the left of you. Then twist your left hip down as you turn to your right, dropping your left hip to the ground. This will stretch the side of your left hip and your left-side abdominal muscles.

The cobra not only works the front of the hips but also stretches the abdominal and back muscles. By increasing the flexibility of these areas, they'll be less likely to tear when sharply twisting and turning in a grappling competition.

The Cobra

Lie facedown on the ground, then rest your palms on the floor in front of your chest. Proper positioning will allow you to easily push your upper body off the ground.

Push yourself up with your hands, keeping your hips relaxed and on the ground. This allows your stomach muscles to receive the best stretch.

Raise your chin until you can feel the tension in the front of your neck, then hold the position.

In a grappling match, twisting an opponent's shoulder can lead to a tapout because the shoulder can only twist so far before causing extreme pain or injury. By increasing your shoulder flexibility, you increase the time and space, i.e., the range of motion, in which you can execute an escape. If your shoulder can handle three more inches of twist, then you have three more inches in which you can escape and not tap out.

Wing Stretch

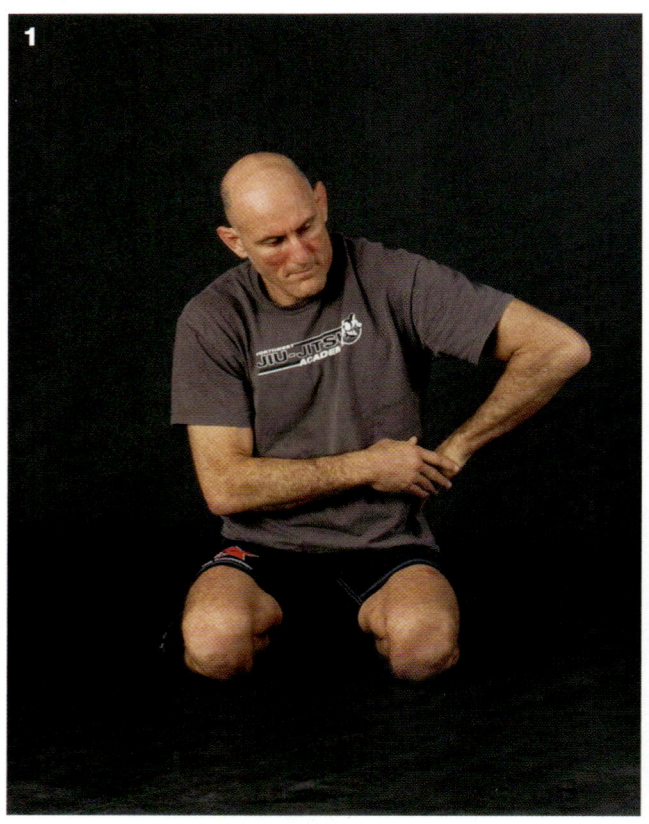

Kneeling on the ground, place your left pinkie finger and palm downward on your left hip.

Use your right hand to gently pull your left elbow forward, stretching your left shoulder.

Like the wing stretch, the *kimura* stretch is a simple way to develop the flexibility needed to survive the kimura shoulder lock because it mimics the motion of the shoulder lock. Developing flexibility at that angle will give you more space to move and more time to escape. Of course, if you feel sharp pain in a real competition, tap out.

Kimura Stretch

Begin on the ground, lying on your left side.

Place your left elbow out and bend it toward the ceiling at a 90-degree angle from your body.

Reach over with your right hand and grip your left hand from behind. This is where your opponent would grip your wrist in a kimura submission.

Using your right hand, gently press your left hand down to the ground in front of your stomach. Try to maintain the 90-degree angle for a ball-joint shoulder stretch.

The Americana stretch, like the kimura stretch, mimics the angle of the Americana attack. The stretch is also a simple way to develop shoulder and tendon flexibility.

Americana Stretch

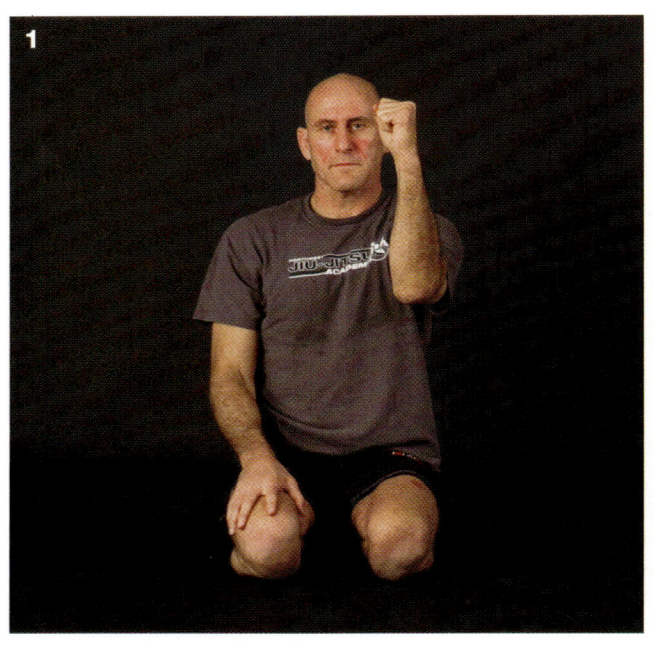

1. Kneeling on the ground, hold your left arm up with your elbow bent toward the ceiling at a 90-degree angle. Your fist should be level with your face.

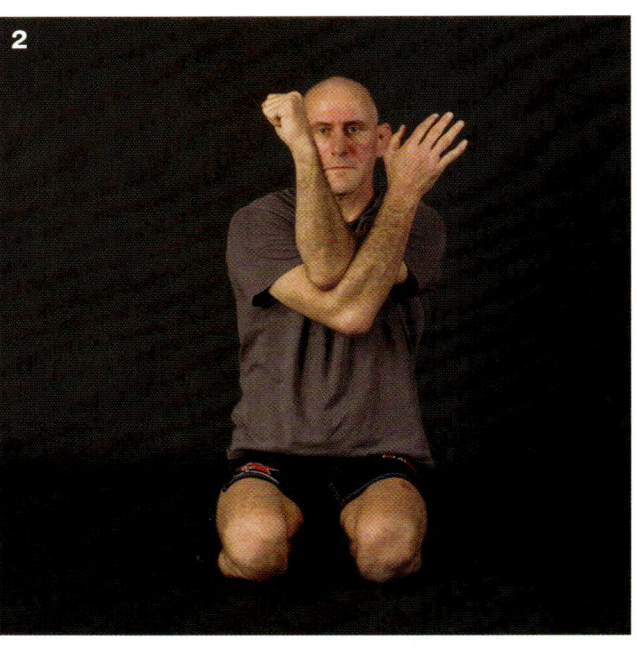

2. Place your right elbow underneath your left elbow with your right palm facing you.

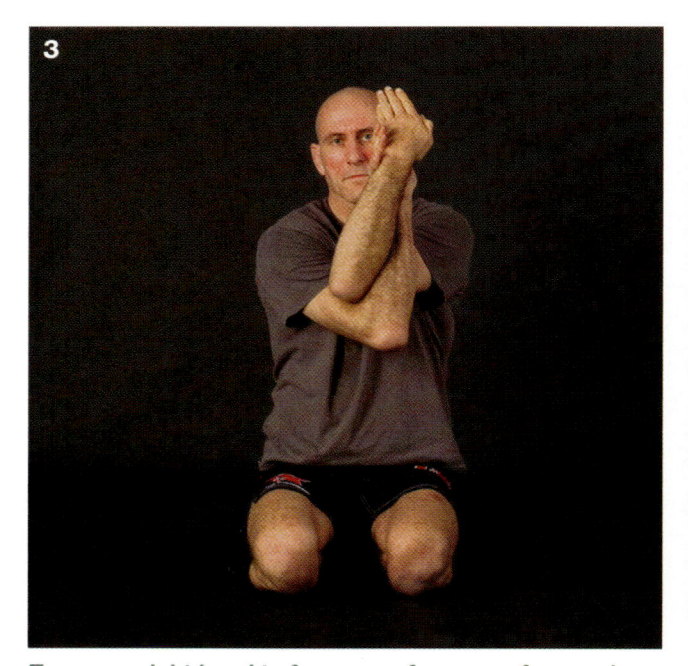

3. Turn your right hand to face away from your face and reach around your left hand.

4. Use your right hand to pull your left hand to the ground, keeping your head and body up in good posture. This stretches your arm at the same angle as the Americana shoulder lock.

Stretching your wrist is also important because it not only improves your wrist's flexibility but also improves your elbow's. During competition, your hand can get caught in the fabric of your opponent's uniform and a little flexibility can help you escape. The wrist stretch can easily be performed throughout the day.

Wrist Stretch

From a sitting position, bring your left wrist into your chest with your left palm facing to the left.

Use your right palm to press against your left hand as you pull your left wrist to your chest.

Neck muscles are frequently used during grappling, making them extremely important. As the attacker, you might press your head into the opponent's body to move or control him. While defending, your opponent might grab and twist your neck. In general, grappling strengthens the neck muscles, but this kind of strengthening also tightens the muscles. Tight neck muscles create stability for the head and keep your neck from being twisted. By performing flexibility exercises, you ensure that you maintain the mobility of this body part, which not only helps you avoid injury but also complements the increased strength of the muscles.

Neck Twist

Kneel on the ground with both elbows resting in front of you. Cup your face with your hands to support your head and allow your neck to relax.

Use your hands to turn your head to the left. Keep your head and neck relaxed.

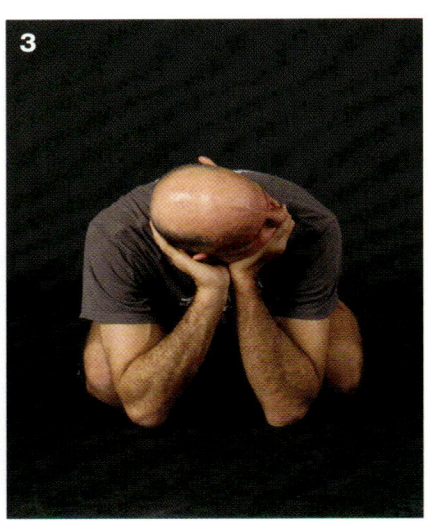

Gently twist your head to the left and then to the right.

The pull-down gently works the back of the neck by allowing gravity to pull your head down. This is especially useful in a grappling match when an opponent tries to "stack" you by pushing your feet over your head to create pressure on the neck. Another variation of this stretch is the "plow stretch," which specifically mimics being stacked but doesn't require a partner.

The Pull-Down

Gently clasp your hands behind your head and allow the weight of your arms to stretch your neck downward, without bending your torso forward.

The side neck pull also mimics stacking, but this time, the head is on the side. When performing this stretch, hold onto your foot with an anchor hand so your shoulder can't rise up and make the stretch useless.

Side Neck Pull

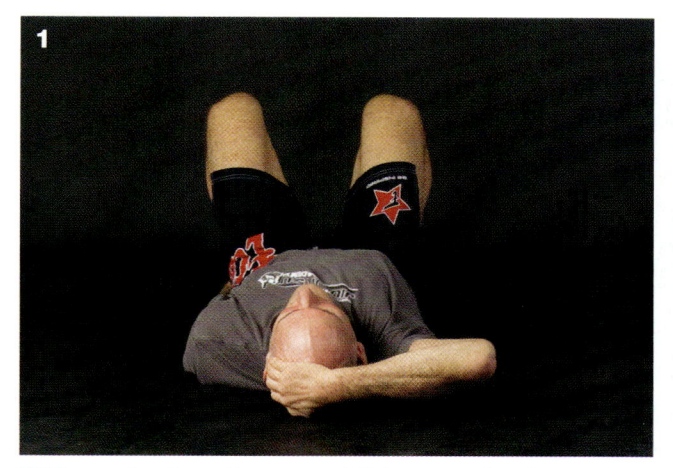

With your back on the ground, bring your feet in as close as possible to your rear end. Hold your left ankle with your left hand as you reach over the top of your head with your right hand.

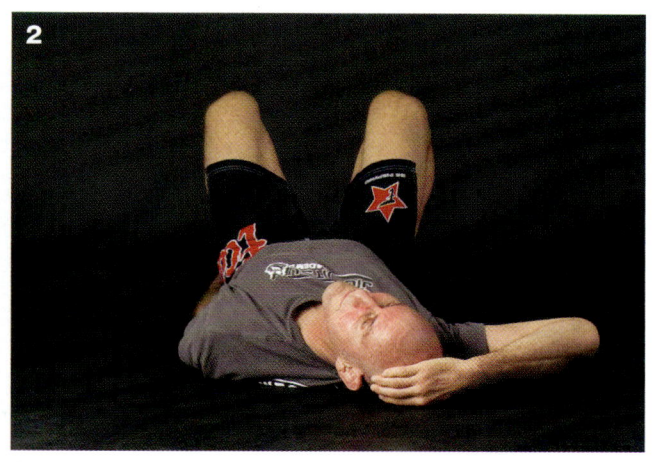

Staying relaxed, use your right hand to gently pull your head to your right shoulder. Maintain a grip on your left ankle with your left hand to stretch the left side of your neck.

The backbend stretches the neck, back and abdomen by arching your hips to the sky, but it must be done carefully to avoid straining the neck or lower back. This kind of stretch not only helps competitors avoid back injuries but is also a good exercise for improving your game, especially when you need to lift an opponent into the air and create a bridge movement to escape.

Backbend

Lie with your back on the ground. Pull your feet close to your rear end and place your palms on the ground just past your shoulders.

**Pushing with your palms and the balls of your feet, lift your hips high into the air as you gently roll the top of your head onto the ground to stretch your neck.
You can make the move easier on your neck by bearing more weight on your hands.**

The stomach is an overlooked area that you need to stretch, and the side stretch is a good exercise for loosening up the side abdominal muscles and rib cage. This limberness will come in handy when you are either trying to twist and escape or twist and take someone down. It will also prevent muscle tears to the sides, but as always, remember to execute the stretch with control.

Side Stretch

Sit on your left side and lock your left elbow with your left hand perpendicular to your legs.

Pull your right foot in, placing it in front of your left knee. Keeping your left arm locked straight, relax the left side of your stomach and lower it to the ground.

A good stretch for the lower body is the modified hurdler stretch, which works the hamstrings. Hamstrings are used for takedowns, jumping, lunging, guarding, gripping and pulling to the guard. Basically, you use them a lot. Limber hamstrings prevent muscle pulls and tears, and it aids other movements like hip stretches.

Modified Hurdler Stretch

Sitting on the ground, place your left leg straight forward. Cross your right ankle just above your left knee.

Start to roll your hips forward, leaning down onto your left leg. This forces your right ankle into your left knee, which prohibits your left knee from bending and diminishing the stretch on your left hamstring.

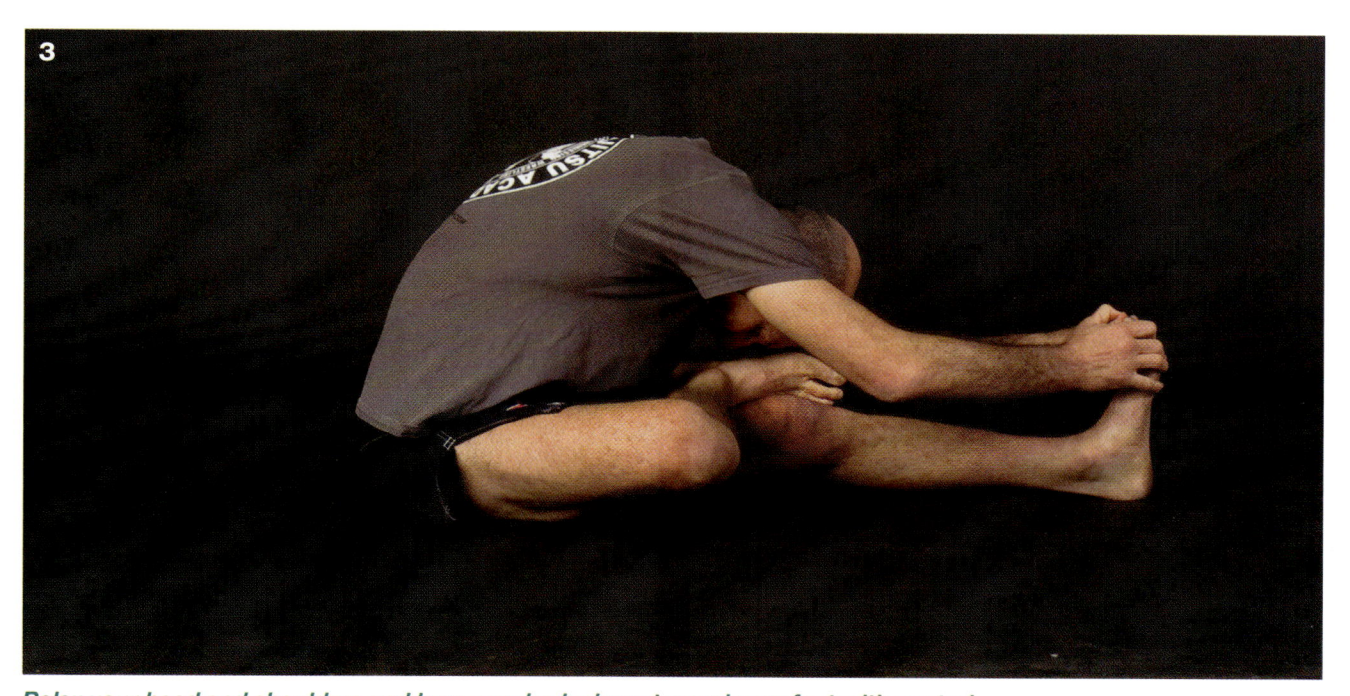

Relax your head and shoulders and lean your body down toward your foot with control.

If you want to stretch intelligently, you must use your time efficiently. One way to do this is to stretch after training. You need to cool down anyway, and stretching while your body is hot is the best time to improve your flexibility. Another method of time conservation is stretching at home, such as when you're watching television or reading this book.

Improving Your Grappling Endurance

At the start of a competition, most grapplers perform at their maximum potential. However, by the end of the match, they perform their techniques with the precision of a less experienced grappler. Their skill level drops because their bodies just can't execute the same caliber of techniques with as much precision when fatigued. So how do you find a way to stay fresh and not tire?

The answer is through developing endurance. Often, competitors take their competition endurance for granted or completely misunderstand it. They assume that if they can train for an hour straight without rest, then they'll be able to compete in a five-minute match with ease, which is false. A lot of grapplers aren't used to channeling the explosive strength required for competition and handling the pressure and adrenaline that comes from performing in front of a crowd. Therefore, they must train specifically to increase their competition-relevant endurance and stamina.

Of course, the fastest way to improve your grappling endurance is through high-intensity grappling, but this increases your risk of injury. Instead, it's better to perform relevant endurance exercises. To do this, envision how you grapple and then apply it to your off-the-mat workout. For example, instead of running 90 minutes at a steady pace, run 90 minutes at an uneven pace that mimics the unpredictable starts and stops of a real match. First, do a good warm-up that might include a steady 30-minute run for general endurance. Then, do irregular sprints by running up a staircase. You could even swim in a pool. At this point, you want to try to recreate the starts and stops of a tournament by exercising at full force for 30 to 60 seconds and then giving yourself insufficient time to rest in between.

Insufficient rest is crucial because that's what happens in competition—you never get enough time to recover your strength before you have to fight at full power again. This type of exercise is known as "anaerobic" training because you are operating your muscles without enough oxygen. They are in a state of "oxygen debt."

A good way to increase your endurance while in oxygen debt is through deficit training—or more specifically, energy-deficit training. Much like the "King of the Hill" game mentioned earlier, energy-deficit training makes use of fresh partners to push tired partners into action in hard and unpredictable ways.

The best way to train with an energy deficit is by facing several partners who rotate in one at a time to spar with a defender that is not allowed to take a break. Some examples of energy-deficit scenarios include the following:

- Every three minutes, a new, fresh opponent rotates in and you start a new match, taking no rest between matches. This is the same scenario I faced in "King of the Hill."

- Every two minutes, a new, fresh opponent takes the place of your existing opponent and assumes the exact same position as the person he is replacing.

- Every two minutes, a new, fresh opponent attacks you from behind regardless of the position you are in, literally jumping into the match and freeing your previous opponent to leave the mat.

Remember, deficit training is about how much you want to win. It prepares you for when you need to dig deep the most: when you are losing the match, when time is running out or when you are completely out of energy. All the preparation, all your classes and all the effort to sign up and show up at the tournament is on the line in those few moments. (People rarely experience this in normal training because they can always tap and start over.) When the end of the match is in sight, you must gather all you have and break through the barriers your opponent has placed in your way. Coming back from a deficit is how you prove that you're a champion, which is something you must train for over and over and over.

It's also important to note that there's the actual loss of endurance, and then there's how you react to it. Continuing to fight as best you can, even though your endurance is dropping, can be the deciding factor between winning and loosing. That's why it's a good idea not only to increase your endurance but also to mentally prepare for the loss of it.

When Rigan Machado thought that one of his students was overreacting to oxygen debt and feeling claustrophobic from being trapped beneath him, he would cover the student's mouth with his gi. While his intentions were positive, I can say from firsthand experience that it was a terrible and frightening feeling. He would watch while students panicked beneath his tight control and not let them tap out. He forced students to learn that their feeling of suffocation was just that—a feeling and not a fact. After a hard training match, he would make students lie on the ground with their gi covering their faces so they would become comfortable with the feeling that they didn't have enough air. Now when I feel like I am going to pass out and need more air, I count to 10 in my mind and the fear passes. Machado's tough training gave me the mental endurance that allows me to keep fighting.

Martial artists must learn to distinguish between discomfort and physical injury. You must also be able to tell the difference between running out of air and feeling like you're running out of air. In all my years of training and competing, I have never seen someone pass out on the mat because of exhaustion. But I have watched a thousand times as people have stopped grappling, reporting that they can't continue because of exhaustion. That is the mind giving up, not the body.

Remember that in martial arts, pain is mandatory but suffering is optional. Pain and discomfort are physical sensations—suffering is a mental reaction you place over those physical sensations. When you are out of breath, you are simply that—out of breath in oxygen debt and needing more air. It sucks, but you are not passing out or dying—it just feels that way. You must learn to ignore those feelings and continue to do your best, which is why energy-deficit training is so important for mental preparation.

Mental control can also help conceal how tired you are. In a competition match, visible fatigue, like gasping for air, can give your opponent encouragement to fight harder while appearing as if you are not tired can demoralize your opponent. My training partners Jake Shields and Gilbert Melendez are masters at this—they seem to get stronger and more energetic the more tired they get, and it really wears down their opponents.

One way to hide your fatigue in competition is to wait for a pause in the action, then draw a deep breath and let it out even slower than it came in. Shorter inhales and longer exhales have the effect of calming your breathing down (similar to briefly inhaling and then singing or chanting, which requires a much longer, slower exhale and is calming to the body). Another good trick when you are out of breath and panting is to take a breath in and then lengthen your exhale by uttering a series of short, quick "chh chh chh" sounds. Brazilian fighters use this technique. It causes you to lengthen each exhale, which gets your breathing back under control.

Remember, in a competition, you will never feel rested enough before having to make another explosive move, so be disciplined in your endurance homework.

Athletic Performance and Your Grappling Diet

In computer programming, they say "garbage in, garbage out." It is also true in terms of what you eat and your athletic performance. Grappling is unique among sports because it is a total body exercise, and for the body to operate fully, competitors try to feed their body the best fuel possible. It's important that you think about what you eat and that you recognize that improvements in your diet can mean more energy for training and competition, less time off because of illness and even fewer injuries.

Before looking at your diet, let's look at what can happen because of what you drink, or more specifically, what you don't drink. One of the biggest nutritional problems that grapplers face is chronic dehydration, which is a lack of water in your system. It can cause fatigue, overheating and muscle tears because soft tissues do not have enough lubrication. Dehydration is a big concern for grapplers because of the high amount of sweating that occurs on the mat, especially if a competitor is training in a heavy and hot gi.

To combat this problem, drink between three to four liters of water a day, especially if you are training hard for a competition. If you don't have enough water, your muscles will not function properly because your blood will become thicker and harder for your heart to pump. And without blood flow, your muscles cannot get the oxygen and other nutrients they need to function properly. Think of water as the oil that helps run a well-tuned machine—your body. By drinking water at regular intervals throughout the day, especially before, during and after workout sessions, you optimize your body's ability to physically perform.

Water vs. Other Drinks

Just because you substitute another fluid for water doesn't mean that you are rehydrating yourself. It's not just fluid you need; it is water specifically. In general, it's better to minimize your intake of soft drinks and sports drinks with high fructose corn syrup and other processed sweeteners. These drinks give you a short-term energy boost that causes an eventual crash in your energy level. Fresh fruit and vegetable juices are ideal because they give you excellent nutrients. But remember that in the end, you should always rely on good old water.

In regards to food, it's important to consider what you put inside your body because, believe it or not, the digestive process uses up a lot of your body's energy. Think about it: After a large meal, don't you usually feel tired? That's because your body is busy transferring energy through the blood to your stomach and intestines in order to digest the food you just ate.

Natural, fresh foods like fruits and vegetables are easy for your body to digest because they have not had their enzymes destroyed during the cooking process. In contrast, processed or synthetic foods, which would include any food that comes in a box or a bag and whose ingredients contain a long list of chemicals you cannot pronounce, are difficult to digest because they have lost their natural enzymes during the cooking process. They also often contain artificial additives for color, texture and taste, and can have preservatives—all of which are not easy for your body to digest.

Grapplers, like most athletes, need to consume a balanced diet of protein for muscle cell growth and recovery, and carbohydrates and healthy fats for energy usage. Whether you realize it or not, the food you eat and when you eat it can greatly affect how you train. When you work out, your body uses a lot of energy, which reduces your glycogen stores. If you don't replenish those after you train, then you will experience an overall lower energy level and will not have power for your next training session. Likewise, if you eat dinner late at night, your full stomach may affect how soundly you sleep

Benefits of Vegetarianism and Veganism

Well-balanced proteins are good for the body, but high cholesterol foods such as meats and cheeses are also strong contributors to blockage of the arteries. Anyone diagnosed with a clinical problem of high cholesterol or other heart disease is told to eliminate fatty animal products from their diet, including cheeses and high fat meats. The buildup of plaque in your circulatory system that is caused by cholesterol, besides being unhealthy and a major cause of heart attacks, is an obstruction of the system that carries blood around your body. That is the blood that you, as a competitor, need flowing full force when you are exercising and competing. Any blockage of the blood flow means less oxygen to the muscles, poorer performance and a slower recovery. Nonanimal products, including grains, vegetables, legumes, fruit, etc., are entirely cholesterol free, so they do not contribute to the buildup of plaque in your arteries.

Also, many people notice that when they consume dairy products, they feel a slight congestion in their chest. This is because most humans are to one degree or another lactose intolerant, and this has an effect when you consume cow's milk. So consuming less dairy, especially in the weeks and days before a competition, can result in clearer nasal passages and less phlegm in the lungs—these are both crucial factors in being able to breathe well during heavy exercise.

Meats and dairy also contain high concentrations of pesticide residues from the many thousands of pounds of food that cows consume as they are fattened for slaughter. Those pesticides, as well as antibiotics and other drugs, are fed to farm animals to keep them alive under what are often the most inhumane of conditions. These man-made "additives" are then stored in their tissues and passed directly into your body when you consume meat and dairy. This can be mitigated to some extent by consuming only hormone, antibiotic and pesticide-free organic and "free range" products.

by tending to cause excessive dreaming, and this can make you tired the next day. Your diet plays an important role in your game, and that affects your competition.

It is important to note that many top BJJ and submission-grappling competitors in the world adhere to a vegetarian (no meat) or vegan (no animal products) diet. The Gracie family is known for the "Gracie Diet," developed by Carlos Gracie Sr. over the course of his lifetime. It is largely a vegetarian diet and involves a combination of fats, oils and vegetables, cereals, sweet and acidic fruits, bananas, milk and an optional small amount of animal-based protein like fish or chicken.

Obviously, the phenomenal track record of Gracie fighters over the last century suggests that the diet works. I and many of the fighters I have trained notice that reducing meat and dairy intake and switching to a good balance of soy, vegetables, fruits, grains, etc. has helped our athletic performance and overall energy level. In my case, I've eliminated meat and dairy from my diet and have been a strict vegetarian for more than 20 years. However, I encourage you to do what works best for your body. Consult a nutritionist, keep a log of what food you eat and see whether it affects your performance. Experiment by weaning yourself off certain products like meat or dairy. Review your diet and consider what you think is the worst thing you consume—too many sweets, processed or fast food, meat, dairy or eating too much in general—and alter it to see whether it changes how you feel physically about your game. But ultimately, the decision is always up to you.

Coping With Injury

If you find yourself injured, remember the two basic rules for speeding up your recovery time:

- Maintain blood flow.
- Do not aggravate or injure the area again.

Maintaining the blood flow in and out of the injured area is crucial because hurt tissues need nutrients to heal, and those nutrients are carried to the wounded area by your blood. When you are hurt, the affected area tends to swell, causing a blood traffic jam that obstructs the free flow of blood. In order to combat this typical physiological reaction, apply a cold pack to the area immediately. I recommend that you purchase a rubber cold pack with a plastic screw on its lid—they are available at any drugstore. Fill 40 percent of the cold pack with rubbing alcohol and 60 percent with water, then store it in a freezer. The mixture will harden into a snowlike slush, which makes it more flexible and able to conform to the injured body part. It will also be really cold, so don't hold the cold pack directly against your skin for too long.

Also, remember that you must intersperse periods of cold with periods of warmth. If you use cold alone, you will bring down the swelling, but you will also contract the blood vessels to a point at which circulation slows down. I recommend that you alternate between 10 minutes with the cold pack and 10 minutes with a warm pack, always beginning and ending with cold. This hot-and-cold switch will act as a gentle massage, drawing blood in and forcing it away from the affected area and ensuring that nutrients are reaching the injured tissues.

The second rule of a speedy recovery is to not re-injure yourself. Don't train before you are fully healed and resist the temptation to keep testing the injury by moving your arm or leg. This is obvious, but it is an extremely common scenario—I've even done it myself. So when you first feel OK enough to train, remember that your injury is most likely not fully healed. In fact, the hurt body part is weak even if the fighter feels eager to jump back onto the mat and train. My strong advice is that injured grapplers should pay attention to their body. Wait until you feel you can safely train again, then extend your recovery period for another two weeks. If you miss a competition, then you miss it. There will be others. You don't want to create a situation in which you now have a chronic weakness or reoccuring injury for the rest of your life.

With that said, I want to also mention that it may be possible to continue training when you are hurt. This is because it's possible to modify the way in which you spar with your partners to accommodate certain injuries. The risk is possible, but it does require careful consideration and can prove beneficial in the long run.

For example, when I was a blue belt, I traveled with my coach, Rigan Machado, and another student to train with Carlos Gracie Jr. in Rio de Janeiro, Brazil. On the fourth day of my eight-day trip, I twisted my elbow while attempting a sweep. The pain was sharp, and there was some swelling, which I immediately iced, but the next day I found that I couldn't use my arm for training. However, before I could think about quitting, I remembered that Jean Jacques Machado was born with only one finger on his left hand. To society, it was an obvious handicap, but it had never stopped him from training or becoming a champion among grapplers. I thought to myself: If Jean Jacques Machado can train with almost no fingers on one hand for his whole life, I could certainly train using only one arm for a few days.

Of course, if I was going to train injured, then I was going to do it smartly by not aggravating or hurting my arm again. I trained by gripping my gi with my hurt arm and not using it to perform any techniques. This meant that I had to fight in my guard and with my legs, which was terribly frustrating at first because I was easy to beat. Still, after two days of training with one arm, an interesting thing began to happen. I was spending so much time fighting from my guard that my guard and my legwork started to improve. In fact, my guard was not getting passed anymore. By the third day of training, my guard seemed invincible against other blue belts, and on my last day of training, when my arm felt good enough to use again, my attacks and sweeps from my guard came alive. I had made a huge leap forward, and I still feel the benefits of that training in my game today. Thank goodness I hurt my arm!

Now I want to clearly point out that our rule from the previous chapter still applies: Avoid injury at any cost! However, if it happens despite your best efforts, then take a moment to consider whether this is an opportunity for you to focus on a new part of your game and be creative. I don't recommend that you take this risk with any injury, especially if training might aggravate or re-injure it. In my case, I knew that I could train by only fighting from my guard and keeping my arm gripped to my gi, which meant my elbow remained close to my body. With a finger injury, it may be possible to tape your hand up and bind your fingers completely. With an ankle injury, it may be possible to tape it and not spar from a standing position but start every training match in the guard.

If you find, however, that your injury prevents you from training, then don't train. Also, never compete if you are hurt because you can't perform effectively unless each limb is working 100 percent. Remember that the bane of every competitor is an injury that keeps him from the mat, and that is why you should be careful. Injuries slow down progress and may even stop it completely.

Section III

FOCUSING ON THE GOAL

Competition-Specific Training and Strategies

Chapter 6
Game Plans

In the last section, we discussed what you should always be doing to make yourself a better overall grappler. Now let's look at how you can focus those attributes on the competition specifically.

When you step onto the competition mat, you should have specific "game plans" for how you will start the match and what your overall goal will be once you hit the ground. Similar to when you begin a trip in your car, your game plan is like a list of directions. You never know whether your car will break down, whether roads will be closed, or how weather conditions will turn out, but you are more likely to arrive at your destination if you start with a specific set of directions, even if you have to modify them along the way.

To help illustrate my point, I'm going to use a story that John Will likes to tell about an instructor who taught at a kickboxing seminar. The instructor invited two students to spar with each other. The fighters traded blows for the first round but neither of them scored any authoritative strikes. The instructor then took each fighter aside for a moment. He told the first fighter that he was doing a good job and generally encouraged him to keep it up. To the second fighter, the instructor said that, if he landed a blow square on his opponent's nose, the instructor would give him $50. In other words, he gave the second fighter a specific game plan.

Sure enough, not long into the second round, the second fighter landed that blow square on the nose of the first fighter. What changed was that the second fighter went from generally trying to hit any part of his opponent to having a specific target to hit. With that specific game plan, he was able to succeed.

In grappling terms, this means that if one grappler is simply going with the flow to see what moves he can execute against a grappler who is focused on completing a very specific game plan, the second grappler will have a better chance of winning.

But game plans are a bit more complicated than that. A competition match is a fluid and organic fight between you and a person, who is a variable that you can't control, and this is why you need a fluid and multifaceted plan of attack. In this chapter, we'll discuss the breakdown of a game plan, especially your starting game plan, your overall game plan (between the start and finish of a match) and the game plan you should use if you need to restart the match.

Blocking Your Opponent's Plan

Before we talk about your initial game plan, let's look at blocking your opponent's ability to execute his game plan. This involves how you stand and how you defend against his attempts to grab you or take you down. Denying your opponent a way to successfully start the fight will open the door for you to execute your starting plan or even your overall game plan.

In both Brazilian jiu-jitsu and submission grappling, competition matches always begin with both fighters standing at a distance. In Brazilian jiu-jitsu, the ability to grab the uniform and halt or redirect your opponent's forward motion for a takedown allows you to safely stand a bit closer to your opponent and a bit straighter up than you would in submission grappling. In both formats, you should assume a stance with one foot forward and the other foot back while standing on the ball of your back foot, ready to launch forward or sprawl backward. You should have one hand lightly extended to grasp your opponent, but you should not be so committed to that grab that your arm is easily pulled away from you.

Proper BJJ Starting Stance

David Meyer stands with one foot back and his elbows in, making it hard for an opponent to grab his arms.

Meyer and Adam Treanor face each other, ready to attack. Notice how neither is exposing their arms for a grab.

When fighting in submission grappling, you must keep more space between you and your opponent. This is because you cannot as easily block a takedown attempt by grabbing your opponent's uniform.

Proper Submission-Grappling Starting Stance

David Meyer stands with one foot back, arms in, and crouches low, ready to shoot in or sprawl backward.

Both Meyer and his opponent Adam Treanor are ready to take advantage of opportunities for a takedown.

What these stances should reveal is that generally a competitor's goal in Brazilian jiu-jitsu is to prevent a grip and in submission grappling to prevent the opponent from making a takedown. However, at the same time, your evasions against these moves should give you the opportunity to get the grips and takedowns that you want to initiate your game plan.

In order to do that, you need to know how to deny your opponent's opening moves. In Brazilian jiu-jitsu, it's especially important to know how to deny a grip because you're wearing a uniform. The best way to do this is to deflect an opponent's hands through misdirection as he attempts to grab you.

Misdirection

David Meyer (right) and Adam Treanor face each other at close range.

Treanor shoots out with his left hand to grab at Meyer's lapel.

Meyer uses his right hand to deflect Treanor's left hand.

Treanor then uses his right hand to reach for Meyer's lapel, but Meyer deflects it using his own left hand.

Before a competition, you should spend some time drilling for misdirection. Remember that you not only want to use your hands to deny your opponent the grips he is seeking but also want to do evasive body maneuvers. These movements include stepping laterally or twisting to the side with the misdirection.

If, despite all your preparation, your opponent does manage to grip your BJJ uniform, then you need to be ready with some moves to free yourself from his hold.

Training for Competition: Brazilian Jiu-Jitsu and Submission Grappling

Breaking the Grip: Lapel

Adam Treanor succeeds in grabbing David Meyer's lapel with his left hand.

Meyer brings his hips forward and lays both his hands over the top of Treanor's hand.

Meyer pushes downward strongly with his hands and jerks his neck up, causing his lapel to move upward.

Meyer continues to push his hands down on Treanor's fingers and stretch his neck up until the lapel is completely free.

Breaking the Grip: Sleeve

Adam Treanor succeeds in grabbing David Meyer's right sleeve with his left hand.

Meyer drops his right hand down toward the center of his body.

Meyer then lifts his right knee and turns his hips to his left, dropping his right knee across the top of Treanor's wrist.

Meyer drops his weight forward and presses down with his shin while he pulls his sleeve up and away to the left, breaking Treanor's grip.

Grips can also lead to takedowns, which is why its equally important to prevent your opponent from grabbing your lapel. Besides keeping your upper body from being grabbed, you also must pay attention to your lower body, specifically your pants. This is because your opponent can just as easily take you down by grabbing them as he can with the lapel.

Breaking the Grip: Pants

Adam Treanor (left) succeeds in grabbing David Meyer's right pant leg with his left hand. Wrapping his right hand around Treanor's gripping hand, Meyer wraps his own fingers underneath his opponent's to get his hand in between Treanor's grip and his own pant's leg.

Then Meyer pulls up strongly with his right hand and he steps down strongly with his right leg to break the grip.

As I mentioned earlier, often BJJ competitors need to be aware of how their opponents can grip a uniform for a takedown. However, even if your opponent fails to successfully grip your uniform, he can still bring you to the ground. Therefore, it is also important that you are able to block his takedown entry.

Takedown Defense With a Gi

1 Adam Treanor (left) plans to shoot in for David Meyer's leg.

2 When Treanor goes in for a takedown, Meyer holds him back. Meyer uses his right hand to hold his opponent's collar and his left hand to block Treanor's right arm.

3 Meyer then steps back with his left leg to stay out of Treanor's reach.

If there is no gi to grab, then it is more difficult to halt your opponent's entry. This means that your primary defense will be your body movement. You can, of course, move side to side, but if someone has shot in quickly and is beginning to grab your legs, the strongest defense is to jump your legs back behind you and sprawl.

Takedown Defense With No Gi: Sprawl

Adam Treanor (left) prepares for the shoot.

Treanor lowers his level and shoots forward to initiate the match with a double-leg takedown.

Treanor penetrates deeply in an attempt to use his hands to trap David Meyer's legs behind the knees.

Meyer jumps his legs back, changing his body from a vertical to horizontal position as quickly as he can. He drops his weight heavily onto one hip as he twists down onto Treanor's shoulder.

Meyer then circles around behind Treanor to set up attacks.

The example on the opposite page shows how to sprawl against a double-leg takedown, but some grapplers know that it can be easier to get a hold of a single leg instead. When someone shoots for your lead leg, it is sometimes impossible to sprawl away before he grabs it. If your leg has been caught, here is an effective defense against being taken down.

Single-Leg Takedown Defense

1. Adam Treanor (right) prepares to shoot in on David Meyer.

2. Treanor moves in quickly and gets a hold of Meyer's left leg.

3. Before Meyer can sprawl, Treanor drives Meyer's weight onto Meyer's right leg. He then lifts Meyer's left leg into the air, which puts Meyer in danger of being taken to the ground.

4. Meyer uses his right hand to hold Treanor's head down and away from Meyer's body. As he circles his left foot out from between Treanor's legs, Meyer uses his foot to hook the outside of Treanor's right leg.

5. Meyer then jumps his right leg back for balance as well as to create space between him and his opponent. He also uses his shin to block Treanor from stepping in closer.

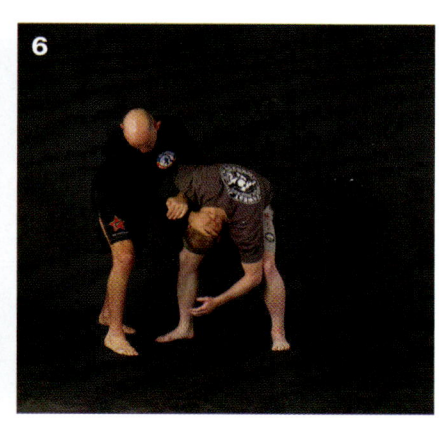

6. Placing his left hand on his right wrist, Meyer executes a figure-4 lock. He pushes down on his opponent's head with his hands as he kicks his left leg back and to the ground, breaking Treanor's grip.

Before the competition, you should practice your takedown defenses by having your partners lightly and repeatedly shoot in for double- and single-leg takedowns. Practice sprawling and twisting your hip onto their shoulders, or let your partners catch a leg so you can test your ability to free it.

It is important to realize that some people in competition do not want to shoot in for a takedown; rather, they want to pull you into their guard for a sweep or finish. This can be harder to do in submission grappling because there is no uniform to pull you in with. Ideally, you'll be able to break any grips your opponent might make before he can try to pull you down. But if you do get pulled toward the guard, here is a good way to stay standing.

Staying Out of the Guard

Adam Treanor (left) succeeds in getting a hold of David Meyer's sleeve.

He goes to the ground, attempting to drag Meyer down into his guard.

To stay out of the guard, Meyer steps in slightly with his feet to keep from falling forward onto his knees. He also keeps his elbows on his hips, which prevents his arms from being pulled forward into a triangle or armbar, making it impossible for Treanor to place his feet on Meyer's hips to effect a sweep. Now, Meyer is free to initiate a guard pass.

As you can see, blocking your opponent's ability to initiate and carry out his starting game plan involves the following:

- evading your opponent's attempt at grips
- breaking free of those grips
- blocking your opponent's attempts to shoot in
- sprawling to defend against a takedown
- preventing yourself from being pulled into someone's guard

If you can do all that, you are ready to look at how you can start the match with the confidence you need to execute your own game plan.

Your Starting Game Plan

You can't know in advance how the match will actually unfold or end, but you do know exactly how the match will begin. All grappling competition matches begin with both fighters standing, and this allows you to create a specific game plan for how you will start the competition.

Because you are standing, your starting game plan depends on what techniques you are good at doing on your feet. If you have a wrestling background, your starting game plan will likely involve a takedown. If your takedowns are weak, then you probably will want to pull someone down to the guard.

Your starting game plan will also be determined by what you are good at on the ground. If you are better grappling on top, you will either want to take your opponent down or possibly pull him to your guard for an immediate sweep to get you on top. If you fight better overall from your guard, you may want to pull your partner down into your guard and hold him there for submissions. The key is to identify one or two specific moves or steps that you are good at executing and that are likely to put you in a good position for success. It also should go without saying that these moves shouldn't leave you in a terrible position if they fail.

The reason you want to have one or two moves is that you want to have a follow-up plan in case the first move doesn't work or is countered. In a competition, first moves often "fail," but that doesn't mean the move is a "failure." Because the move will force your opponent to commit his body to a reaction, your second move should capitalize on it so you can still execute your game plan. Basically, the first move feeds the second move—they are not separate moves but rather a combination. If the first move succeeds in taking down the opponent, then great, but if not, you're already set up for your second move, which not only gives you a focus on how to start the match but also options.

BJJ Starting Game Plan

In this game plan, David Meyer (right) wants to take his opponent to the ground and still be on top. To do that, Meyer initiates the match by grabbing onto Adam Treanor's right sleeve with his left hand and onto the left lapel with his right hand. He inches his foot forward, causing Treanor to think he can shoot in to grab it for a takedown.

As Treanor steps forward, Meyer snaps Treanor down to the ground with both hands while stepping back. The reason he does this is to prevent Treanor from grabbing his legs.

With Treanor on the ground, Meyer drops his body on top of his opponent, releasing his original grips and achieving his ultimate goal.

BJJ Starting Game Plan: Variation

1 David Meyer (right) initiates the match by gripping Adam Treanor's right sleeve with his left hand and left lapel with his right hand. Even though he inches his foot forward, Treanor resists being snapped down to the ground. Meyer quickly realizes this and moves on to his second move.

2 Meyer pulls Treanor forward and up onto the balls of his feet to do his second game-plan move.

3 He bends his knees, steps in with his right foot and pivots his body in front of and just below Treanor.

4 He continues to pull Treanor forward and off his feet to execute a judo throw.

5 Once Treanor is on Meyer's back, Meyer drops his right shoulder and rolls Treanor to the ground.

6 With Treanor off his back, Meyer recovers his posture so as not to be pulled forward and off-balance when Treanor lands on the ground. Now, Meyer can drop down on top of Treanor, achieving his ultimate starting goal.

Even though the two above game plans demonstrate a first move followed by a potential second, it's important to remember that competitions are fluid, starts are quick and game plans should not be set in stone. For example, if the situation calls for it, a competitor might have to change his game plans, meaning that "Step 2" in a game plan doesn't always have to be the backup move. Instead, it can become the main game plan.

It's also necessary to note that the above game plans won't work in submission grappling because they involve grips on a uniform. However, that doesn't mean all game plans are exclusive to Brazilian jiu-jitsu or to submission grappling; instead, some game plans are plausible in both formats.

The following game plan does not require a high level of skill to execute, which is good for grapplers who don't have wrestling takedown skills. (See next page.)

BJJ or Submission-Grappling Game Plan

1. David Meyer grips Adam Treanor's right sleeve or wrist (if there is no gi) with his left hand.

2. Meyer pulls Treanor's arm strongly down toward his left foot. If the opponent falls to his knees, then this move is complete, but it's unlikely this will happen.

3. It's more likely that Treanor will push off his front foot to pull his arm back. Meyer takes advantage of this reaction and lets go of his opponent's hand.

4. As Treanor's right hand retracts, Meyer shoots in low, reaching his left hand around the outside of Treanor's right heel.

5. Meyer falls forward to his knees and places his head on the inside of Treanor's right leg.

6. Meyer then holds Treanor's foot in place as he pushes his head to the left and down into Treanor's knee.

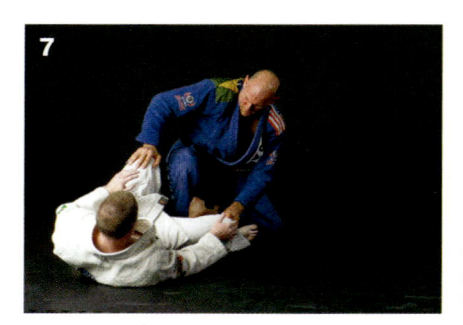

7. As Treanor falls to the side, Meyer rises up in position to begin passing Treanor's guard.

I hope that you're noticing that in all the game plans, the competitor (you) wants to initiate the match. At its simplest terms, your starting game plan is your starting move because you not only dictate your first action but also dictate your opponent's first reaction.

Initiating the match doesn't always have to be offensive. For example, you can bait the opponent by starting out with what seems like a defensive or sloppy move, i.e., letting the opponent grab your wrist. The important distinction is that you know the move is set up while your opponent doesn't.

Baiting the Opponent

1 David Meyer (right) lets his right hand drift out in front of Adam Treanor, giving him the opportunity to grab at it.

2 Treanor takes the bait and grips the right wrist.

3 Meyer quickly springs into action. He brings his right elbow forward to touch Treanor's left elbow. This uses leverage to pry his wrist free. At the same time, Meyer reaches with his left hand to control Treanor's right wrist.

4 Meyer then steps forward with his right foot as he pulls Treanor toward him. Meyer reaches his right arm under Treanor's left arm, and Meyer hugs his chest close to Treanor's arm so Treanor cannot pull his arm away. This is called an arm drag.

5 Meyer bends forward, pressuring Treanor's arm and making him stand up and pull back to maintain his balance.

6 Meyer suddenly lets go of Treanor's arm, allowing Treanor's upper body to pop back up, while Meyer stays low and shoots in to grab Treanor's left leg for a single-leg takedown.

7 Meyer drives Treanor back onto his right leg, which makes Treanor's left leg light and easy to lift.

8 Meyer then spins hard to the right as he uses the right side of his head to press down into Treanor's hip.

9 Because of the pressure downward and the twist, Treanor cannot adjust his balance and is forced to fall.

Training for Competition: Brazilian Jiu-Jitsu and Submission Grappling

Because I often prefer to be on top, many of my starting game plans help me get into that position. However, it's important to also know how you can pull to your guard and then end up on top. While this may be easier to do in Brazilian jiu-jitsu because of the gi, the following game plans are still useful in submission grappling:

Open Guard to Sweep

David Meyer (left) uses his right hand to grab Adam Treanor's left sleeve. He also uses his left hand to grab Treanor's lapel behind the neck.

Then Meyer jumps forward with only his feet and hangs from Treanor's uniform, dropping all his weight to the ground.

This not only helps Meyer get down on the ground in an open guard but also helps him drag Treanor down with him.

To prevent his opponent from posting, Meyer pulls Treanor's left arm forward. He also lifts his left foot in order to knock Treanor off-balance and make him roll.

As Treanor falls to his back, Meyer rolls over, staying on Treanor's left side while twisting his right knee forward and out of Treanor's legs.

Meyer finishes the move on Treanor's side in side control.

120

It is possible that with the previous move, your opponent will stay standing and resist being dragged down. Now it's time for that contingency move I mentioned, taking advantage of your opponent's reaction.

Guard to Sweep Contingency Plan

David Meyer (left) uses his right hand to grab Adam Treanor's left sleeve and his left hand to grab Treanor's lapel behind his neck.

Meyer then jumps his feet forward and hangs his weight from his grips on Treanor's uniform.

Treanor resists being pulled down and presses hard with his feet to remain standing.

Meyer then places his left foot in front of Treanor's hips and places his right heel on the side, behind Treanor's right heel.

Pushing with his left foot and pulling back with his right heel, Meyer forces his opponent to fall backward.

As Treanor falls, Meyer uses that momentum to pull himself up. He also pushes off the ground with his right hand to come onto one knee.

Now, Meyer is on top and ready to initiate a guard pass.

It's also possible to fight from your guard, which is preferable if you are very skilled in that position. Of course, you can always initiate the match by attempting to pull an opponent immediately into your guard, but it's better if you attempt a fake takedown. The reason for this is because it not only means you don't need to find a grip with which to pull someone down, but it also appears more aggressive to the referee.

Faking a Takedown to Pull to the Guard

1. David Meyer (right) and Adam Treanor square off.

2. Meyer lowers his level and shoots forward for a double-leg takedown, or so it seems.

3. As Treanor sprawls, Meyer stops his forward momentum and places his left elbow on the ground to support his and Treanor's weight.

4. Meyer then turns onto his left hip and brings his legs around to the right and underneath Treanor.

5. Because Treanor ends up sitting on Meyer's feet in the butterfly guard, Meyer can then initiate his guard attacks.

Game Plans and Points

A starting game plan ensures that you are able to take the initiative in the match. It is designed to place you in the position in which you are strongest to fight from. Your starting game plan can involve a quick finish or a way to score points, but it doesn't have to because that isn't its main purpose. Instead, playing the points is the skill you use throughout the match, so that in each decision you make, you are considering whether you have the best chance of getting the most possible points. The best fighters have a good starting game plan and know how to play the points. I'll discuss how to play the points in greater detail in the next chapter.

How to Restart the Match After the Clock Stops

Sometimes during a competition match, the referee may call a temporary stop to the action. There are several reasons for this, such as the fight is too close to the edge of the mat, a competitor is injured or bleeding and the referee wants to investigate, or the fight's stalled—the competitors are stuck in one position and can't seem to break out of it. Especially in cases like the last, the referee will call a timeout. If he does, remember that you must remain frozen in your exact position until told to move, but the chances are that the referee will ask both fighters to break position and restart the match from a standing position.

What does this mean?

It's time to implement your starting game plan again.

Some things to note about restarting game plans is that you need to initiate the match again with the same level of aggression that you first began. No matter how tired you are, actively engage your opponent as soon as the referee says, "Go!" Because the time has already passed and the end is near, this aggression and initiation may impress the referee, who might have to decide the winner based on a potential tie at the match's conclusion. This energetic display of endurance can also send an important and disheartening message to your opponent, which is that you aren't as tired as he probably is.

Additionally, re-initiating your game plan means that you can change your position, which is good especially if you were in a bad one. What often happens in a restart is that both fighters immediately clinch and return to their same stalled position on the ground.

Returning to a Stall

1

In this example, Adam Treanor is in David Meyer's closed guard. The referee notes that both fighters are stalled and can't (or won't) act, so he breaks up the action.

2

With both fighters standing, the referee restarts the match.

3

Meyer grips Treanor.

4

Meyer pulls Treanor back down to the ground.

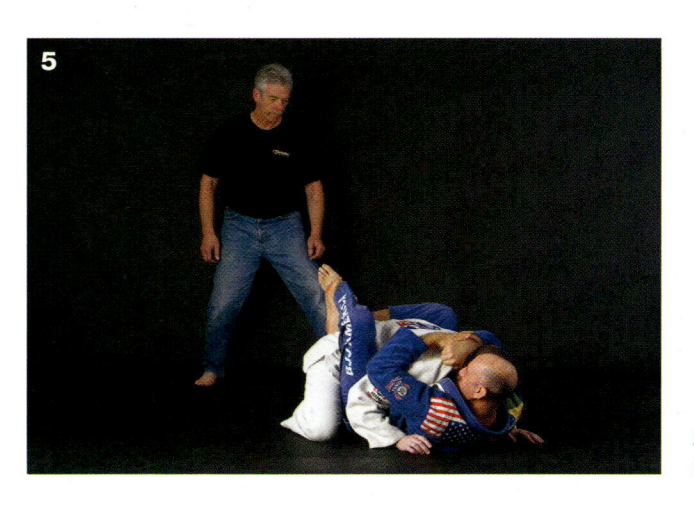

5

Meyer closes his guard, returning to the same position that the referee just broke up.

Of course, if you find the stalled position to your liking (perhaps you are ahead on points, using up the clock or were in a dominant position), then by all means let yourself go there again. If, however, you were on the losing end of the stall, it is crucial that you not let yourself fall back into that same position. Change the pattern of the fight, and do not follow the same steps that got you into the stalled position in the first place. This is technically your "restarting" game plan—a plan that does not end in the stalled position. Here is an example:

Restart Game Plan

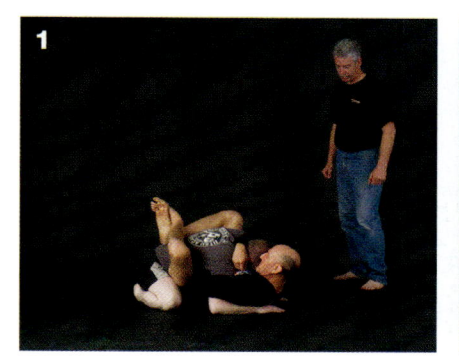

Adam Treanor (top) and David Meyer are stalled in the closed guard.

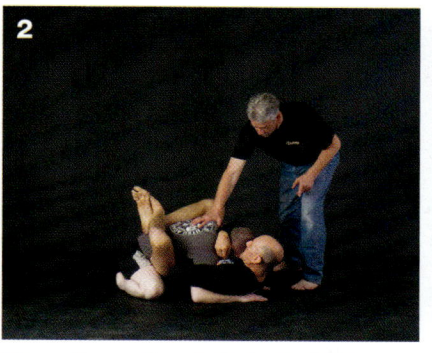

The referee signals to both fighters to stop the action and stand up.

Meyer unlocks his guard.

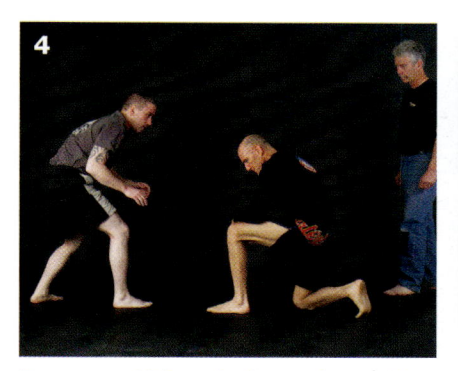

Treanor and Meyer both stand up, with Meyer staying intentionally at a close distance to set up an immediate takedown when the referee restarts the fight.

The referee signals to continue.

Rather than pull Treanor back into his guard or give Treanor time to initiate a game plan, Meyer immediately shoots in on Treanor for the low single-leg takedown.

Meyer traps Treanor's right heel.

Meyer presses his head to the left, causing Treanor to fall, and Meyer scores two points for the takedown.

As you can see, every time there is a break in the action called by the referee, it is a chance for you to jump out ahead in the fight and take the initiative when the fight starts again. Being aggressive in this way will impress the referee and wear down your opponent, and may just get you where you need to be to win the fight.

Practice Starting From Standing

As you've probably noticed, starting game plans and restarting game plans all begin from a standing position. Oftentimes, regular practice matches between students in a BJJ or submission-grappling school begin with both fighters on their knees on the ground. There are several reasons for this: More people can train on the mat at the same time, and it reduces injuries associated with takedowns and falls. Unfortunately, this means that many novice competitors come to a tournament without any takedown or throw experience that are essential at the start of a real match.

The fact of the matter is that it's important for you to feel comfortable standing. If you are not comfortable, then you get tense, waste a lot of energy, and you may not be able to execute your starting game plan. So if you do not spend a lot of time starting matches from a standing position at your school, you need to devote some concentrated time to that in the weeks before a competition. Otherwise, when you step onto the competition mat, your opponents may initiate their plan, drawing you into their plan, which is of course their area of strength.

Your Overall Game Plan

Your starting game plan is contingent on the moves that you'll execute whenever you are standing. However, most grappling matches generally end up on the ground, which is where most of the action takes place. This is why you need to develop an overall game plan to account for the time from when you hit the ground after the match's start to the match's end.

An overall game plan simply entails identifying your best position and the specific ways you can get there from every other possible grappling position. For example, if you prefer to be on top in side control, then you want to have at least one good takedown, one good sweep and one good guard pass that gets you there; this covers your standing, bottom and top position.

To continue with that example, you would create a list of statements, such as:

- I will try my favorite takedown. If it succeeds, I will be ready to pass the guard.

- I will then try my favorite guard pass until I get into side control.

- If I am taken down, I will get back to my guard and try my favorite sweep. If it succeeds, I will be back on top and ready to pass the guard.

- I will then try my favorite guard pass until I get to side control.

Your overall game plan needs to be very specific. It must tie all points together like a road map because at no point in the match do you want to simply grapple for the sake of grappling. You are more likely to succeed if you have a specific plan you are trying to execute. And even if you are not succeeding, you will at least be more likely to initiate action, causing your opponent to react and counter instead of executing his own strategies.

So ask yourself: "What is my favorite position?" Once you can answer that, ask, "Do I have a way to get there from every position?" If the answer is no, then your task is to develop paths to that position by talking to your instructor, other students or just thinking it through on your own.

Once you think you have your overall game plan worked out, spend a few weeks trying to implement it in training. See whether you can execute it. Notice how having a particular task in mind actually helps your training. As you improve, start your practice matches in different positions—including bad ones—and see whether you can still bring the fight back to your game plan and under your control. Once you get familiar with fighting based on a plan, you will see how it gives you a focus that brings you an advantage over people who are fighting without one.

Chapter 7
Learning to Use the Points and Clock

Having a game plan is important, but doing well in competition involves skills that go beyond simply knowing how to set up and execute techniques. A grappling competition revolves around an entire set of rules, and as I have said, the rules are like a third fighter on the mat. They can hand you a win or a loss. But other than knowing what the rules are, how can you actively engage the rules to work in your favor? One important way to do that is to understand how to play the points and play the clock to your advantage.

A competitor who "plays the points" during a match knows what the point score is, how to use specific positions to rack up more points and how to keep his opponent from doing the same. If the competitor also "plays the clock," then he is conscious of how much time is left, when to explode if behind on points, or when (and how) to stall if ahead on points. As you can see, paying close attention to the points and the clock will help you take the appropriate actions, and this can be crucial in winning a match.

How to Play the Points

Most people fight a grappling match as a blind attempt to make any advance they can, whether it leads to a submission or a point. Generally, a lot of competitors don't think about how they can engineer the points toward a victory, or how to use that knowledge to decide what game plan, move or position to execute. That's why, as a knowledgeable grappler, you should know the point system of a specific tournament in advance, and you should practice stringing together moves that tally the greatest number of points for you to implement at the match. To illustrate how much it pays to play the points, take a look at the following two photo sequences (See Pages 129 to 131.):

Playing the Points Ineffectively

1

David Meyer (left) is in the open guard, and Adam Treanor attempts to pass it.

2

Meyer sweeps his opponent off-balance.

3

Because he succeeds in the sweep, Meyer achieves two points. However, he attempts to get four more points by achieving the mount.

4

Because he is not yet in solid position, Meyer loses his position and isn't awarded the points.

5

Meyer finishes the sweep in Treanor's open guard.

Most people would look at the previous sequence and think that I played the points well because I earned two. But is that true? It is true that I successfully swept Adam Treanor, earning two points and reversing our positions. But by attempting the mount while in motion, I not only gave up the possibility of a better ending position but also missed an opportunity to earn more points.

Let's consider a different approach:

Playing the Points Effectively

1 David Meyer (left) begins in his open guard with Adam Treanor attempting to pass it. He uses his right hand to control Treanor's left sleeve.

2 Using his left arm as an underhook to lift Treanor's right arm and his left foot to lift Treanor's right leg, Meyer rolls to the right. This throws his opponent off-balance.

3 This time, Meyer leaves his left foot intentionally behind when Treanor falls.

4 He finishes the sweep (earning two points) and allows Treanor to trap his left leg in a half-guard. Even though things might look bad, Meyer retains an underhook with his left arm for control.

David Meyer

5 Then Meyer crosses his right arm to the right side of Treanor's head and turns to his right side.

6 Meyer uses his left hand to help free his left leg.

7 Freeing his left leg, Meyer establishes side control and is awarded three points for the guard pass.

8 Treanor fights to regain his guard by placing his feet on the ground to lift his hips to create space and lift Meyer up.

9 With both of Treanor's feet on the mat, Meyer takes the opportunity to mount.

10 Meyer completes the mount and is awarded four points.

In the example on the previous page, I executed the same sweep, but rather than try for a possible mount and end in Treanor's guard, I allow my leg to be caught in Treanor's half-guard. I get two points for my sweep, but I'm in a strong position to pass the guard and get an additional three points, bringing my total to five. And as soon as I establish my side control, I seize the opportunity to mount from my strong position to earn another four points, bringing my total to nine. That is seven more points than if I had just tried and failed to achieve the mount from my sweep. This is an example of how thinking positions through in advance can help you decide how to move during the match in order to play the points.

Another way to play the points is to identify an advantageous position and repeatedly cause it to occur. However, the only way to score these points is if it does not appear obvious to the referee that you're setting your opponent up in this way. This prevents competitors from repeatedly racking up an infinite number of points.

Playing the Points Through Repetition

David Meyer stands in Adam Treanor's open guard.

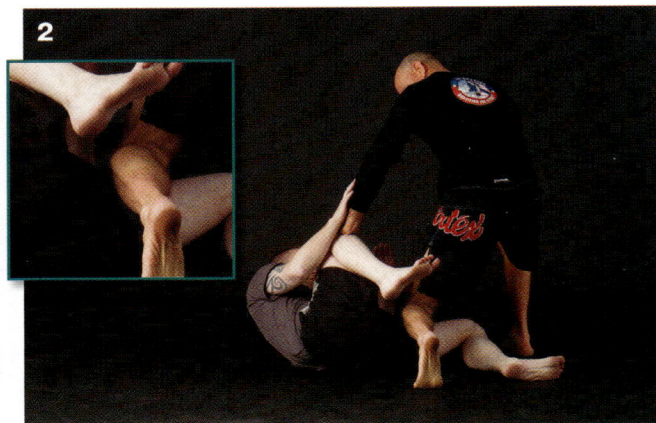

Meyer twists to the right, dropping his left knee over Treanor's left thigh.

Meyer then drops his left hip to the ground.

Meyer continues to move to the right to draw his left foot free. Then he turns to hold Treanor in side control. The guard pass earns him three points.

David Meyer

5 Noting that Treanor's overall guard defense appears weak, Meyer allows his left leg to drift out to his left.

6 Treanor takes the bait and seizes the chance to catch Meyer in the half-guard.

7 Crossing his right arm to the right side of Treanor's head, Meyer turns to his right side.

8 He uses his left elbow to help free his left leg.

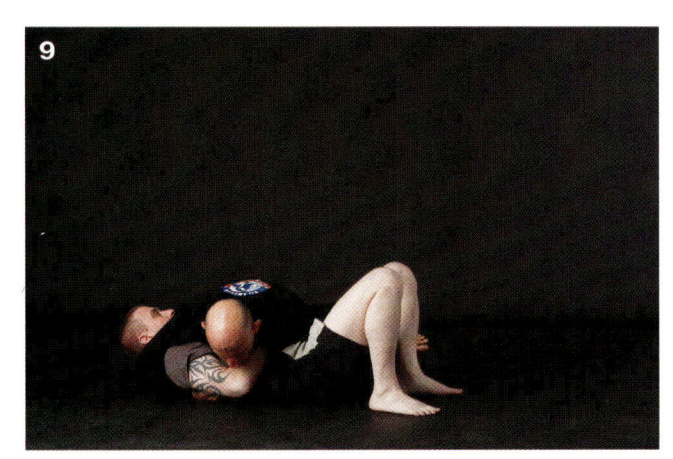

9 Meyer finishes in side control and is awarded another three points for passing the guard again.

Another way to play the points is to recognize positions that lead to movements, which your opponent does not expect. These surprise transitions not only are difficult for your opponent to stop but also can earn points. Take, for example, a transition between the mount and a knee to the stomach. By achieving the mount, you've already scored four points, but by abandoning the mount and moving to the knee on the stomach, you earn two more. These surprise moves are only possible if you consciously look out for them during a match.

Playing the Points Through Surprise Transitions

1. Beginning in the north-south position, David Meyer is on top of Adam Treanor. He places both his hands palm up under Treanor's shoulders.

2. Gripping Treanor's uniform, Meyer jumps to his feet and slides Treanor's shoulders back and up.

3. Continuing to pull up and back on Treanor's shoulders, Meyer collapses his knees and sits to the ground.

4. Meyer then places his heels around Treanor's hips and is awarded four points for back control.

Keep in mind that playing the points not only is an understanding of how you can think ahead to gain more points for yourself but also is an understanding of how you can strategically give away points to your opponent if you have to, but not enough points so that he will win the match.

Consider that you might be ahead on points but growing very tired toward the end of the match. If your opponent has more energy, you might be in danger of a finishing hold, or perhaps of having your opponent catch you and pass you on points. Most fighters in this situation would simply hold on to whatever position they are in as hard as they can.

It may, however, make sense to allow your opponent to score some points, but in a way that puts your opponent in a position that you can defend more effectively until time runs out.

For example, if you have passed someone's guard and are ahead by three points, you can allow your opponent to put you in his guard, an act for which he receives no points, and you can stall there as the match nears its end. You can even let him sweep you for two points if you have to, so long as you feel assured of landing in your own guard. You will then still be ahead by one point if you can hold them in your guard for the remainder of the match.

There are scenarios of how to play the points that involve amassing more points or knowing when to give them away. You need to become sensitive to the point system in your training so you can start to speak the language of points. The easiest way to do this is to have short practice matches that start in a variety of positions. The goal is to be the first partner to score five points. You can begin with one fighter in the guard or one fighter on the mount. This will cause you both to think about the points and how to make points your focus, rather than by just concentrating on submissions.

Point-Deficit Practice

When you amass and give points away, it's safe to assume that you are in control of a fight. But what if you're behind on points? Even if you are, you can still be in control, which is why it pays to know how to play the points even when you are behind.

The best way to prepare for these scenarios is to practice training with a point deficit. Like the energy-deficit situations in Chapter 5, point-deficit training pits you against a partner who is "ahead" by a specific number of points while you only have a short amount of time to recover points or achieve a finishing hold. By having this restriction, you'll learn to fight differently than if you were just training for general skill.

There are an infinite number of point-deficit scenarios and variations, but here are some that I recommend you practice and that follow the general BJJ point system:

- Your partner is mounted, and you are losing by two points with two minutes left. In this scenario, your partner can attempt a finish or just stall until time runs out. So what do you do? Remember, referees do not award points for escaping the mount, which means you not only have to escape the mount but also have to pass the guard to earn three points. You can also try to submit your opponent with something like a quick foot lock.

- Your partner is in your closed guard, and you are losing by three points with two minutes left. In this scenario, your partner can either stall or attempt to pass the guard—earning points. (Generally, it is best if he stalls, forcing you to work hard to initiate action.) You need to finish your opponent from inside your guard, or you must sweep your opponent. The sweep will only earn you two points, which means that you must follow up the move with a surprise finish or by passing the guard.

- You partner has full control of your back with both "hooks in," meaning his heels are in front of your hips. The points are tied, and there are two minutes left. In this scenario, you must escape your opponent's back control, then find a way to quickly finish your opponent or score a point.

- You are on the mount, but you are losing by two points with two minutes left. In this scenario, you have the dominant position, but you are still losing the fight. This mean you must either finish your opponent, dismount and achieve a knee on the stomach, or let your opponent recover the half-guard before passing his guard for points. (See illustration below.)

Point-Deficit Scenario: Two Points and Two Minutes Left

1. David Meyer starts on the mount position, but he's still down by two points with two minutes left.

2. Even though Meyer tries to create opportunities for an armbar or choke finish, Adam Treanor remains defensive and time is running out.

3. Meyer then changes position by sliding his left knee forward and swinging his left foot over Treanor's right knee and across Treanor's belt line.

4. Holding his opponent down in the knee-on-stomach position, Meyer earns two points. Now the fighters are tied. If Meyer is able, he can attempt to remount his opponent or try an armbar or choke-hold finish from his current position. But even if he doesn't earn more points, the match will end in a tie. If this is the case, Meyer's dominant position at the end may give him an edge when it comes to the referee's decision.

- Your partner is in your butterfly guard and is ahead by three points with one minute left. Because sweeping him will only get you two points, you must sweep and pass his guard or just finish him. (See illustration below.)

Point-Deficit Scenario: Three Points and One Minute Left

1 Adam Treanor begins in David Meyer's butterfly guard. He is ahead by three points with one minute left.

2 Meyer uses his hands to make space by pushing Treanor's head away.

3 He then sits up onto his left elbow, pressing his head against Treanor's chest.

4 Using his left hand to post on the ground, Meyer has a quick decision to make. He could back his feet away and square off on his knees, but this won't earn him points.

5 Instead, Meyer pulls his legs out behind him and immediately drives forward with his head, causing Treanor to fall back for the sweep. Meyer earns two points.

6 Because he's still behind by one point, Meyer cartwheels over Treanor's legs for an immediate guard pass.

7 He lands on Treanor's left side, establishing side control and earning another three points with 15 seconds left. If neither fighter submits, Meyer wins the match.

The deficit-point scenarios you can train for are infinite, but it is important that you choose some and practice them. This will give you practice in fighting when behind on points. I recommend that the point deficit not be more than five and that the time not be more than two minutes.

Playing the Clock by Stalling

As you now know, playing the points refers to understanding how to earn points, give them away and recover them during a match. However, in order to do that effectively, you need to know how to balance playing the points against the allotted match time. Understanding the passage of time is crucial because it not only helps you pace yourself, slow down and stall when ahead on points but also helps you pick up the pace and explode when behind on them. This is why it's just as important to know how to "play the clock."

Perhaps you're wondering whether it's possible to pay attention to the clock while focusing on your game plans, the points and all the other elements of a grappling match?

The answer is "Yes." Many tournaments keep a clock on the score table so fighters can see it. However, the best way to remain conscious of the time throughout the match is through a corner coach, a friend or someone who not only will keep you updated on the remaining time but also will not be afraid to shout out or ask the scorekeeper how much time is left.

One of the best ways to play the clock when you're ahead on points is to stall. This is because it tires out your opponent and keeps him from earning points while time runs out. Stalling is also a great way to save your energy, which is especially useful if you have more matches to fight that day.

The basic rule when stalling in a competition is to appear as if you are attempting to advance the fight. The reason behind this is that if the referee senses a fighter is stalling, he will demand action, restart the match or deduct a point from the offending fighter.

If you are in a control position and ahead on points, you should take the opportunity to tire your opponent out. After all, the ball is in your court, and he has to move. Think of your energy level as the gasoline gauge on a car dashboard. Both you and your opponent have emptying fuel tanks, but if you are in a superior position, you can empty your opponent's tank quicker than yours because he must struggle to escape. This is a wise use of time that draws you closer to victory and also wears your opponent down for a possible finishing hold. This stalling tactic is known as "cooking the fight" because your opponent is trapped like food in an oven—he is going soft under all the heat and pressure of the match.

Stalling when you are in top control is easiest because, by definition, your opponent can't easily change positions, making it easier for you to hold yours. But there is a danger to stalling in a top control position because it is also easier for the referee to see that you are not initiating any attacks or new positions. You need to pretend not to stall, and this takes some practice to do effectively.

The way to appear as if you are trying to move the match forward when you are actually stalling in a control position is to feign small aggressive moves or position alterations. These actions make it seem like you are trying to achieve a goal—a finish, pass, sweep, etc. If you appear to be exerting energy to move the fight forward toward a better position or finishing hold, you will able to continue your stall without the referee breaking up the fight or penalizing you.

There are many ways to feign aggressive movements. You can focus your attack on a limb like the arm. You can vary the distance of your knees by bringing them in close and spreading them away to give the referee the impression that you are attempting techniques. In the end, it adds to the sense of action. The referee should believe that you are aggressively looking for new ways to attack, when in reality, you're keeping a careful balance of control so that your opponent can't escape and time can pass.

Stalling in a Top Control Position Scenario, No. 1

David Meyer is in side control, and Adam Treanor's right arm is caught around Meyer's head.

Meyer attempts to trap Treanor's arm in an arm lock.

As Treanor moves to defend his arm, Meyer continues to grab and attack it. Of course, if given the opportunity, Meyer will capture the arm for the finish, but Treanor's defense is good. Instead, Meyer continues to bother the arm, making it appear as if he is trying to execute a move.

Stalling in a Top Control Position Scenario, No. 2

Because he is on the mount and ahead on points, David Meyer decides to stall.

He presses down on Adam Treanor's arm, appearing to set up an arm lock. By attempting finishing moves, Meyer encourages Treanor to defend himself, which strengthens the illusion of action.

Treanor pulls his right arm in toward his own chest for defense.

Meyer then inserts his left hand across Treanor's neck to choke him with his collar.

Treanor defends it, so Meyer inserts his right hand across Treanor's neck for another choke.

Treanor continues to defend, so Meyer lowers his entire mount position to change the pressure and give the appearance of movement.

Making movements while in a control position can give the appearance of motion and allow you to stall for time. But you can only stall for so long in a single position, so using transitions to other control positions when on top is really the best way to stall for time, give the appearance of action and tire out your opponent.

Stalling in Multiple Control Positions

1
David Meyer begins in side control and is ahead on points, so he decides to stall.

2
Meyer turns to his left side, lifting his right leg to indicate that he is looking to mount. If Adam Treanor does not defend, Meyer will mount. That's why Treanor lifts his right knee to defend himself.

3
Meyer then rolls to his right side, faces Treanor's head and uses his left hand to choke, using Treanor's lapel.

4
As Treanor pushes at Meyer and tries to escape, Meyer rotates his left hip to the ground and begins to circle his legs toward Treanor's head.

5
Meyer moves his right hand as he changes to the north-south position.

6
Meyer then locks down in a north-south position for a moment, before he begins other movements as he stays on top.

As I mentioned earlier, stalling on top is easiest to do because you are in a control position. However, it is also possible to stall from a more neutral position like when you are in an opponent's guard. When stalling in a closed or open butterfly guard, you need to stay close to the opponent's body to avoid any attacks. Lean forward, keep your chest down, and place your hands on the sides of the opponent's ribs and your elbows on the sides of his hips. Try to stop any hip movement to keep your opponent from creating space. It's also slightly more difficult to stall in a butterfly guard because your opponent can use his shins to push you away.

Stalling From the Closed Guard

David Meyer is in Adam Treanor's closed guard, blocking Treanor's arms from attacking him.

Meyer moves his hips as far forward as possible while dropping his head and chest onto Treanor's stomach. Meyer also places his hands on the outside of Treanor's ribs to keep them hidden—he doesn't want Treanor to grab them. Finally, Meyer also locks his elbows on the ground, pulling tightly against his own knees.

This position holds Treanor in tight. Notice how there is no way for him to move away, create space or launch an effective attack.

Stalling From the Butterfly Guard

David Meyer starts in Adam Treanor's butterfly guard, sitting on Treanor's feet.

Meyer drops his head and chest down, keeps his hands tight in along the side of Treanor's ribs, and keeps his elbows in tight and on the ground beside Treanor's hips.

Now Treanor can't move away, create space or launch an effective counterattack.

Because the positions illustrated above are static, it's difficult to stall for long in the closed or butterfly guard. There are few attacks you can execute from inside someone's guard, which means that you won't be able to fake aggression like you can from a control position. Ultimately, the real activity you'll need to do is pass the guard, which by definition is not stalling.

In addition to stalling from a top control position or when in an opponent's guard, it's possible to stall if you've pulled an opponent into your guard and are ahead on points. This generally means that you'll frequently break the defender's posture, causing him to fall forward on you. When the opponent can't regain his posture, you also deny him the opportunity to pass the guard.

It's important to note that breaking your opponent's posture is a safe and effective way to tire him out and eat up time on the clock because he must struggle first to regain his posture before passing the guard. Additionally, holding your partner down in bad posture allows you to set up, or appear to be setting up, attacks such as arm locks and chokes, all of which perpetuate your stall.

Breaking Posture

1

David Meyer begins on his back with Adam Treanor in his closed guard.

2

As Treanor reaches forward to control Meyer's upper body, Meyer circles both his hands up from his stomach.

3

Meyer continues to sweep his hands up and around while he simultaneously pulls his heels into Treanor's back. This causes Treanor to lose posture and fall forward.

4

As Treanor falls forward, Meyer locks his hands together, hugging Treanor close behind Treanor's neck.

5

Meyer then temporarily unlocks his feet while he slides his hips back and climbs his legs high across Treanor's back.

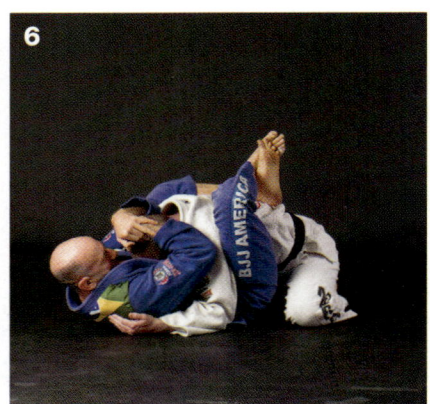

6

Meyer then recrosses his legs high on Treanor's back, maintaining hold of Treanor's head. This makes it very difficult for Treanor to regain the posture needed to pass the guard.

You can stall from your butterfly guard, as well, but this takes a bit more skill because your opponent can move more freely and can potentially pass your guard. However, like in the other example, you can't feign indefinitely because the referee will warn and then penalize you. You can, however, mix these stall tactics with attacks on your opponent's arms and neck to continue giving the appearance of action.

Stalling From Butterfly Guard Scenario, No. 1

David Meyer begins on his back with Adam Treanor in his butterfly guard.

Meyer sits up, bringing his arms above Treanor's arms.

Meyer wraps his arms over the top of Treanor's arms, pulling Treanor's elbows tightly against his sides.

Meyer then lies back, trapping both Treanor's arms and making it impossible for Treanor to easily rise back up.

145

Stalling From the Butterfly Guard Scenario, No. 2

1

David Meyer starts on his back with Adam Treanor in his butterfly guard.

2

Meyer sits up.

3

Meyer reaches his arms underneath Treanor's arms and clasps his hands together high up behind Treanor's shoulders.

4

Meyer then lies back, pulling Treanor down. Meyer keeps his hands clasped together, pulling high on Treanor's back and making it hard for Treanor to rise up and regain his posture.

Beyond stalling from a control position and stalling from the top and the bottom in the guard, there is one more general position you might want to stall from when grappling on the ground, and that is when you are pinned on the bottom and not in control. This could happen if your guard is passed, you are swept and now trapped on the bottom. This seems counterintuitive. Why would you want to stall when you are trapped on the bottom? Why wouldn't you want to escape? The answer is the same reason you would ever want to stall—you are ahead on points.

The most basic way to stall when trapped on bottom is to either bear-hug your opponent or block your opponent from changing and advancing his positions. For example, when your opponent is in side control, you want to use your hands and knees to block his ability to mount and/or transition to a knee-on-stomach position. This effectively freezes the opponent from making more points.

So to sum up, you can stall from any position on the ground, top or bottom. You can also practice stalling with your partner in your own guard, stalling while in your partner's guard, stalling when pinning your partner, or when you are pinned under your partner. A good stalling drill is to start in any position, top or bottom. You are "ahead" by three points and want to stall with 90 seconds left while your training partner tries to move to make up the point deficit. Not only does this drill teach you how to stall but also gets you to think about how to make up (or hold onto) points.

How to Stall While Standing

Stalling while on the ground is easier to do than while standing because the referee expects to see moments of inaction on the ground while entangled fighters take time to rest and set up attacks. In contrast, stalling while standing is harder to conceal because the referee expects you to take the fight to the ground as quickly as possible.

The most obvious way to stall while on your feet is to circle around the mat or back away from your opponent. Of course, this type of stalling is easy for the referee to recognize. This is why you should avoid it unless there are just seconds left in the match, you are ahead in points and there is not enough time for the referee to deduct points.

Circling the Mat

In this example, David Meyer (left) keeps his distance from Adam Treanor.

As Treanor moves forward, Meyer circles to the left.

Treanor resets his stance and prepares to shoot in, but Meyer circles to the left again.

Each time Treanor prepares to shoot, Meyer circles away.

If you are in a situation in which more than 20 seconds remain in a fight and are ahead by at least two points, then you can redirect the opponent's attacks. You engage the opponent at a closer range, visibly look like you are not running from a fight and sidestep/redirect/deflect the attack. Note that stalling at such a close distance requires that you have confidence in your takedown defense skills just in case.

What's more effective about this stall is that the referee can clearly see that the opponent is being aggressive and that you are not avoiding his actions. However, the opponent's aggression won't earn him points, which is good for you.

Stalling by Misdirection

David Meyer (right) and Adam Treanor close the distance between each other.

When Treanor reaches out to grab at Meyer, Meyer redirects the attack.

He circles to the side to appear as if he is looking for his own angle to shoot in at.

Treanor then shoots in again.

Meyer again misdirects Treanor's arms.

Meyer circles to the side.

Another way to stall at a closer-standing range is to move in for the clinch and tie up the opponent in that way. There are two basic ways to clinch an opponent: the single-handed "neck tie" and the underhook. The former is effective because it blocks the opponent from moving forward while giving you a point from which to control his balance and movement. The latter is effective because it controls your opponent's movement effectively by preventing him from moving forward or backward.

The "Neck Tie" Clinch

David Meyer (right) uses his right hand to hold behind Adam Treanor's neck. Meyer drops his right elbow directly in front of Treanor's chest, blocking Treanor's ability to shoot in and grab Meyer's legs.

As Treanor moves forward, Meyer steps back and pivots, using his right hand to redirect Treanor's motion and maintain a safe distance.

Underhook Clinch

David Meyer places his right arm under Adam Treanor's left arm for an underhook, holding high onto Treanor's shoulder. If Treanor lifts his left arm to attempt to free it, Meyer can circle to Treanor's back. Holding Treanor in this way makes it very difficult for Treanor to shoot in for any leg attack as Meyer lifts his arm, and Treanor must overhook Meyer's arm to keep Meyer from ducking under and getting his back, which just stalls the fight further.

Whether you stall from a distance or from a clinch, you must have confidence in your balance skills and your skill to avoid takedowns or you run the risk of being taken off your feet and giving away two points. In fact, if you find that you are the competitor behind on points and your opponent is stalling, then the only thing you can do is succeed in taking him down or pulling him into your guard. A good way to practice this is through training matches. Both partners should begin on their feet; one person must stall while the other only has 90 seconds to score a takedown.

How to Break a Stall on the Ground

There are many ways to break a stall while on the ground. However, breaking a good and effective stall can be quite difficult, which is why it takes even more practice than learning how to stall itself.

In a competition, it might make sense first to look at the referee and communicate with your eyes that you are frustrated with the stalling tactic of your opponent. This might get the referee to break the stall for you. You can't rely on that though, so you need to know how to do it yourself. Let's look at some of the common positions in which you might be trapped with your opponent stalling.

One place you might find yourself trapped is in your opponent's closed guard. The first thing you must do is regain your posture if you have lost it. If you are being held down by your opponent and cannot lift your head up to regain your posture, press the top of your head into your opponent's jaw, driving your weight down and into him as much as possible. This will generally cause your opponent to no longer want to pull you down but to push you away to escape the crush on his jaw. At the same time, you now have the chance to back away and regain your posture in the closed guard.

Once you have recovered your posture in the closed guard, you need to break the stall, and sometimes the only way to do that is to stand up and use gravity to open your partner's crossed legs. The following is an example on how to recover your posture in any grappling format.

Recovering Your Posture

Adam Treanor stalls with David Meyer in his closed guard.

To break the stall, Meyer grabs at Treanor's collar near the neck. (If this is a submission-grappling match, Meyer would grab Treanor's neck.) Then he presses his knuckles into his opponent's neck to prevent Treanor from breaking his posture again.

3 Meyer uses his right hand to press down on Treanor's waistline so Treanor cannot lift his hips and execute an armbar against Meyer's extended left arm.

4 Meyer then rises to his feet with his elbows close to his own hips. This prevents Treanor from unlocking his feet and possibly controlling Meyer's hips.

5 Meyer looks upward to maintain good posture. He also uses his leg strength to lift Treanor into the air.

6 Meyer then uses one hand to press down against Treanor's knee as he bounces his hips up and down to shake Treanor's feet loose.

7 Once Treanor loosens his grip and starts to fall, Meyer bends his legs and drops Treanor, taking a stable stance with his elbows on his knees to defend against sweeps and upper-body attacks.

Another common stall position is when someone is stalling in your closed guard. This can be difficult to break because you have the ground behind you and can't move as effectively. However, it is possible to get out of the stall, and the following is a good example:

Breaking the Stall: Closed Guard

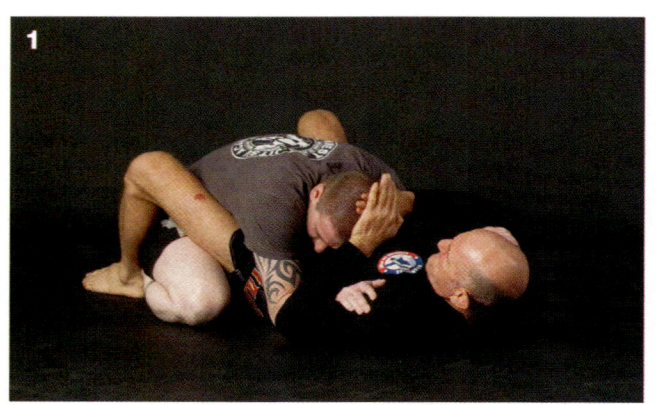

1

David Meyer holds Adam Treanor in the closed-guard position. Because Treanor has more points, he is stalling.

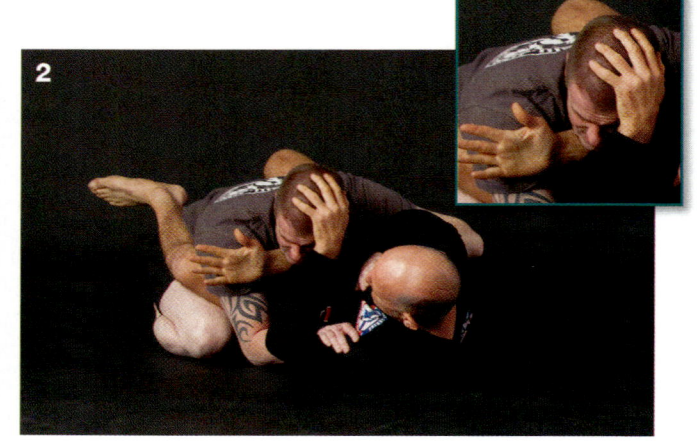

2

Meyer uses both hands to push Treanor's head to the left. He also lifts it up. Then he puts his right wrist across Treanor's neck to apply pressure.

3

As Treanor backs away from the pressure on his neck, Meyer unlocks his feet and places them on the ground.

4

While holding Treanor away with his right hand, Meyer sits up onto his left elbow.

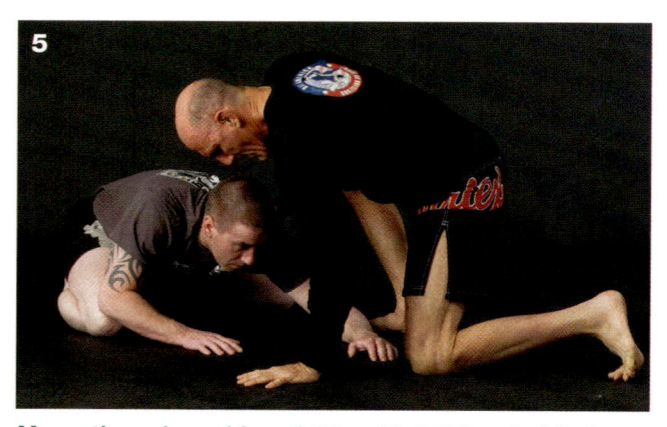

5

Meyer then places his weight on his left hand while he slides his hips and legs back and away from Treanor.

When someone is stalling in your butterfly guard, it is somewhat easier to break than from your closed guard. However, that doesn't mean there aren't any difficulties. Make sure that you don't give your opponent an opportunity to pass the guard by using your hands to push away and block his shoulders from doing so.

Breaking the Stall: Butterfly Guard

1 David Meyer begins on his back with Adam Treanor ahead on points and stalling in Meyer's butterfly guard.

2 Meyer digs his straightened fingers on his left hand underneath Treanor's right armpit.

3 Meyer then uses his right hand to clasp the top of his left hand. He lifts his own left elbow to pry Treanor's right arm free.

4 Meyer continues to pull hard on Treanor's right elbow, threatening to hyperextend it in an armbar.

5 Treanor defends his arm by passing his hand out from Meyer's hand. Meyer pulls his opponent's arm across his body, setting up a possible sweep.

6 Treanor pulls back, drawing his arm free. This releases Meyer from the stall, leaving him free to move and attack.

Baiting Your Opponent to Escape a Stall or Bad Position

Despite all the methods for breaking stalls in various positions, sometimes the only way to break an effective stall is to give your opponent such a good opportunity to execute a finishing hold or sweep that they willingly take the bait and change the position for you. This allows you a chance to escape and continue to fight.

I want to emphasize that exposing yourself to a sweep or finishing hold can be risky, but if you know what you are doing, it can be effective. The reason for this is that when you are intentionally offering a chance to your opponent to execute a sweep or finishing hold, you have the benefit of being prepared for the move he is about to execute. This puts you in control because you are the "puppet master"—pulling your opponent's strings and causing him to make predictable movements.

Let's look at some common bad positions you may find yourself in, but this time, we'll look at some effective ways to bait your opponent into executing an attack, which you will use to escape.

A common bad position in Brazilian jiu-jitsu and submission grappling is when you find yourself in the closed guard. If you are in your opponent's closed guard and he is ahead on points and not allowing you to open his legs, you can use an armbar as bait to escape the position.

Baiting With an Armbar in the Closed Guard

David Meyer is in Adam Treanor's closed guard. Treanor is ahead in points and stalling.

Meyer appears to unwittingly move his left elbow up the centerline to Treanor's stomach. This "frees" Treanor's hip.

Because his right hip is free, Treanor believes he has the opportunity to get his right leg over Meyer's head and execute an armbar. He unlocks his feet and places his left foot on Meyer's left hip.

He then swings his right leg over Meyer's head to catch Meyer's left arm in an armbar. However, Meyer is waiting for him to do this. When Treanor swings, Meyer keeps his left arm bent, and inch by inch, he pulls his left elbow back from between Treanor's legs.

Meyer has escaped the armbar, and Treanor's closed guard is now open, freeing Meyer to move.

If your opponent does not take the bait and does not attempt the armbar, it may be because he does not yet feel strong enough in his position to execute the move. If this is the case, you can bait him to cross his legs higher on your back and use that as a way to open his guard.

Breaking the Closed Guard Stall

1. David Meyer is in Adam Treanor's closed guard. Treanor is ahead on points and stalling.

2. Meyer keeps his head low and in bad posture, bringing his elbows toward each other, which gives Treanor the opportunity to climb his legs higher on Meyer's back to better hold Meyer down and set up armbars and triangles.

3. Treanor grips his legs high across Meyer's back.

4. Meyer then pushes forward, rolling Treanor onto his neck and lifting Treanor's hips off the ground.

5. Meyer lifts his hips high while he keeps his head low, placing his right foot directly in front of his left foot on the same line as Treanor's spine.

6. Taking advantage of the space between Treanor's legs, Meyer then sits back on his left foot, bending his right knee and inserting his right knee up and through the space.

7. Meyer then uses his right knee and shin to push forward as he pulls his shoulders back, forcing Treanor's legs to open.

Another way to bait an opponent to end a stall in the closed guard is to give him a sense that he can successfully sweep you to obtain a better position, thus tricking him into deciding to open his legs without you forcing him to do so.

Sweeping Through the Closed Guard

1 David Meyer is in Adam Treanor's closed guard. Treanor is ahead in points and stalling.

2 Meyer moves his left knee to the center behind Treanor's spine and steps up with his right foot.

3 Seeing an opportunity for the scissor sweep, Treanor elects to unlock his legs. He swings his hips out to the left and prepares to use his legs to sweep Meyer.

4 As Treanor begins to use his legs for the sweep, Meyer relaxes his lower body, allowing his legs to be swept yet maintaining the position of his upper body facing down.

5 As Treanor completes the sweep of Meyer's legs, Meyer allows his body to twist, with his stomach facing up yet his shoulders still attempting to remain facing down.

6 Meyer then quickly recovers the downward-facing position of his hips and is on Treanor's side.

7 Meyer completes the move by establishing side control. This not only breaks the guard stall but also earns Meyer three points for the guard pass.

Frequently, an opponent might stall if he is ahead in points and has you pinned in a control position. If you are unable to execute an escape, your only option may be to offer him a positional advancement, such as moving into the mount position, which is often just too good for him to refuse.

From Bottom Side Control: Bait to Mount, No. 1

David Meyer is trapped in bottom side control with Adam Treanor on top, stalling. Meyer lets his left foot drift away, which lowers his left knee and signals an opportunity for Treanor to mount.

Treanor takes the opportunity to step over Meyer to the mount. As Treanor moves, Meyer pulls his right knee up close and catches Treanor's left leg on his right shin.

Meyer continues to pull his right knee in tight, and Treanor's left leg naturally slides down onto Meyer's right foot.

Meyer then uses his right foot to lift Treanor's left leg and lower body, making space for Meyer's left knee to come in tight.

Meyer sets Treanor on his feet, ending in the butterfly guard.

Baiting an opponent to mount creates an opportunity to block the mount as well as have your opponent end up in the guard where you can continue to fight more effectively. Here is another example of a way to bait an opponent into the mount position and turn the result in your favor.

From Bottom Side Control: Bait to Mount, No. 2

1. David Meyer is trapped in side control with Adam Treanor on top and stalling.

2. Meyer lets his right foot drift away, which lowers his right knee and signals an opportunity for Treanor to mount.

3. As Treanor steps over Meyer with his right leg, Meyer turns to his right side and uses his right elbow to help shove his own right knee under Treanor's left knee.

4. Treanor is now on Meyer's right foot.

5. Meyer then slides his hips to the right, turns onto his left side and slides his left knee under Treanor's right knee.

6. Treanor finishes in Meyer's butterfly guard.

While baiting an opponent to mount works well, sometimes an opponent won't take the opportunity because he is comfortable in side control, feels secure or is winning the fight. In cases like these, you can bait him to put his knee on your stomach, which is a smaller change in position than him transitioning to the mount.

From Bottom Side Control: Bait to Knee-on-Stomach Position

David Meyer is trapped in side control with Adam Treanor on top and stalling.

Meyer lets his right leg drift away but keeps his left knee up. This lets Treanor believe that he might be able to put a knee on Meyer's stomach.

Treanor places his right knee on Meyer's stomach and rises up to apply pressure. However, Meyer reaches across his own body with his left hand and holds the top of Treanor's right heel.

Meyer then turns to his right side, causing Treanor's right knee to drop to the ground. Meyer pulls on Treanor's right heel with his left hand and presses his left elbow into Treanor's right thigh.

Meyer rises up on his right elbow while he continues to pull on Treanor's right heel, causing Treanor to fall to the right and Meyer to come out on top.

In these previous examples, we examined how you can be trapped on the bottom in side control but are still able to bait an opponent to change positions, improve your own position and end a stall. However, your opponent might be too secure in his point lead and simply won't release a good position. If this is the case, it is time to up the ante and offer your opponent the best prize of all: a finishing hold that will end the fight immediately. Few fighters can resist an opportunity to make their opponent tap out.

From Bottom Side Control: Baiting the Armbar, No. 1

David Meyer is trapped in side control with Adam Treanor on top and stalling.

Meyer reaches his right hand out from in front of his chest and lays it across Treanor's left ear and on Treanor's back. This exposes Meyer's arm for an armbar.

As Treanor grips Meyer's right arm to set up an armbar, Meyer turns onto his left side and presses his right biceps hard into the side of Treanor's head. This tricks the opponent into flattening Meyer down again because he doesn't want him to rise to his knees.

However, in order to flatten him on the ground, Treanor needs to push off his own knees or feet, creating the perfect opening for Meyer to slide his hips away and slip his left knee underneath Treanor.

Meyer slides his hips away from Treanor to make space and brings his left leg all the way through, wrapping his legs around Treanor in the closed guard.

While it's possible for a competitor to offer his opponent a chance at an armbar and use that as a way to bring the opponent back into his closed guard, this same setup can be used to offer an armbar and then roll the opponent over, resulting in a complete reversal of the position.

From Bottom Side Control: Baiting the Armbar, No. 2

1

David Meyer is trapped in side control with Adam Treanor on top and stalling.

2

Meyer reaches his right hand out from in front of his chest and lays it along Treanor's left ear and on Treanor's back. This exposes Meyer's arm for an armbar.

3

As Treanor grips Meyer's right arm to set up the armbar, Meyer turns onto his left side and presses his right biceps hard into the side or Treanor's head. This tricks the opponent into flattening Meyer down again because he doesn't want him to rise to his knees.

4

As Treanor pushes him back to the ground, Meyer uses his right arm to grab and hold Treanor's back. Then he uses his left hand to push on the front of Treanor's right hip.

5

Meyer pulls with his right hand and uses his left hand to guide Treanor's hips over his own hips.

6

Meyer rolls to his right and ends up in side control on top of Treanor.

The two previous examples show variations of the same setup—it just depends on what you're able to do. Note that because you are pinned on the bottom, the "armbar bait No. 2" isn't considered a sweep and will not earn you two points. The referees or scorekeepers don't reward you for dramatic escapes from bad positions. However, if you manage to get into a good position, you can work to finish your opponent or score points to catch up and win the fight.

The most risky armbar attempt is when you're on your back and the opponent has mounted you, meaning he is sitting on your chest. Only attempt this armbar if you cannot execute any mount escape, are proficient, and you are down in points and time is running out. If all these factors add up, then this maneuver is the perfect way to not only end the stall but also escape.

From Bottom Mount: Failed Mount Escape to Armbar

1 David Meyer is trapped in the mount with Adam Treanor on him and stalling.

2 Meyer turns to his right and lets his left arm drift up toward Treanor's chest.

3 Treanor sees a perfect opportunity for an armbar, so he places his left foot on the ground in front of Meyer's stomach and prepares to bring his right leg over Meyer's head for the finish.

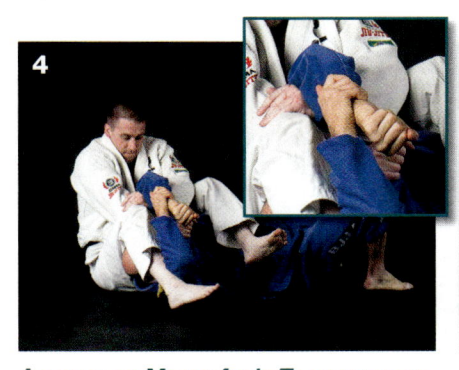

4 As soon as Meyer feels Treanor move and begin to swing his right leg over Meyer's head, Meyer clasps his right forearm over his left and aligns both his forearms so that they make one solid bar. As Treanor's leg comes around Meyer's head, Meyer lifts his arms like a shield so that his elbows and wrists all go above his head.

5 Meyer's arms stop the motion of Treanor's right leg, blocking it entirely from passing over Meyer's head. Meyer then lifts his head up.

6 Without Treanor's right leg on his head to stop him, Meyer is able to turn to his left.

7 Meyer then recovers to his knees inside Treanor's closed guard.

How to Use Aggressive Mat Control

In a competition in which the fighters are so evenly matched that the points are tied and there is little time left, the referee will award victory to whoever he thinks fought most aggressively. For this reason, it is very important to not just remain aggressive throughout the fight but also to fight even more aggressively in the last minutes and seconds. This is because those last moments remain most current in the referee's mind, and they will probably be the deciding factor in his judgment, if the referee needs to decide the winner.

This bears repeating: The last minutes and seconds of the match will have more influence on the referee's decision than the first minutes and seconds. This is why the last use of playing the clock that we will discuss is to realize when time is almost out and the points are tied. Now it's time to put on a show to win the referee's decision.

Frequently, if the points are tied at the end of the match, the referee stands both fighters up because someone is stalling or there has been little action. It's also possible that both fighters have stood the entire match, with neither grappler able to execute a takedown. In those last seconds spent standing, showing aggressive mat control may be your only way to demonstrate to the referee why you should win.

Mat control is the ability to move your opponent around the mat so that even if neither fighter executes a takedown, it is clear that you are more in control and being more aggressive. You can show the referee this quite simply, such as in continually pushing your opponent backward.

Mat Control

David Meyer (right) and Adam Treanor are tied with seconds left at the end of the match.

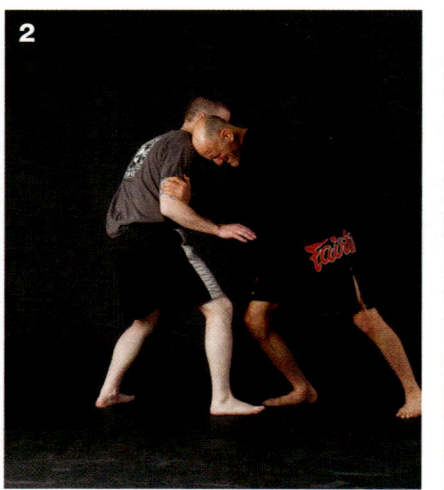

Meyer drops his shoulder into Treanor's chest and creates a solid base with his left foot back.

He then drives Treanor backward, and if possible, he drives him out of bounds. This demonstrates to the referee Meyer's physical power and aggressive mat control.

Remember that in the last seconds of a match, your aggressiveness isn't a matter of skill but of show. You want the referee to see that you physically dominate the opponent, even if all you're doing is pushing him around.

If you cannot push your opponent backward and out of bounds, it's likely because he is as strong and pushing back with equal or greater force. If this is the case, you should learn how to redirect that force to spin him around and out of bounds.

Mat Control: Redirection

Adam Treanor (right) blocks David Meyer's ability to move forward and drive him backward.

Meyer suddenly stops resisting Treanor's push and twists to his right. He simultaneously steps back, causing Treanor to spin forward.

Ready for this reaction, Meyer brings Treanor fully around, maintains momentum and pushes Treanor back and out of bounds.

Essentially what you're doing is sumo wrestling, and this technique can be practiced before competition. It's even a good warm-up to do before training.

The basic "sumo" drill is this: Create a square or circle on the mat with clear boundaries. Face your partner in the center of the mat. Both of you should attempt to force the other's knee or hand to touch the ground or cause any part of the opponent's body to step or fall outside the boundaries. If both of you fall outside the boundary, the loser is whoever touched outside first. This drill is a great way to practice aggressive mat control and is directly translatable to a real grappling match.

Interview with **Bas Rutten**
MMA Veteran and Champion

Q: What type of exercises do you recommend for strength training and conditioning?

A: I like to combine power with conditioning—jumping over a bag that lies on the ground from left to right, kettlebell swings, push-ups, kicking a bag, abs, sprawls, hitting a bag while standing, sprints, biceps with kettlebells—just like in a real fight. I usually take 12 exercises like those and do them for 30 seconds each, [totaling] six minutes. After seven rounds of that kind of workout, you are done! Another killer is a treadmill exercise that I do. I warm up for 10 minutes at 11 miles per hour. (That may seem too fast, but trust me, I have friends who go faster.) After that, I go back to 9 mph and put the incline all the way up, as high as I can. I let the machine run between my legs before I jump on there for 45 seconds and off to rest for 30 seconds. Try and see if you can do that 10 times—it's a nightmare! This will also make you mentally very strong.

Q: How do you like to warm up before a match?

A: Hard, hard, hard! My friends freak out when I do 10 rounds and two minutes of full-power [blows] on the Thai pads. I also do many sprawls and sit-ups so that my abs are warmed up—I don't think a lot of people realize how important that is. If your abs fill with lactic acid, your lungs won't be able to fully expand, which means you run out of gas. Remember, after the warm-up, you have to stretch everything really well and that includes your abs.

Q: Do you have specific training methods you use to prepare for a competition (specific drills or scenarios)?

A: I think the key to success is to be relaxed, so I listen to calm music, play nonviolent video games like *Tetris*, tell jokes and do other funny stuff. If I have people in my dressing room who yell or scream that I "have to kill my opponent," then I send them away. I try to save the aggression for the fight, but that's still "controlled" aggression. I just let it out at the moment I need to be aggressive, then I can relax right away again. If you fight with emotions, you make mistakes. I like to play mind games also, which subtly enrages my opponent. This way he'll want to hurt me really badly and will "load up" his punches so that I can see them coming at me more clearly.

Q: When you start a match, do you have a plan or do you wait to see what the opponent does?

A: Most of the time, I let him make the first move to see what he's up to and to determine his reach. Then I start countering, and later, I start attacking. I watch my opponent's fights to find out what things he always does instead of what things he only did once in his last fight. I try to see if I can find good counters for [my opponent's common moves], and I tell my sparring partners to attack me with them a lot so my counters will come naturally.

Q: Do you think grapplers in competition should go for the submission or pay more attention to the points?

A: That's the same as asking if you want to see boxers go the distance or do you want them to knock their opponents out? Nobody likes a point game. Do you really want to tell people that you are a world grappling champion because you got the title by escaping the guard, going back into the guard, escaping the guard, etc., to get points? No. I think it's much cooler to say that you became a world champion because you submitted all your opponents. Then you show real skill.

Q: What advice would you give to someone who is nervous about competing in grappling?

A: I would ask them, "Why are you nervous?" Really, what's the worst thing that can happen to you? You get submitted and that's it. If you tap out, you won't break anything, and if [you're stuck in a] choke and you tap, then you won't pass out. That's it. If you think about it, it's not that bad. I think the main reason people don't want to lose is because they don't want to do it in front of their friends, family and fans. If you lose, then so be it. Now it's time to really show your friends, family and fans what you're made of by never getting caught in that same submission again. But you should fight for yourself and not for other people. If they complain, then let them do it.

Chapter 8
Taking Risks and Going Against the Norm

Your ability to do well in a competition is almost entirely dependent on the sum of your physical attributes, your skill level, your fighting spirit, your competition-specific knowledge (such as having a game plan), and your ability to use points and the clock. But sometimes that's not enough because your opponent is simply a better overall grappler than you.

It's during times like these that you need one last trick up your sleeve to defeat an opponent. That trick usually comes in one of two forms: 1) It is either some specialty technique or method that you developed and that most grapplers are unfamiliar with, or 2) it is an ability to execute a finishing hold from an unexpected position that can even catch a better grappler by surprise and make him tap out.

Developing a Specialty

The legendary grappler Gene LeBell once told me, "If you're a white belt with a black-belt foot lock and you are fighting someone without a good defense, then you can still win, even if he is better than you." What this means is that you can still beat an opponent who in all other areas is technically more skilled than you; it's just that he happens to have a vulnerability in the one area where you have relative strength. Or perhaps your opponent doesn't realize that in this one area, you've worked hard to develop a particular expertise.

A great example of this is my old friend Eddie Bravo, to whom I taught his first BJJ class many years ago. Early in his grappling career, Bravo decided to focus on some very specific positions and moves; he wanted to develop them to a degree that other grapplers had just never seen. Bravo is an innovator, and he spent years developing a particular finishing hold called the "twister" and a closed guard called the "rubber guard." In regards to the twister, Bravo worked out all the ways he could execute that move from many different positions. In regards to the rubber guard, Bravo's approach is unique in that it involves crossing the legs high on your opponent's shoulders, then grabbing your own feet with your hands to manipulate the position. From this position, Bravo was and is able to execute extremely powerful attacks, including the triangle.

It was these special skills that brought Bravo fame—he was the first American to beat a well-known and skilled Gracie in a grappling competition. Even now, Royler Gracie is a fighter of mythic proportions, and in that 2003 tournament, no fighter had managed to score a single point off of him. Yet, with less than a minute to go, Bravo caught Gracie in a triangle choke and made him tap out.

Now Bravo is an awesome grappler and a top-level black belt by any standard, but most people would never have bet that he would beat Gracie. The key to Bravo's specialty is that he is insanely good not only at his unusual method of fighting but also in drawing people into that unique realm. So it was this perfect combination of unusual, dangerous and relatively unknown attacks that found the crack in Gracie's defense and won Bravo the fight.

Now developing an odd area of expertise can take many years, and it is often done at the expense of developing other solid and well-rounded skills. But you may find that fate itself pushes you in this direction, perhaps because of a particular physical limitation you may have or because of an unusual attribute like long legs or extreme flexibility. The key here is to understand that it is often worthwhile to spend some time developing an unusual move or position for which you have an affinity. You should also consider ways to get there from other, more common grappling positions.

So take a moment to ask yourself whether there is something unique about your body type that could be turned to your advantage? Are you particularly lanky or thick? Are you tall or short? Are you extremely flexible? Or perhaps, there is some position or move you have come across that is unusual and you like it? If the answer to any of these questions is "yes," ask your instructor how you might turn this to your advantage. You can also seek out other competitors with similar unusual attributes and see how they turn it to their advantage. In fact, feel free to copy them.

But even though finding a specialty is worthwhile, I don't suggest that any grappler make it the basis of his entire grappling training. This is because it is always essential to develop a general set of well-rounded skills. You might also face a situation in which you become particularly successful in your specialty, and over the years, other competitors will develop effective counters and variations to it.

Surprise Finishes

Developing an odd area of expertise may not be possible or appropriate for your particular grappling style, but another set of tools you can more easily develop to defeat an otherwise better opponent are surprise entries to finishing holds. The distinction here is that the finishes themselves are not unique or even tricky. Instead, the setup and entry for the move is, and this is why they are surprising.

An example of this is when I participated in a special black-belt BJJ competition in California. My opponent was a Brazilian black belt who lived in Florida and had flown across the country specifically for our match. I felt very confident in my skills, and I fully expected to win the fight.

The match began with us jockeying for position, and within a minute, we ended up on the ground with my opponent in my guard and no points scored. Instead of attempting to pass my guard, he reached around my head with one arm and in front of my neck with the other, grabbing his own sleeves to execute a sleeve-grab choke known by Brazilians as the "Ezekiel." The choke is risky to execute because it leaves the attacking fighter susceptible to a sweep. Both arms are busy with the choke and unable to defend, and this is exactly what happened. I successfully defended the choke, swept my opponent for two points and passed his guard for three more.

At that point, we were grappling so near to the mat's edge that the referee decided to stand us up and restart the match in the middle. Because I had a five-point lead, I decided to spend the remaining minute of the match stalling and immediately pulled my opponent into my closed guard. Instead of resisting my move, he jumped into my closed guard, lying flat on top of me. As I quickly maneuvered to close my legs around him, he was quickly setting up the Ezekiel choke again. Before I could react, he had his sleeves grabbed and the choke locked. For one of the few times in my competition career, I tapped out.

I give credit to my opponent because he beat me with a surprise finish. He set me up by attempting the move early on, and my defense of it led me into a false sense of security. Then he jumped on me as a distraction, which I did not foresee, and set up his surprise attack.

The fact is that Brazilian jiu-jitsu and submission grappling are still young sports in terms of how many competitors are training in them and the skill level of the average competitor. So it is relatively easy to develop attacks that your opponent may not be familiar with, and I recommend you do so.

The only caveat I offer here is that quick attacks that lead to finishing holds that fail can also help an opponent escape or achieve a superior position. For example, if you attempt an armbar from the mount, you may allow your opponent to escape and end in your guard. Also, attempting a foot lock from any position can, if it fails, put you on your back with your opponent on top, in a better position. For these reasons, it is normally better to take your time, establish a good control position, and wear your opponent out somewhat before attempting a submission hold.

But there are times when it does make sense to attempt a surprise finish. If you are safely ahead on points and winning a fight, ending the match sooner rather than later can be good because it will help you save energy for your next match. If your point lead is large enough, it doesn't matter whether your finish fails and your opponent improves his position.

Conversely, if you are faced with a better opponent and are losing a fight by points and are unlikely to catch up, your only hope to win might be a surprising and quick finishing hold.

The basic rule for surprise finishes is that they are by their nature "surprise" finishes. They can come from good positions or bad positions, although it is much easier to set up a surprise finish when you are in the good position, i.e., in control. The trick is to set up the finish without your opponent being prepared to defend it.

The flying triangle is a classic surprise finish. It is generally executed at the beginning of a match when both fighters are standing, or it's executed later when a match is restarted or when a fighter's reactions are slower because of fatigue. It is generally considered a surprise attack because the opponent doesn't expect the competitor to jump at him for the takedown. (See sequence on next page.)

Flying Triangle

1. *During a restart, David Meyer (right) and Adam Treanor start the match again on their feet. Meyer holds Treanor's right elbow with his left hand and Treanor's right lapel with his right hand.*

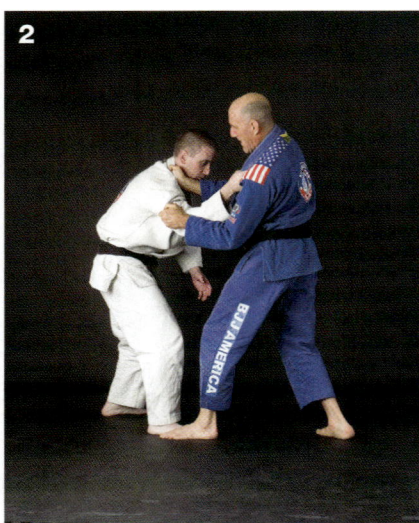

2. *Meyer steps forward and just to the outside of Treanor's right foot with his left foot.*

3. *Meyer pulls Treanor's uniform to jump into the air and swing his right leg over his opponent's left arm and onto his opponent's left shoulder.*

4. *Meyer then jumps his left leg up and under Treanor's right armpit.*

5. *He leans back, being careful to tuck his chin into his chest as his weight bends Treanor downward and brings them both to the ground.*

6. *Meyer squeezes his knees together and holds Treanor's head down with his right hand as he adjusts the lock with his legs to secure the triangle. As with all triangles, Meyer forces Treanor to tap by lifting his hips and pulling down on his opponent's head.*

Another classic surprise finish from a standing position is the flying armbar. When executing this move in training or in competition, you must be careful not to injure your opponent's arm before he has a chance to tap. This is because if you really do catch the opponent by surprise, you can accidentally hyperextend his elbow when you both hit the ground. The impact jars you and the opponent, which can increase pressure on the arm; so be careful.

Flying Armbar

1. While in a standing position, David Meyer (left) uses his left hand to hold onto Adam Treanor's right elbow. He uses his right hand to grip Treanor's left collar close to the opponent's neck.

2. Meyer steps forward with his left foot.

3. He then jumps his right leg high and under Treanor's left armpit. Note: Getting the right leg high is key to the success of this move.

4. While leaning back, Meyer lets his left leg fly over Treanor's right shoulder and head.

5. Meyer then finishes the move with his left knee bent over Treanor's head, pulling Treanor toward the ground. As he releases his right hand's grip on Treanor's lapel, Meyer is careful to keep his chin tucked to his chest so his head hits the ground softly. He then forces his opponent to tap by gripping the right wrist and arching his hips forward to create pressure on Treanor's right elbow.

Both the flying triangle and flying armbar are surprise finishes that go straight from the standing position into the finishing hold. However, if either attack fails, then you'll need to fight from your back using the guard. A fighter with a good guard might even make this part of his game plan because if the surprise attack works, then great. But if not, then the competitor is fighting in his strongest position.

If you want to avoid pulling to your guard, another surprise finish from a standing position is to shoot in for a low single-leg takedown followed by an immediate foot lock. The opening move isn't the surprise finish. Instead, it is the setup for an immediate and successful takedown.

Single-Leg Takedown and Foot Lock

1. David Meyer (right) and Adam Treanor begin on their feet. If Treanor's right foot is forward, Meyer will put his own left foot forward and visa versa.

2. Meyer crouches down. He drops his right knee to the ground as he places his right hand on the ground in front of his opponent. Then Meyer reaches around his opponent's right heel with his left hand.

3. Because his left heel is trapped, Treanor can't sprawl his leg back. For the takedown, Meyer brings his left ear to the inside of Treanor's right shin.

4. Using his right hand on the ground as a base, Meyer presses the left side of his head against Treanor's right shin, forcing him to the ground.

172

As Treanor falls, Meyer maintains control of Treanor's right heel with his left arm and rises up momentarily to his feet.

He stands up just enough to let his right knee come forward and rise up between Treanor's legs. Meyer simultaneously pulls Treanor's right foot into his left armpit.

Meyer then falls to his left side and squeezes his knees together as he encircles Treanor's right foot with his left arm—he tries to get as close to Treanor's ankle as possible. Using his right hand to hold the top of his own left wrist for support, Meyer pushes his hips forward and arches his shoulders backward to stretch Treanor's toes away from the front of Treanor's shin. This forces the opponent to tap out.

If this takedown fails, you will likely either have your opponent sprawled on top of you or you will simply need to rise to your feet again and continue standing. Either scenario is a good way to initiate the match or restart it in a standing position.

Like in the previous example, foot locks are ideal surprise finishes as long as they are legally allowed by the rules in your competition and divisions. As mentioned in Chapter 1, foot locks are dangerous to execute because the defender may twist or roll to escape the undue pressure placed on the foot and ankle. If untrained, the opponent can seriously injure his own knee. Beyond potential injury, foot locks also can take you from a strategic good position to a bad position. For example, a competitor can go from a top position to a bottom position if the foot lock fails, meaning he must struggle to get back on top.

In recognizing these potential drawbacks, a foot lock as a surprise finish is ideal when you can't seem to pass the guard, and are behind on points and time is running out. In these circumstances, it is particularly effective because your opponent is often so focused on keeping you from passing the guard that he is not prepared to defend his feet from attack. Obviously, as a surprise finish, you need to execute a foot lock quickly to work, but again, be careful not to injure your opponent and pay attention to the rules.

Foot Twist From an Open Guard

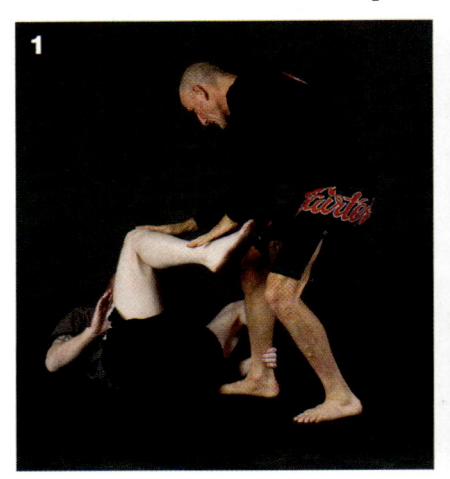

1. With little time left and behind in points, David Meyer decides to risk a surprise attack while standing in Adam Treanor's open guard. Meyer places his right foot between Treanor's feet and moves in close enough so that Treanor's right foot is near his left hip.

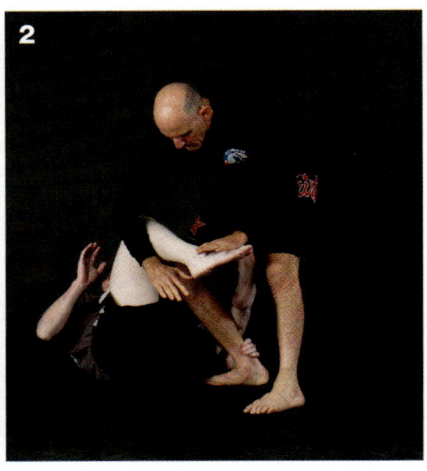

2. Meyer turns quickly to his left and circles his right arm around Treanor's right foot.

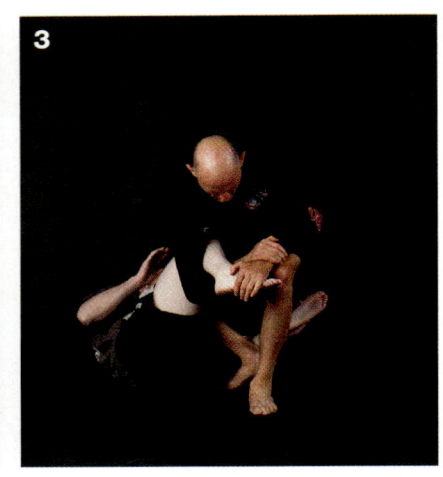

3. As he holds the top of Treanor's right foot with his left hand, Meyer grabs his left wrist with his right hand for a figure-4 lock.

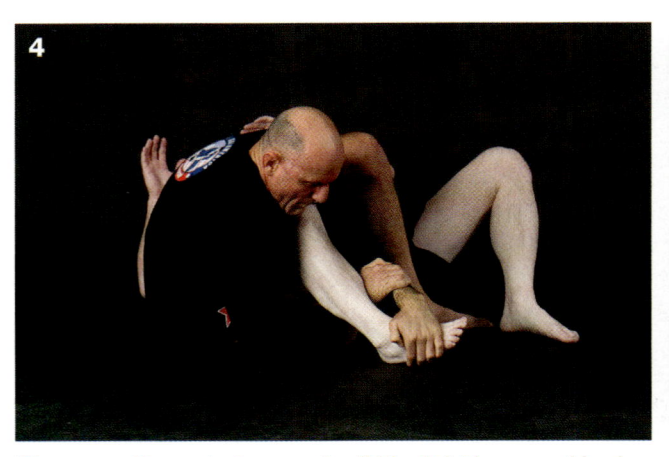

4. Meyer continues to turn and roll his right knee and body over the top of Treanor's right leg.

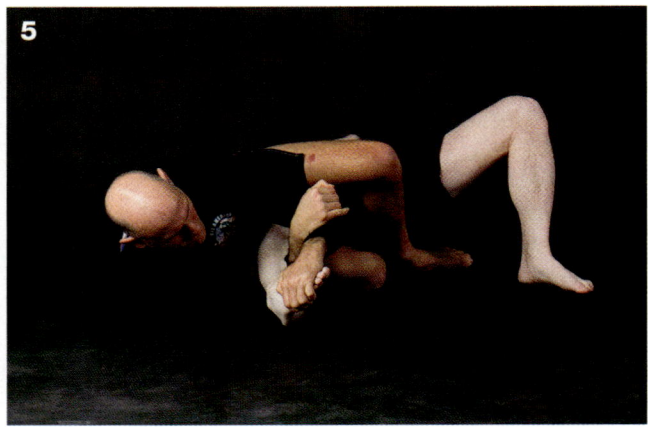

5. Meyer finishes by squeezing his knees together and twisting the toes of Treanor's right foot to the left and back toward Treanor's body to force a tapout.

David Meyer

Foot Lock While Kneeling in an Open Guard

1

In a common scenario, David Meyer kneels in the open guard with his left knee on the ground and his right knee facing up.

2

As Adam Treanor's right shin is across Meyer's hips, Meyer presses forward with his right knee and slides his left foot tightly under his own body.

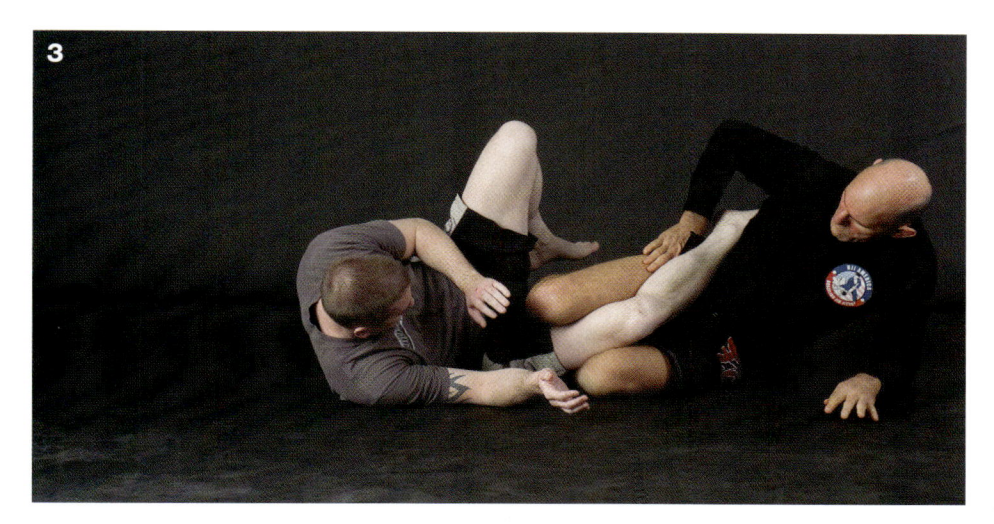

3

Meyer then falls onto his left side, squeezing his knees together around Treanor's right leg. He encircles his opponent's right foot with his own right arm, getting as close as possible to Treanor's ankle.

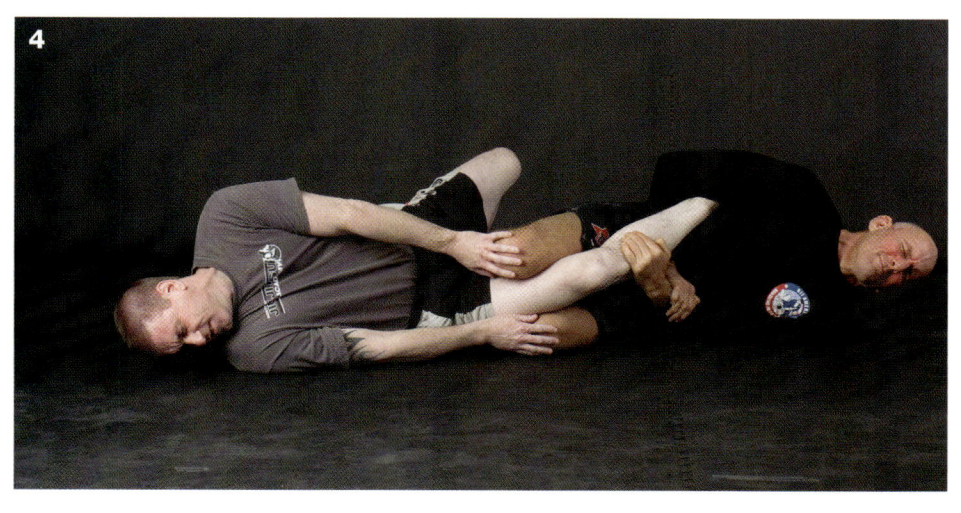

4

Meyer uses his right hand to hold the top of his left wrist, creating a figure-4 lock. Then Meyer lies back, pushing his hips forward and arching his back to stretch Treanor's toes away from the front of the shin to get the tapout.

Foot locks are also effective from other positions. In side control, for instance, a foot lock is particularly effective because the opponent is pinned on the bottom, is more concerned about blocking the mount, choke or armbar attacks, and generally not paying attention to his feet.

Foot Lock From Side Control

David Meyer is in side control with Adam Treanor on his left side.

Bringing his left shin onto Treanor's stomach, Meyer gets ready to do a knee-on-the-stomach position from a crouching knee.

Treanor immediately turns to his left to defend and push Meyer's left knee off his stomach.

Keeping his opponent occupied, Meyer tries the same technique with his right knee.

Meyer then brings his left knee under Treanor's left knee. He also lifts Treanor's left foot up into his own left armpit.

Falling back onto his right side, Meyer uses his left arm to encircle his opponent's left ankle. He squeezes his knees together to control the left leg and uses his right hand to hold the left wrist, creating a figure-4 lock. Meyer then pushes his hips forward and arches backward to stretch Treanor's toes away from the front of the shin. This forces him to tap out.

In addition to foot locks, armbars are also effective surprise finishes. Fighters tend to be more cautious and weary of armbars because they are more common moves, but they can be skillfully set up so that your opponent does not see them coming.

Here is an example of a surprise armbar finish from side control. In this move, the opponent is not prepared for the armbar attack because your weight is on him and because there is no sign that you are about to do anything with his arm.

Snap Armbar From Side Control

David Meyer is in side control on Adam Treanor's left side. He sneaks his left wrist under Treanor's left wrist, keeping his weight down so as not to give any indication that Treanor's left arm is under any threat.

Still keeping his chest down, Meyer circles his right knee over Treanor's head while pivoting on his left knee and bringing his left foot under Treanor's left shoulder.

Meyer then sits close to Treanor's left shoulder and sweeps his left knee up to the sky, which pries Treanor's left elbow away from Treanor's side.

Meyer squeezes his knees together to control Treanor's left arm and sits back for an armbar.

Surprise finishes are possible while standing, passing the guard or when in top positions. But you can also execute surprise finishes when your opponent is in your guard. This does require some skill because anybody in your guard realizes that they are in danger of armbars and triangles, so how you set them up is extremely important.

Here is an example of one of my favorite surprise entries into the triangle from the guard:

Triangle From the Closed Guard

1

David Meyer begins on his back with Adam Treanor in his guard. Meyer holds Treanor's left elbow or sleeve with his right hand and Treanor's left lapel with his left hand.

2

Meyer slides his body slightly away from Treanor and onto his right side.

3

Meyer drops his left knee over Treanor's right elbow and lays his shin horizontally across Treanor's body, similar to the position you might use for the scissor sweep, except Treanor's right arm is trapped by Meyer's left shin. Meyer pulls Treanor's left arm away from Treanor's body and presses into Treanor's right arm with Meyer's left shin. This makes Treanor want to pull his right arm out and bring it back to where it can provide support for his left arm.

4

As Treanor draws his right arm back to free it, Meyer follows it with his left shin, and the moment that Treanor's right hand is away from his body, Meyer circles his left shin over Treanor's neck, leaving Treanor's left arm trapped between Meyer's legs.

5

Meyer then squeezes his knees close together and locks his right knee over his left foot for the triangle.

6

Meyer pulls down on Treanor's head as Meyer lifts his hips to get the tapout.

One final example of a surprise finish is a rolling legbar from the "turtle" position in which you are on your hands and knees and your opponent has circled around to your side. This position is fairly common, especially if you've failed in a takedown attempt in which your opponent sprawled away and then circled around you.

As with any legbar (knee lock) attack, you must be cautious. Don't put too much pressure on your opponent's knee before he has the opportunity to tap out. Knee locks are particularly dangerous in this regard because the opponent frequently does not feel pain until there is an injury. So you must be wary of two things: holding your opponent in the finishing position, and giving the opponent or referee the time needed to tap out or stop the fight because he sees that the knee is in danger.

Rolling Legbar From the Turtle Position

1

David Meyer is in the turtle position and Adam Treanor is at his right side. To keep his opponent from grabbing his limbs or jumping onto his back for control, Meyer keeps his arms and legs in tight.

2

Meyer inserts his right foot between Treanor's legs and crosses his right foot over Treanor's left calf.

3

Meyer then extends his left leg out and tucks his right shoulder in, lifting his hips in the air.

4

Rolling over his right shoulder, Meyer uses his right arm to reach under his legs and encircle Treanor's left leg.

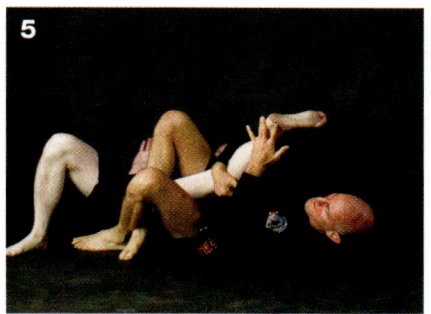

5

As he finishes the roll, Meyer grabs Treanor's left foot and extends his leg with both of his own hands.

6

Meyer then lies on his left side, squeezes his knees together to immobilize Treanor's left leg and holds Treanor's left heel with both his hands. Meyer slowly arches his hips forward as he pulls back with his feet and hands for the tapout.

This leg lock is not only useful as a surprise finish but also can disorient your opponent and help you recover from the turtle position to a more neutral position or even a superior position on the ground.

Surprise finishes can occur from many different positions. They are not a substitute for your general grappling skills, but they can be that one risk you can take that allows you to win the match when your overall skills are just not enough.

Chapter 9
Good Match Coaching, "The Eye in the Sky"

An important factor in having the best chance possible at winning is the quality of your corner coach. Your corner coach is the person who gives you directions and information during the competition match. Your corner coach pays attention to the details that you and your opponent can't see, like your opponent's moves and strategies, the score and time remaining. The corner coach also gives you verbal encouragement and support, which can be vital at certain points in the match.

Ideally, your normal instructor would be your corner coach because he has a lot of competition experience and knows your game, strengths and weaknesses best. But if there are many competitors from your school, it is just not possible for your instructor to be in everyone's corner for every match. That's why it's more common to ask a fellow student to be your corner coach.

I was fortunate to have my instructor, Rigan Machado, as my corner coach for most of my important fights. For example, in 1996, I competed in the then largest BJJ competition in the United States. At the time, I was a brown belt, chosen specifically to represent the Machado team in a "superfight" against Rickson Gracie's top American brown-belt Mark Eccard. Our two schools were the powerhouses of the sport, and I felt a tremendous amount of pride and pressure riding on my shoulders.

During the match, I remember how the auditorium fell silent. Because my guard was my strongest game, I immediately enacted the game plan my coach and I had worked out—pull my opponent to my guard—and immediately attempted a sweep. But Eccard's balance was awesome and passing the guard was his best game. We were in a technical standoff, which is why, after an initial exchange, the chess match began.

I can still remember hearing Machado's words so clearly from where he was on the sidelines. He instructed me perfectly on every detail of Eccard's attacks. And I also remember hearing Gracie's perfect coaching for Eccard. It was as if Gracie could read my mind; he seemed to always know what I was trying to set up.

I have never in my life seen or experienced a higher level of coaching that day with Machado and Gracie—and on that day, their warriors fought to a zero/zero tie. In a controversial decision that took more than 10 minutes beneath a chorus of shouting, the referee gave the victory to Eccard for having spent more time "on top," trying to pass my guard. However, both he and I agreed, it was as dead-even a match as anybody could ever have.

Of course, you may not have the luxury of being the recipient of such intense corner coaching, but that's OK. The truth is that you just need to know what to look for in a coach and what to ask for.

What You Need From Your Corner Coach

Good corner coaching is mostly encouragement and a little bit of information and instruction. Often that encouragement is simply to be told that you are doing well. In addition, just knowing that there is someone watching and supporting you can be very important, especially if your match is extremely tough.

In regards to technical advice, it's ideal to find someone you trust, who understands the sport and who knows your game, like your instructor, fellow classmate or training partner. When you have found this person, let him know your game plan in advance so that he can guide you. In addition, your corner coach can remind you to get back on track, if necessary. Frequently in the heat of the fight, you might be drawn into your opponent's plan, and it is important to have a corner coach to call you back to your strategy, even with the words, "Get back to your game plan." In this way, the corner coach not only puts you back in control of the match but also doesn't give away your game plan to the opponent.

One of your corner coach's most important jobs is to keep you informed on the points. He should alert you each time the referee awards points to you or your competitor. So you will always know who is winning the match and by how much, thus helping you to guide your strategy on how to play the points.

It is also equally important for your corner coach to inform you if the referee has not awarded you points. For example, if you pass the guard and your opponent is not yet fully under control, the referee may award an advantage point rather than an actual point. It is crucial to know this so you do not change positions until you actually score. It is also important to know if your opponent has not been awarded points. For example, if the opponent passes the guard and you know the referee has yet to award points, then you can keep expending energy to push him back into the full- or half-guard. However, if you know the referee did award points for the pass, then you can take a breath, consolidate your energy and move onto your strategies to escape from the bottom.

Your corner coach not only should keep you updated on the points but also on how much time is left in the match. I suggest that you ask your corner coach to tell you each time you cross a minute marker—for example, five minutes left, four minutes left, etc. This, along with a knowledge of the points, will allow you to know whether you are behind and must wildy explode before the clock expires. It will also let you know whether you are winning and should stall or whether you need to show aggressive mat control when the points are even.

If you are behind on points and time is running out, your corner coach should encourage you to take risks, such as baiting your opponent to escape a position or in trying for a surprise finish. During the heat of a fight, it's easy to focus on defending against a particular attack, thus forgetting that you are down on points and going to lose anyway. Through your corner coach, you might be able to know when to take a risk, earning you the victory instead.

Your corner coach's last important job is to be your advocate with the referee. This might mean politely protesting to the referee if he has made a bad call, pointing out things to the referee such as illegal moves by your opponent that the official can't see, and most important, making sure the referee is correctly awarding points to you.

For the most part, referees do their best, but they are of course human. Chances are that they've been on the mat for hours without a real break by the time your match starts. As they tire, referees can miss awarding points, especially if something happens quickly. For example, a fighter might take his opponent down, fall into the opponent's open guard, and as the opponent struggles to recover, the fighter might be able to hop straight over the opponent's guard to the mount. Many referees will award two points for the takedown and then four points for the mount. But the referee might forget to give three points for the guard pass. Another common error is when a fighter sweeps his opponent and ends up directly in the mount. Sometimes the referee will award four points for the mount but forget to award two points for the sweep that got the fighter there. Mistakes happen, and your corner coach is there to politely but firmly let officials know at the moment the mistake occurs.

These refereeing mistakes can be very easy to make, so the corner coach needs to watch closely, and if a mistake occurs, he must quickly and politely inform the referee that a mistake has been made. So to sum it up, when you ask someone to be your corner coach, ask them to:

- encourage you,
- remind you to stay with your game plan if you get off track,
- keep you updated on the score and points,
- let you know when time is running out and if you should stall or explode, and
- watch closely and advocate for you if the referee is not seeing something he should or not scoring your match properly.

If You Are a Corner Coach

Just as you ask one of your friends to be your corner coach, he may ask you to be his corner coach. If you agree to help, you should, of course, do what we have discussed. But I also want to offer you some more detailed advice to make you a better corner coach for your friends and teammates.

The most important thing a coach can do for a fighter is give him encouragement, support, read his problems and help the fighter overcome them.

I have found that speaking in the plural helps: "Let's finish strong" or "We can get out of this" may sound funny, but some people really like the feeling of not being alone on the mat. Encouraging a pinned fighter with something like "I know you are tired, but we can get out of this" is equally helpful. Or the following encouragement might help for a fighter on top: "Keep your position. You have two more minutes, and this fight is yours."

Telling a fighter when he is doing something positive is also a good idea. Phrases like "Good pressure, keep your weight on him" give the competitor good instruction while revealing no details of your attack setups or game plan to the opponent. (The opponent already knows the competitor's weight is on him.)

In addition, let your competitor know that the opponent is more tired than he is. Whether this is true is of no significance. Instead, it's a mental boost for your fighter to believe that the opponent is in worse shape.

Do note that in telling your fighter that the opponent is tired is not meant to frustrate the opponent. I believe it is absolutely unacceptable and unsportsmanlike for a corner coach to say things designed to frustrate and anger the opponent. Perhaps the corner coach might not mean for his remarks to be inflammatory, but saying things like "That guy is no good" or "His guard sucks; pass it" degrade the opponent rather than bolster your fighter.

But in this one case in which you are encouraging your fighter by telling him the opponent is tired is supportive and can energize him. I've never had an opponent complain, and in fact, sometimes he believes it to be true himself, which is even better.

Effective Corner-Coach Phrases

- Let's finish strong.
- We can get out of this.
- I know you're tired, but we can get out of this.
- Keep your position. You have (____) minutes, and this fight is yours.
- Good pressure, keep your weight on him (in reference to an effective technique or move).
- He's tired! We've got him!
- Play your game.

What Not to Do as a Corner Coach

There are certain mistakes corner coaches make time and again, and I want to make sure that you avoid them. One big mistake is that the coach forgets to coach toward the specific skills of the individual fighters. The corner coach is instructing the fighter to do things that the fighter can't execute.

Each competitor has a specific set of skills, physical attributes and past experience he brings to a competition. As the corner coach, you must cater your comments to these factors. One would expect a fan to get excited and scream useless encouragement to fighters, which is exactly what coaches should not do. It doesn't make sense to yell at a fighter to execute a move, even the right move, if your fighter does not know or is not proficient at that move. Your coaching must revolve around your fighter and your fighter's knowledge and skills.

I have seen many instances in which corner coaches in competition yell at their fighters to "Take him down!" They urge the fighter to execute a takedown, even though that fighter does not have good takedown skills compared to his opponent. The problem is that the coach is saying what he would do, but clearly, these words are not helping the lesser-skilled fighter.

A better way to handle this situation would be if the corner coach says something like "Shoot the takedown and pull to guard" or "Push him off the mat." Remember, your task as a corner coach is not to just give instructions but to also give instructions that are relevant and useful to your fighter based on his knowledge and skills.

Another big mistake coaches make is that they attempt to "puppet" the fighter. In other words, they shout command after command to get the fighter to do the obvious or control his every move. If your fighter is in someone's guard, he doesn't need you to yell, "Pass the guard." He knows that is his task. If the fighter is stuck on bottom, they don't need you to yell, "Put him back in your guard." Obviously, he is trying to escape, which may include putting his opponent back into his guard. It is not valuable for a corner coach to shout obvious technical instructions. Saying things that are not helpful might cause a fighter to stop listening to important information.

The worst occurrence is when a corner coach sees an opportunity for his fighter to take advantage of and yells, "Get the triangle." Sometimes, I think coaches forget that the opponent can hear them, too. Every detail you give your fighter is also a potential warning or even an instruction for the opponent, so be careful. Make sure that your instructions don't needlessly tip off the opponent to what your fighter is trying to do.

Keeping in mind that both fighters hear the instructions, there are a few instances in which defensive instructions can be useful. For example, if a corner coach sees a specific sweep or attack coming, he can warn the fighter with a quick line like "Base-out with your right foot" or "Chin down." Letting a fighter know that he is being set up is helpful defensive coaching, and it doesn't tip off the opponent who is well aware of what he is attempting.

My last piece of advice on how to be a good corner coach is to remind you that, as passionate as you are about the match, you will not help your fighter by getting excited and screaming. In fact, it's easier for your fighter to distinguish your voice if you speak clearly, calmly and loudly under the roar of the screaming audience. As the corner coach, you are the clear mind, the "eye in the sky," the fighter's bonus perspective and experience.

So remember, if you don't have to, say nothing and just let the fighter concentrate on the match. But if needed, give the competitor calm, infrequent interjections—mostly made up of encouragement—useful facts about time and points and the occasional specific instruction on technique.

Interview with **Cesar Gracie**
BJJ Expert

Q: In your opinion, what is the value of participating in a competition?
A: I definitely think [competing] is a good thing. It gets [you] focused on getting better. It gives [you] motivation and ultimately it sets a goal. I feel that people who do compete get better faster than people who don't.

Q: What do you think about the differences between *gi* and no-gi matches?
A: I think it's just [personal] preference. I do believe that you are going to have to be a little more technical as a competitor when you do gi competitions because your escapes have to be better. You can't rely on slipping out of [holds] as much. It's also harder to escape from some positions, which is going to give you a little bit more technique. I think that the gi-less competitions are probably going to give you more speed, but in the end, both formats are important because they bring in different elements. Ultimately, I think you should compete in both, but other than that, it is a matter of preference.

Q: What specific advice do you have for grapplers about to go into competition?
A: If you are competing for something that has a lot of meaning—the world championships or something—then you definitely need to watch your training and diet as well as make sure you are well-rested. Whatever way you prepare to do it, you need to put it all together in the weeks before the competition. This way, when the competition comes, you are going to be at 100 percent.

Q: Do you have any advice for coaches?
A: I think the best thing that I can tell a coach is to really get to know the game of the fighter you are coaching. Know your fighter. Know what his strengths are. Know what his weaknesses are. Know when he is going to break so you can encourage him. Know in what spots he does well and when he is most comfortable. Have a vision for your fighter about what the opponent is trying to do, then try to line things up so that your guy can win. It's like a chess game—you are out there trying to tell your guy where to move his pieces. Because I've grown up with Brazilian *jiu-jitsu*, I've had the privilege of training with some of the best coaches in the world at a lot of schools, and I know the difference between a good coach and a bad coach. Sometimes coaches make mistakes. They put too much pressure on a student also to win, and suddenly, jiu-jitsu is not fun for the student. It's become a chore, and at that point, the student doesn't even want to train. I've seen coaches destroy so many students who should have been really good. The students' only problem was that they didn't have a coach to train them properly.

Q: Why do people do worse in competition than in the gym?
A: The mental game—because they fall apart. When people are expected to win and things don't go their way, they think, "Hey, I'm not taking this guy down as easy as I should be." They start to lock up more and more mentally until they can't do anything right. They are so focused that things aren't going their way that they can't think clearly on how to win. At the academy, there is no pressure. People just naturally do the right thing.

Q: What advice do you have for competitors stressed about losing?
A: The way to get rid of that [feeling] is first to tell yourself to accept the fact that you are going to lose a lot. The best BJJ people in the world who I know lost a lot, and then they got good. They just kept throwing themselves out there [into competition] over and over again until they finally conquered their own fears and their own [internal] pressure to perform at the level that they [originally] wanted to.

Q: What is the "right" attitude to have in competition?
A: I remember I [was coaching] Nathan Diaz and Gilbert Melendez—they were purple belts at the time—and they were going against a couple of really good guys that were black belts and were some of the top guys from a particular school. My guys were not expected to beat them in competition, but [Diaz and Melendez] took in that warrior spirit—which is the correct attitude to win—to not give up and overcome their opponents with skill. If you don't give up, you can mentally break somebody else because you're going to show them that you're here to stay and are just going to keep coming. I've seen guys that are not supposed to win, but guess what? Their coaches didn't tell them that [probability], so they won anyway.

Section IV

THE PAYOFF
Final Preparation and Competition Day

Chapter 10
Tying It All Together

You now have a lot of information on things you can practice that are specific to competition and will help you perform better. You also know you need a starting, restarting and overall game plan, as well as the ability to know how to block your opponent's game plan, play the points and clock, and practice training from a point deficit from many different positions. In addition, you know you should be able to stall and break stalls, develop surprise finishes and find a good corner coach to help you in each match.

These things can be practiced as part of your normal training, regardless of how near or far you are from the next competition date. But there is one last important step that will tie it all together and that you should practice in the four weeks leading up to the competition. That step is to conduct practice competition matches at your school. These matches are designed to let you practice all the things we've discussed in the book but in such a way that puts you under pressure and simulates the adrenaline release you will feel during a real competition.

Practice vs. Competition

The release of adrenaline is part of an entire physiological reaction when you feel fear and stress. It can work for you or against you. It can power up or deplete your muscles' energy. It can sharpen or narrow your attention. In fact, the biggest factor that can render years of martial arts experience absolutely ineffective is adrenaline, which is why it's important to recognize and learn how to direct it in competition.

When someone is scared or under pressure, an entire series of complex physiological reactions occur. Adrenaline is released, a person's heart rate rises, and he experiences tunnel vision and a sense of the world moving slowly. The person might even experience something known as "reptile brain" in which complex speech and physical dexterity give way to short, hard-wired movements and words. People who have ever had a street fight probably know what I mean.

Of course, a grappling tournament is no street fight but it does involve the rush of adrenaline. If you are a novice competitor, you might begin your fighting career like a crazed person who thrashes at anything that moves, unnecessarily tiring yourself out while missing all kinds of strategic opportunities. However, as you compete, you'll learn how to control that uncontrollable rush. In essence, you'll end your fighting career like a jet pilot who is calm, clear-minded, emotionally unshakeable and always focused on the task at hand. The way to begin this process is to recreate some of that stress and excitement in the comfort of your own school during the weeks leading up to a competition through practice matches.

Practice Competition Matches

In the four weeks leading up to a tournament, create practice competition matches to tune up your body for specific competition strategies. These practice matches are simply matches at your school where you start standing and fight exactly like you would during the competition. Ideally, a third person should act as the referee by awarding points and making calls. Your fellow students should also watch from the side of the mat, cheering you or your opponent on to recreate the noise from an actual audience. I recommend that you extend the match time to one minute longer than the actual competition match time because it will build endurance, and actual competitions always feel longer than they are.

Practice matches also give you a chance to practice listening to the instructions of your corner coach as you fight. If your instructor is not going to be at the tournament, you should have the person who has agreed to be your coach practice his role. That way, a practice competition match not only helps you and your opponent prepare for game day but also gives the corner coach some practice.

One point of caution: Make sure that all fighters warm up thoroughly and demonstrate control in the practice matches. The reason for this is that when a competitor is truly trying to win while people cheer him on, a referee makes calls and corner coaches mete out advice, the chances for injuries greatly increase. So please be careful.

Train Your Weak Spots

It is crucial in the weeks leading up to a competition that you not only train your strong spots but also your weak spots. Even if you are better overall than your opponent, the one chance he has to beat you is if there is a crack in your armor.

For example, if you are heading toward a competition in which foot locks or kneebars are allowed and you don't have a good defense against those techniques, it would be a good idea for you to find training partners who attack legs so you can make your mistakes in training and not in the competition. Even if you don't have partners who can execute these particular attacks well, ask them to at least try because this will sharpen your awareness of the danger.

Another example: Perhaps you have a problem passing the guard. Ask your instructor (if you have one) to show you better ways to pass or stay out of someone's guard. The temptation before a competition is to practice your strong points, but don't forget to spend some time on your weak points, as well.

So what is your weakest area? Are there moves you tend to fall victim to again and again? Ask your instructors and training partners for their thoughts. Whatever they say, you should probably work on to strengthen. Perhaps you have bad posture when passing the guard, or perhaps you are too defensive. Perhaps you leave your arms out and vulnerable to attack or you are easily taken down.

For most grapplers, the weakest spot is a defense against foot and leg attacks. There are a number of reasons for this. First, many grapplers come from high-school wrestling or judo backgrounds, neither of which allow such attacks. Second, many BJJ and grappling schools discourage such foot and leg attacks because they have a high injury rate.

When I began participating in submission grappling, the sport and tournaments were still quite new. I knew that as a BJJ black belt, my biggest danger was coming up against a less skilled grappler who had fast foot and leg attacks. Other than that, I was extremely confident in my skills. I worked with my partners Rick Williams, Ryan Gregg and Andy Wang, who were all experts in foot and leg attacks. As a result, I added these attacks to my arsenal and have never been tapped out by a foot or leg attack in a tournament.

If you are fighting in a division in which foot and leg locks are legal, you should address this weakness. The best way to develop a good defense against foot and leg attacks is to train with people, as I did, who know them and will try them but who have excellent control.

Foot Lock From the Open Guard

1. David Meyer is standing in Adam Treanor's open guard. Treanor makes a mistake and allows his right foot to lie alongside Meyer's left hip.

2. Meyer uses his left elbow to pin Treanor's ankle alongside Meyer's left hip.

3. Meyer then sits back, capturing Treanors right leg between his own thighs.

4. Meyer places his left foot in front of Treanor's right hip, preventing Treanor from coming forward. Meyer turns to his left side, squeezes his thighs tightly together to hold Treanor's leg in place, and arches his hips forward and shoulder backward, causing Treanor's right ankle to hyperextend.

If you get caught in a legbar, foot-lock or heel-hook position, buy yourself some time to escape by holding onto one of your opponent's hands. It is almost impossible for the opponent to finish any leg attack if he only has one hand to use. However, note that you must do this before the attack "locks."

The best cure for foot and leg attacks is to prevent them before they happen. The following sequences explain how to avoid some of these attacks and escape them, if needed.

Foot-Lock Escape, No. 1

1

David Meyer (bottom) makes a mistake, leaving his right foot alongside Adam Treanor's left hip. This exposes him to a possible foot lock.

2

Treanor uses his left arm to encircle Meyer's right ankle, preparing for the foot lock.

3

Meyer sees that his foot is caught by Treanor's left arm and immediately slides his hips to his left as he twists his right heel to the left while bending his right leg.

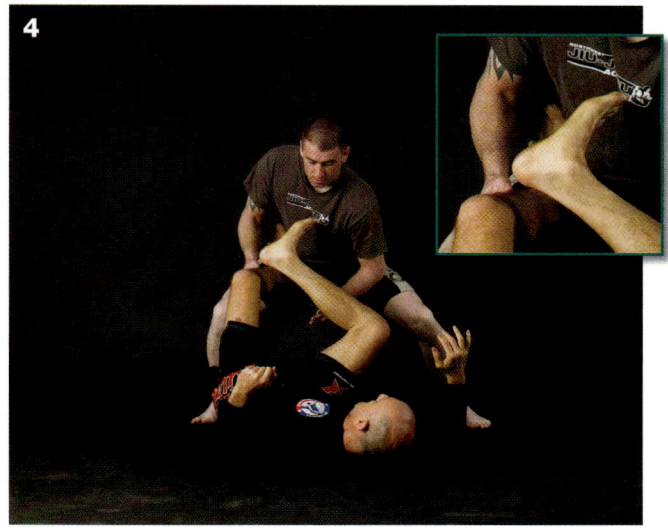

4

With his right heel in front of Treanor's body, Meyer uses his left foot to push on Treanor's chest and free his own right foot entirely, thereby avoiding the foot-lock attack.

Training for Competition: Brazilian Jiu-Jitsu and Submission Grappling

This reaction of twisting the heel free is the most basic way to slip out of a foot lock before it occurs. Practice this movement again and again with your partner so that your body will instinctively know how you need to move in a competition. If, however, your opponent does catch your foot and falls back to apply the lock, you must react quickly with the following escape or you will lose the match:

Foot-Lock Escape, No. 2

Adam Treanor (left) traps David Meyer's left foot against his right hip.

Treanor falls back and is about to squeeze his knees tight and arch his back for the finish.

Before Treanor can do that, Meyer reaches forward with his right hand and holds Treanor's right shoulder from behind. Meyer then pushes his left foot deeper and past Treanor. This is called "putting on the boot" because Meyer is pressing his foot as if he is pushing it into a boot. This motion ensures that Treanor will have a hold on Meyer's calf but not on Meyer's ankle.

With Meyer's ankle behind Treanor, Treanor cannot arch and hyperextend it. Meyer then posts with his left hand on the ground and rises his hips in the air and forward.

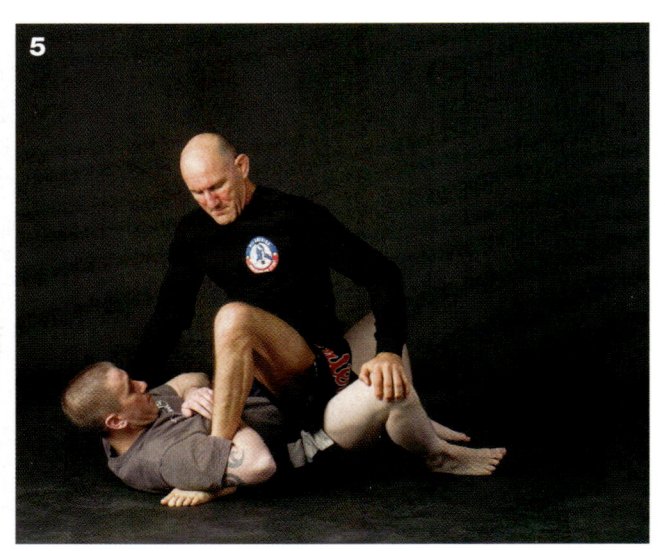

Meyer comes forward over Treanor's left knee and is seated on top of Treanor's body in a dominant position; his left foot is no longer in danger of the foot lock.

If your foot is caught, then you must execute an escape. But you need to understand that your opponent is going to execute a foot lock or a heel hook—two very different locks. A foot lock stretches your toes back and hyperextends your ankle in a straight movement. A heel hook twists your foot to the side, mainly twisting the knee instead of the ankle. If you are caught in a heel hook, then the following is the best escape to use:

Heel-Hook Escape

David Meyer (bottom) makes the mistake of leaving his left foot alongside Adam Treanor's right hip.

Treanor falls to the ground in the same position as a foot lock, but then he reaches back with his right forearm and catches Meyer's left heel.

Treanor then squeezes his thighs together to hold Meyer's left leg in place and attempts to twist Meyer's left heel to Treanor's left side.

Meyer feels that this is a heel hook, not a foot lock, and as Treanor twists Meyer's heel, Meyer turns his entire body to the right, escaping the pain Treanor is trying to create.

Treanor rolls, still attempting to create pressure on Meyer's heel and knee. As Meyer rolls onto his back, he pulls his right leg in and begins to press on Treanor's body.

Meyer pushes with his right foot and slides his body back, thereby freeing his left foot from Treanor's grip.

Like any problem, the best defense is prevention, so simply having partners who frequently attempt foot and leg attacks will make you aware of a problem before it develops as well as teach you how to defend against it. You should do light sparring with a continual flow in which both competitors constantly and lightly attack the feet and legs. This will help build up your reactions to these attacks without risking injury.

Chapter 11
The Final Week

After weeks and months of preparation, there is little you can do in the last week before the event to improve your performance on competition day. The days before the competition are no longer about training, conditioning or anything else. They're about letting your body heal and getting your head together for the tournament day.

However, there are a few things you can do in that last week that will hurt your chances of winning, and it's important to know what they are and how to avoid them.

Don't Overtrain

In 1993 before there were any BJJ competitions in the United States, I was a BJJ blue belt and my coach Rigan Machado wanted me to enter a local judo championship with him. We trained hard the week before, and I wanted to be in particularly good shape because I not only was entering the tournament as a "black belt" but also was unfamiliar with the rules of judo.

On the day before the tournament, I wrestled extra hard and even climbed up and down a rope at a local gym several times without using my legs to strengthen my grip. Unfortunately for me, the next day my hands were still fatigued, and I could feel my weak and sore grip with each opponent I fought. In the end, my grips were completely burned out and I didn't win. I had overtrained and not given my body the chance to recover properly before the competition.

But I still hadn't learned my lesson when I was prepping for the 2005 Pan-American Games in Los Angeles. As an experienced black belt with many old friends attending the tournament, I really wanted to do well. I trained twice as hard on the mat, ran stairs, lifted weights and pulled a hip muscle just one week before the competition. For the first time, I could not and did not compete in a competition for which I had registered. I was heartbroken.

I tell you these stories because, as excitement builds in the last weeks before a competition, it becomes easier and easier to overtrain and not let your body recover. Coupled with the heightened excitement of an upcoming tournament, this type of training can and often does lead to a higher than usual injury rate. I cannot begin to tell you how disappointing it is to train for a tournament only to get injured in the days leading to the event, or how disappointing it is to walk into a match on competition day only to discover that your body is not 100 percent because of your recent training.

To avoid that, remember to give your body several days to fully recover from hard training. In the days before a competition, your recovery specifically depends on a good diet, drinking a lot of water, stretching and plenty of sleep.

That's why I recommend that your last hard day of training be four days before a tournament. Do not participate in any more practice matches after that day. Instead, just go to class, drill techniques and do only light training like wrestling noncompetitively with classmates. If you can, get in a Jacuzzi to relax your muscles or schedule a moderate sports massage that doesn't cause soreness.

Do not train the day before the tournament and only stretch. If you have nervous energy, go for a light run or swim to work that out and help you sleep during the last night, but don't do anything that will break down your muscles or cause soreness.

Cutting Weight

Before a tournament, you should never cut weight. A person cuts weight by starving himself of food and water and by sweating out the body's moisture. In doing this, the body becomes weak and your muscles become prone to tearing. There is an electrolyte imbalance that affects your brain function and your ability to make quick decisions on the mat.

I do not recommend that any competitor or person attempt to cut weight, even to meet tournament weight requirements. If you happen to be overweight for a certain division after registering for a tournament, try to achieve weight loss through natural means months and weeks before the competition day.

Stressing Out

Even the best fighters can find themselves drained on competition day because of days and nights of worried anticipation. This is very normal, and it is just the ego taking control of variables that you can't control by mentally rehearsing the competition and its outcome. If your mind is in constant fight mode in the final week of training, the constant release of adrenaline will needlessly drain your energy.

I remember when the Pan-American Brazilian Jiu-Jitsu Championship was held in 1995 in Southern California. At the time, I was a purple belt who had recently won a major competition. Unlike in that competition, however, I was going against top Brazilian BJJ purple belts for the first time. I was so nervous during that final week that I came down with a cold.

But I didn't want to give in to the sickness, and I showed up for the competition anyway. Medicated and weak, I stepped onto the mat and was forced to submit by my Brazilian opponent within the first minute. But oddly enough, the moment I lost the match, I suddenly felt much better physically. I was still upset at the outcome, but just knowing that I had no other fights for the day lifted a huge weight off my shoulders. I didn't even feel that sick at all, which meant that the stress had made my fever much worse than it was.

Three years later, I had the opposite experience. After recently receiving my black belt and having participated in a few matches in which I won against experienced grapplers, I prepared for the Pan-American Brazilian Jiu-Jitsu Championship in 1998 in Honolulu. Because of my past matches, I felt confident, relaxed and just took in the sweet Hawaiian air. I didn't put any pressure on myself to train, prepare or grapple before the tournament. On the day of the competition, I took the silver medal, forfeiting in the finals to my own coach, Carlos Machado, who took the gold. Throughout the entire tournament, I felt healthy, strong and just enjoyed myself, which I believe helped me win.

From these experiences, I've realized that stress places a severe drain on the body. It is like a tax and its side effects—poor digestion, lack of sleep, lack of focus, etc.—lower your performance bracket.

The only true key to competition stress reduction is a sincere belief that winning is not everything, there are variables out of your control, and that the fears associated with both don't matter. This is an easier thing to say than to believe, but by continually reminding yourself of it, you can still achieve a positive outcome.

To help you get into the right mind-set, there are things you can do to alleviate stress. They include the following:

- Avoid the temptation to look and see whom you are fighting when the competitor rosters are posted online. Often, people don't show or last-minute changes are made.

- Make a list of everything you will need on the day of the competition—including any help you might need from friends for coaching or driving. Arrange it all in advance so you don't have to worry about it.

- If you are traveling a long distance, be wary about jet lag, and give yourself enough time to adjust, especially in a new time zone. You may have to arrive a day or two before the competition if there is a time difference or a week or two if there are several time zones difference. The best success I personally have with jet lag is in taking a light run on arrival, working up a good sweat and drinking lots of water. Remember, the air conditioning in planes and hotels dehydrates you, so you must rehydrate immediately and constantly. In addition, don't force yourself to adjust to the new time schedule. Instead, get your systems pumping and sleep if you are tired.

- Make yourself comfortable, especially if you are traveling. Travel stress can degrade your energy level by forcing you to sleep in places that are not comfortable or eat foods that are not part of your normal diet. If you have favorite foods, bring them or take the time to find a local store that has them. If you have a favorite pillow, bring it. Hotels can damage your ability to compete if you are not comfortable in bed, so doing whatever it takes to get a good night's sleep is well worth the effort.

If you are still stressed by thinking about the competition, then it can help to visualize how you will perform with some mental preparation. Imagine how you will start the match and how you will execute your game plan. Imagine escaping bad situations and coming out on top and finishing your opponent.

Heighten Your "Bracket"

If you feel particularly stressed about winning before a competition, consider that on any given day, there is the very best you will perform and the very worst. You can think of these two extremes as the top and bottom of a bracket in which the bracket bottom is your worst possible performance and the top part is your best possible performance. The gray area, or the space in between the two extremes, represents all the possibilities of performance for you on any given day.

Your goal in training and practice is to raise your entire bracket higher. This means that you want to raise the worst you could ever do to a level that is not as bad, and you want to raise the best you could do to a level that's even better. Because let's face it, even on a bad day, Michael Jordan won't play that bad. He has a very high performance bracket.

When you apply this to your preparation for a grappling competition, consider that your opponent brings to the match his bracket of performance potential, as well. If his worst performance is still better than your best performance, barring some absolute fluke, you are going to lose. That's not a bad thing. If you were playing Michael Jordan in basketball, for example, wouldn't you learn a lot about the ins and outs of the game, even if you lose?

If your opponent is far superior, keep in mind you do not need to be better overall than he is. You just need to have a high enough bracket so that your very best is better than his very worst. Then just perform at your best and you might win.

You vs. a Superior Opponent

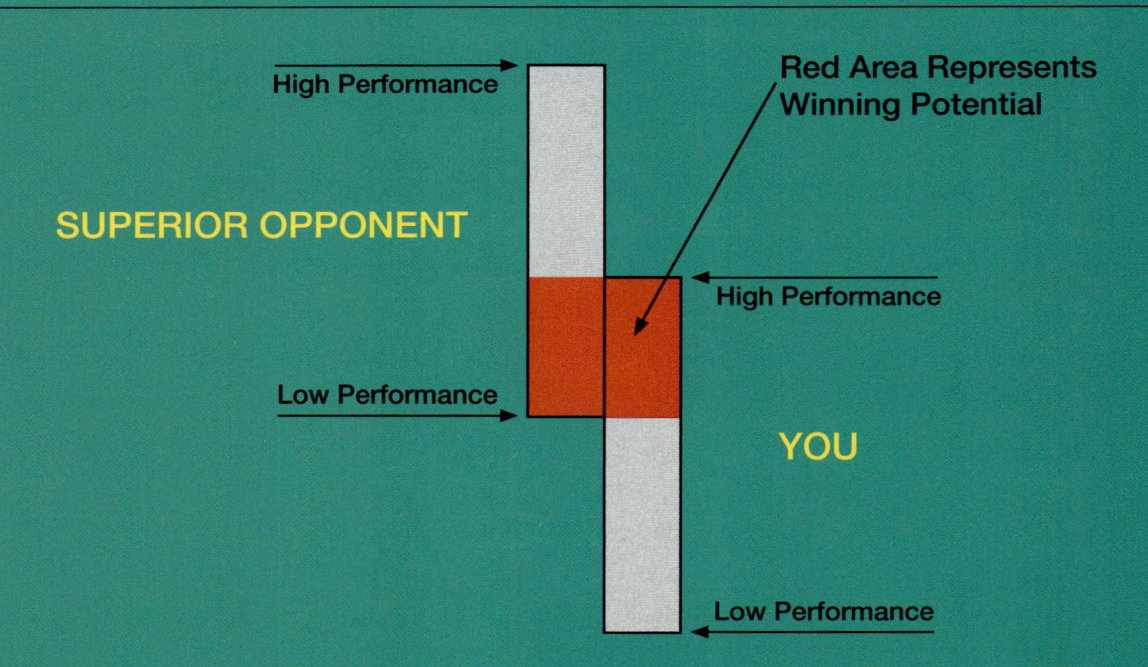

At the same time, if your opponent is far inferior to you, don't be cavalier or overconfident. If the best he might do is above the worst you might do, then you better take the match seriously or risk losing because of an upset.

Because you can't control your opponent's bracket, you can't control who wins. So relax, and perform at the top of your bracket and the rest will take care of itself.

Interview with **Frank Shamrock**
MMA Veteran and Champion

Q: What are your favorite training methods?
A: I'm a huge, huge fan of drilling—not only basic techniques but also turning those [basic] drills into more dynamic, full-body conditioning exercises. [For example], I take sprawls or takedowns or even make reversals and position changing into more speed-oriented stuff. I really like that, especially as I get older.

Q: How do you like to start a match?
A: I go with the flow because the style of submission wrestling that I was [trained in] is more a feeling-type of energy much like judo. I like to feel where the energy goes and convert my style to support it.

Q: As competition day gets closer, how do you train?
A: As the competition gets closer, I just back off from hard grappling and end up doing more play or situational grappling. I break the match down into situations as opposed to one strong, strenuous match. That just [helps me] save my body and tune my mind.

Q: Do you recommend that competitors try to win by submission or win by playing the points?
A: I think it should be all about the finish because that should be the most important thing. But it also depends on what the game [competition match] is for. I was brought up in an entertainment-based system, and the most important thing in that, first off, was to entertain, meaning to try to finish—end of story.

Q: How do you warm up before a match?
A: I warm up my mind first. I visualize and think about what I'm going to do. Then I do a light warm-up for my body. I use the rest of my warm-up time to do situational movements, like technical movements or drilling, and [situational] types of holds. This way, my mind and my body are fused into one unit that is ready to go and grapple. Then I just stay warm until the match. I like to start warming up about 45 minutes before my match so I am really, really warmed up.

Q: Do you have any advice to offer competitors about competition stress?
A: Nerves are a natural part of it and a good part of it because they keep you on edge. You're nervous because there is some fear. Try to figure out a way to overcome those fears of failure, injury, defeat or just fear. I would recommend that a person examine those fears [in training] because it [all comes down] to your training. And all those things can be overcome by exposing yourself to them [in competition].

Chapter 12
Competition Day

Because the outcome of a match depends more on your training than anything else, all you really need to do is show up and compete on the day of the tournament. If you do what you practiced and have a higher performance bracket than your opponent, then you will probably win. Everything else is out of your control, so just relax and have fun.

Otherwise, the following are some things to keep in mind to help you be at your best on competition day.

Uniform

For submission grapplers, make sure you have a dry and warm T-shirt to put on for each match you have that day. It's not so much to increase your performance bracket but to make you more comfortable; it is no fun to wear a cold, wet T-shirt all day. Also, there's a chance your uniform might tear, so it's better to have a replacement.

For BJJ and submission-grappling competitors, have something warm to put on between matches for comfort and to keep your muscles warm. As you get cold, your muscles tighten up, and it's not good for your body or mind to go into a match stiff under any circumstances. Having something warm and comfortable can help you get ready for your next match whether it's minutes or hours away.

For the gentlemen, I recommend that you wear underwear that you're comfortable with people seeing. If you're grappling, your pants might slide down, and it just saves you from having to think about one extra thing on the mat.

Of course, all grapplers should make sure that their uniforms conform to tournament rules before the competition day. But on the day itself, it's a good idea to check one last time.

Eat Breakfast and Lunch

One problem people have on competition day is deciding what and when to eat. They are concerned about what will happen if they have food in their stomach during the match, or sometimes, they are unable to eat at all because of nerves.

My advice is this: Chill out—you are not going to war. It's a competition. When it's over, win or lose, you can go see a movie, so eat what you feel like eating.

When I first began competing, I quickly discovered that, depending on the tournament's size and organization, you might not have your first match until midday or even until that evening. On more than one occasion, I've seen competitors waiting hours for their match while feeling hungry and weak. In the end, they were forced to eat the unhealthy snacks available for purchase at a tournament—if any snacks were available at all.

So on competition day, eat a good breakfast or eat what you normally would eat, which for me is fruit. I find that bananas are an excellent choice because they are high in potassium and other nutrients, which help prevent muscle cramps.

Whatever you choose, don't worry about filling up—just eat normally. Remember, your weight division might fight early in the day, but your open weight class may not start until the evening. That's why it's useful to bring bread, fruits, water or other fluids to the competition as well as some lunch. This could be whatever you normally eat, like a sandwich. I prefer to bring a lunch of vegetable sushi and cut fruit. I also bring nuts and dried fruit to snack on as needed throughout the day. I also suggest that you bring some extra food and drinks for your friends because often when people see what you're eating, they ask if they can have some, too.

Pay special attention to drinking a lot, even if that means you need to run to the bathroom multiple times. Bottled water is a must, but you should also have some sort of electrolyte replacement drink for rehydration that hits the spot in between matches. The major national brands are good, but I prefer healthier fruit drinks infused with natural salts, and that are available at health-food stores.

That reminds me to remind all gentlemen grapplers to have their shoes on in the bathroom. There is no more unsanitary place on the planet than a men's bathroom at a grappling competition. Lots of guys rush in and out, some having just fought, and a few of them might be really bad with their aim.

Bring a Friend

In addition to having a corner coach, it is extremely important to have a friend record your matches on video. This helps you analyze your performance, win or lose.

I strongly advise that you ask a friend or family member to videotape you and your teammates' matches. It is also helpful to have a friend at the tournament to simply look after your personal belongings while you compete, cheer you on and generally be there to help you out with little things like telling you when your division has been called, if you choose to remain outside the building for any reason.

Pre-Competition Jitters

I remember when I arrived with Rigan Machado at my first major judo competition; I confided in him that I was scared. He asked me what specifically scared me. When I thought about it, I realized that I was afraid that a judo black belt would choke me out in front of everybody. Machado smiled at me and then he reached for my shirt collar and asked what I would do if someone was attempting to choke me? I slid my forearm up alongside my face, blocking access to my neck just as I had been taught. Machado smiled and said, "You see? You know the defense. My friend, no one is going to choke you out." His absolute confidence in me was reassuring, and indeed, not only was I not choked out but I also forced several of my opponents to tap out that day.

Despite all my talk on how winning is not the most important thing and how it is just a game, etc., it is natural to feel stressed out and have competition jitters. The truth is that you will survive no matter what happens or how much pressure you feel. In fact, sometimes the only solution to overcome anxieties is to experience the stress, do the competition, face whatever the outcome is, and just amass more competitive experience so that you are less stressed in the future.

Some competitors like to bring music and headphones to listen to relaxing music. That's fine, but make sure that you are aware of when you need to begin warming up for your match.

Many other competitors prefer to spend as little time in the competition arena as possible before their match. Watching the other fights and hearing the crowd cheering may ultimately be more draining than energizing. Obviously, if you are going to go outside the building, you need to talk to the tournament organizers to see when your division is likely to compete. Remember to keep poking your head in just to make sure your name has not been called, or have someone you trust, like your friend or corner coach, give you a five- to 10-minute warning.

If you find that you are scared or if you notice that your body feels weak before your match, just understand that it is because of stress and low levels of adrenaline rather than anything else. Your legs may seem weak, but they are as strong as they ever were. If it helps, remember that you opponent is probably feeling the exact same effects of stress and adrenaline that you are.

Mental Affirmations

Before a competition, you're going to be thinking about something, and if you're like most people, you're going to be stressing out. Instead of thinking negatively, consider some of the following affirmations:

- This is just a game and a tool for growth.
- In just a few minutes, it will be over and I will be the winner.
- My opponent will be more tired than me.
- I have trained hard and I have a right to win.
- My teachers and partners are with me on the mat in every move I make.
- This mat is my house and I will command it.
- I am better than I realize.
- Now is my time to shine.

How to Warm Up

Many competitors say that the first match of the day, whether during practice at your school or at an event, is the hardest. This is because it takes your body a few minutes to get warm and pump blood and nutrients effectively. Once your heart and lungs are pumping, you hit your stride and can continue training or competing for many more minutes. And even though this is true, it's interesting to note how many competitors are hesitant to warm up for a competition match. For some reason, they are more concerned with "saving" energy rather than getting their body pumped up and warmed up.

Now be honest with yourself: If you train for hours on end in your school, do you really think some jumping jacks, push-ups or light running in place will deplete the energy you need for a grappling match? If your answer is: Not a chance, then you are correct. In reality, it's much smarter to warm up to the point of being out of breath and covered with sweat than to not do it. In the time it takes to walk onto the mat and for the referee to start the match, you not only will have caught your breath but you also will be warmed up and ready to push hard again.

At least 15 to 30 minutes before the match, I usually step outside the tournament building to run some wind sprints and get out of breath. You can also skip rope, squat/jump in place or do partner warm-ups like sprawls, leapfrog and pummeling. After my warm-up, I catch my breath on the way into the building so that when I step on the mat, I am sweating, warm and my lungs and heart are ready to pump. In a BJJ competition, I also recommend warming up your grips by squeezing hard on your own lapels and then releasing.

Grip Warm-Up

For a BJJ tournament, warm up your hands by squeezing hard on your lapels, doing at least three sets of 10 repetitions. This will warm up your grips by getting blood pumping to your forearms and fingers before the match.

Training for Competition: Brazilian Jiu-Jitsu and Submission Grappling

Rocking Chair

This simple warm-up is better than it appears. Start standing and then sit back, rolling your feet to touch the ground above your head (1-6). Then roll forward and come to a standing position once again with your hips fully arched forward (7-9). Doing this 20 times at a good pace not only warms the legs and core muscles but also raises the heart rate before the match.

David Meyer

Grappling Leapfrog

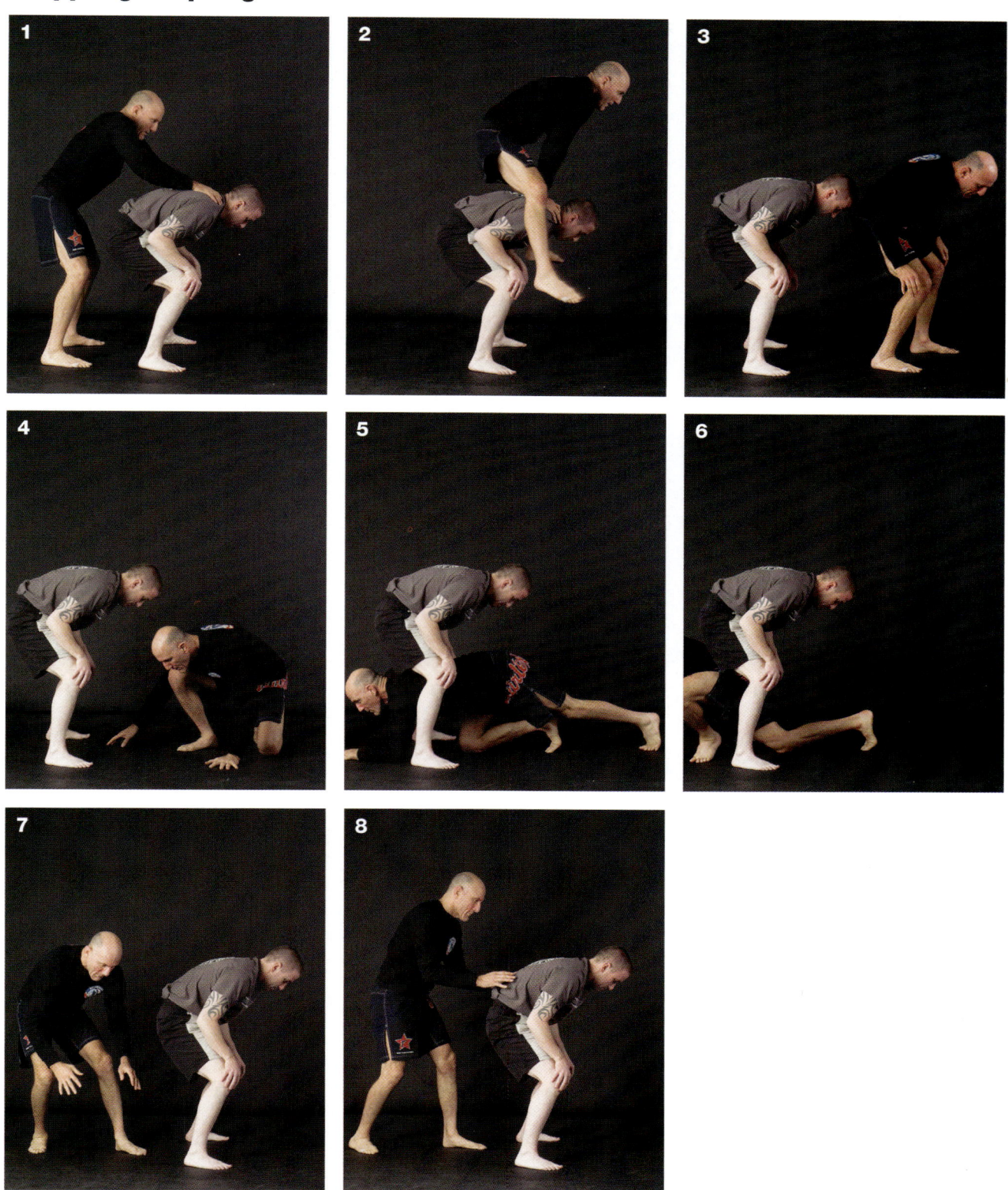

Leapfrog is a simple partner warm-up that will pump blood through your upper and lower body, and increase your heart and respiration rates in preparation for your match (1-8). The motion that you use when you crouch and shoot under the leg is similar to a takedown (4-5). It also makes the exercise more tiring, thus warming you up even more.

Pummeling

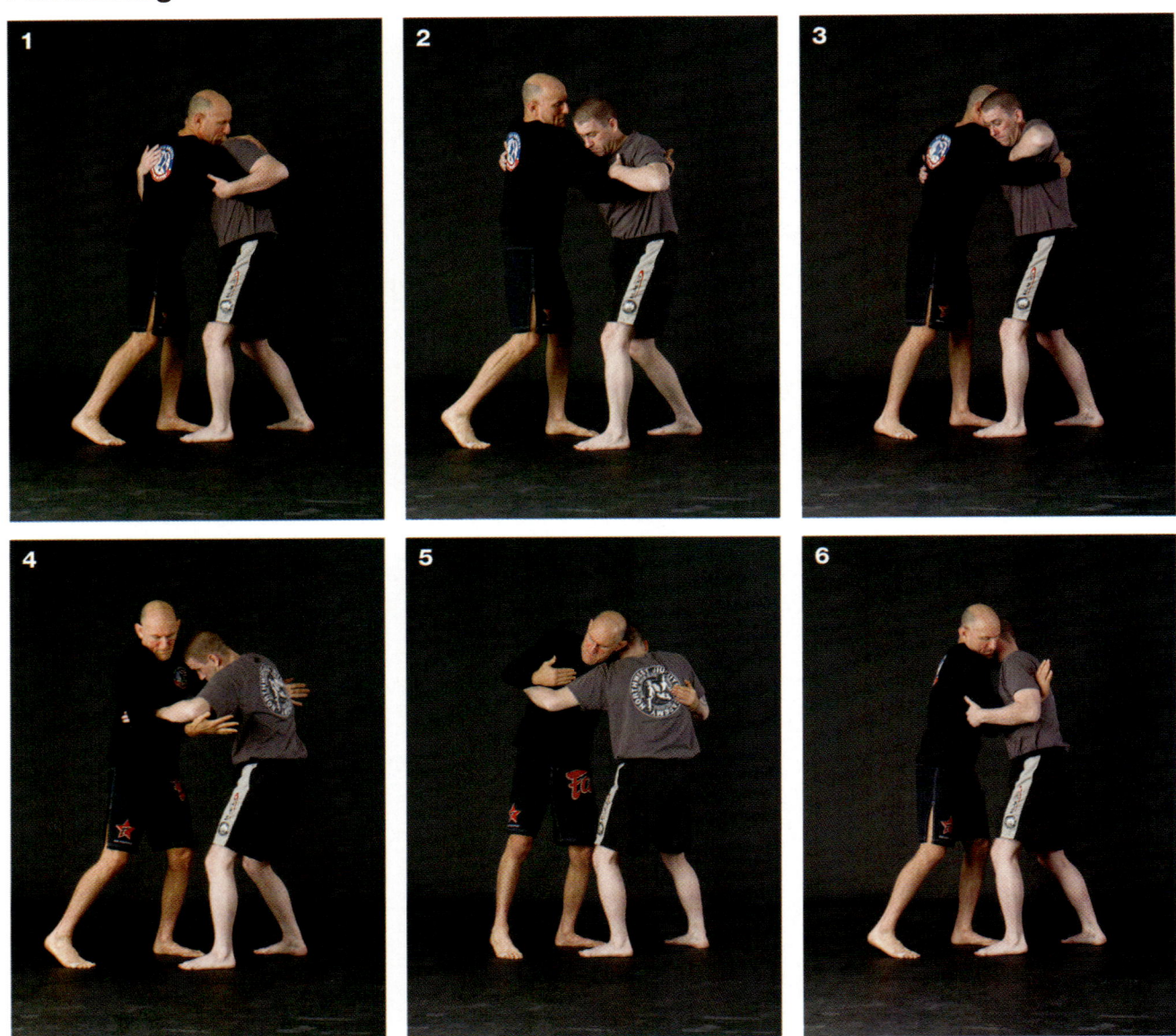

Pummeling is a simple partner warm-up in which both partners begin with their right arms underneath the partners' left arm in the underhook position (1). Both partners then switch positions, digging their left arms under for the underhook (2). The warm-up starts cooperatively, but the partners can begin to resist each other, making it more and more difficult to penetrate their arms for the underhook (3-6). This is an excellent upper-body warm-up. If you have no partner, warm up the upper body by pushing against or bear-hugging a wall or tree.

Once again, the goal is to step onto the mat warmed up, sweaty and after having depleted your first wind. Of course, the difficulty still remains in getting the timing right. Often, competitors receive no information or no correct information about when their division starts fighting. You may find yourself warming up and then sitting for another hour or more. There is no magic answer that I can give you here except for the following two things:

- You are tough. You can warm up or not warm up, cool down or not cool down, and it won't make that much of a difference compared to all the hard work and preparation you've done.

- Your opponent is going through the exact same roller coaster that you are.

So try your best.

Own the Mat With Attitude

When you step onto the mat for a competition, you must be completely confident in yourself and your skills. You need to feel as if you own the mat, and you must be 100 percent convinced of your worthiness to win.

To communicate this feeling to yourself and your opponent, don't shyly step onto the mat. Stride. Take a full lap around its edges to get a feel for its size and texture. This mat is now your mat. When you stand facing your opponent, look him directly in the eyes.

Use body language and your eyes to own the mat. Be firm and make direct eye contact but also be sportsmanlike when you shake hands after receiving instructions from the referee. You're not trying to intimidate your opponent; instead, you're trying to assert that you're there to win, and this should be obvious in every move you make.

Psych Your Opponent Out

Aside from your attitude of owning the mat, there are many other things you can do during a fight to strengthen yourself emotionally while emotionally weakening your opponent. The following are a few ideas:

- Before the match starts, look relaxed, confident and carefree. This generally unnerves an opponent. I like to smile and say hello to my friends in the stands as I move around on the mat waiting for the match to start.

- Whenever there is a break in the action—i.e., the referee restarts the match—always initiate the attack as soon as the referee says, "Go." This is especially important when starting from a standing position. By charging at an opponent as if you are not tired, you may be able to break his spirit. Jean Jacques Machado is a master of this tactic. Machado literally runs toward the opponent, which denies him an extra second to gather energy, concentration or hope.

- Never show an opponent that you are tired. Always control your breath, which you can do by modulating it with deep and slow or choppy exhales. Never pant deeply. If your opponent feels your chest panting, he may be energized with the knowledge that you are tired. But if the opponent is panting and your breath is calm, then this can demoralize even the best of grapplers.

If and when you are pushed to your limits, have no strength left and feel like you can't breathe, remember two things:

- The match will soon be over, and you won't die. In fact, you will forget how weak you felt five minutes after the match ends. So don't allow yourself to be disappointed by giving up.
- Think: "My opponent is more tired than I am." Jean Jacques Machado once told me this mantra, and it works. You must always believe that.

Start One Point Down

If you have a tendency to fight passively, trick yourself by starting your match with a fictional point deficit of one point. This will force you to actively push forward in the match. In fact, a mental point deficit may be the key to your game plan because any good game plan should help you fight aggressively. In thinking you are behind, the game plan may force you to actively hunt for opportunities to make points or force a submission.

Mental visualization is helpful, too. For instance, sometimes I imagine that the opponent has my medal around his neck, and when he taps out, then I can take it back.

Win Fresh, Lose Spent

You should never lose a fight and have energy to spare. If you lost and can't do anything but crawl off the mat, then you tried your hardest and should be commended for it.

If you are completely out of energy and pinned, hold your position, breathe deeply and count to 10. This will allow you to regroup and recover. Remember, even if your opponent is on top, he is more tired than you. You must believe that. In just a few minutes, the match will be over, but your actions in those minutes can create a victory that will stay with you for the rest of your life.

If you are in a bad position, try to work yourself out of it step by step and not with one great explosion. Those explosions drain your energy and can leave you demoralized if they fail.

It is when you are dead tired and losing the match that you discover what you are made of and if you have heart. "Heart" does not exist on a warm sunny day at the beach. "Heart" is what grows when the chips are down and you feel like you are going to die. That is your chance to expand your limits and show yourself as a true warrior. As the Machado brothers say, "When the body says no, the mind says go!" So suck it up and turn the fight around, or die trying.

If, on the other hand, you are ahead in points and winning the fight, then it becomes important for you to attempt to save energy, i.e., finish the match with strength left over. This is especially true if you are in a bracketed tournament in which winning the match will advance you to another fight. Often, by saving energy as you win one fight, you can give yourself a competitive advantage over your opponent in the next fight because he may step on the mat more tired than you.

Chapter 13
Sportsmanship—Win Like a Champion, Lose Like a Warrior

The moment any match is over, it is history. Whether you won or lost, there's nothing more you can do about the outcome, but the competition is far from over. If you are the winner, don't gloat. If you are defeated, don't be bitter. Honor your opponent and move on to improve your game for your next competition.

Honor Your Opponent

In 1998, I became the first American to win a medal at the black-belt level in a BJJ world championship. As a medium-size grappler, I took the bronze medal in the open weight class division, after losing to Mario Sperry—one of the top BJJ fighters in the world and reigning BJJ heavyweight world champion at the time. He was bigger than me and way better than me, but I was not intimidated by him. I stepped out on the mat and executed my game plan, which was to pull him to my guard. Sperry managed to pass my strongest skill in about 10 seconds.

The match continued with Sperry smashing me in side control for several minutes while I defended his choke attempts. I even managed to put him back in my guard, but Sperry smashed through it again. Clearly, he didn't have to work that hard to break my defenses and attacks. He forced me to submit with a choke from side control.

Now to Sperry, I was nothing more than an annoyance that he had to do away with before his final match with the great Roberto "Roleta" Magalhaes, which Sperry ended up winning. However, after our match, Sperry helped me to my feet and raised my hand in the air as if I had won the match. He then gave me a warm hug, told me how hard I was to tap out, apologized for placing his choke across my lip, and then admitted that he did that because he didn't want to get too tired for his next fight in the finals with Magalhaes.

I don't believe he was getting tired at all, but his gesture, words and kindness were extremely gracious, especially from such a respected world champion. It really showed me that he was a champion in more than just his technical skill; he was also a gentleman.

Remember that you can still fight hard and, at the same time, be a good sport. Always play by the rules, and never act in a manner that is demeaning to yourself, your opponent or your teammates. You stand as a representative of your school, your instructor and the sport in general. Take that responsibility seriously and honor it.

Keep the following in mind:

- During the match, follow all the referee's instructions. If you disagree with something, voice it respectfully and then let it go. If need be, take it up with the tournament organizer later.

- Try not to injure your opponent, whether you mean to or not. Be especially aware of this if you have your opponent in a finishing hold.

- Recognize that your opponent mustered up the same courage you did to prepare for and enter a competition. Acknowledge that, win or lose, with honor.

If you are the victor and your hand is raised by the referee, raise your opponent's hand to honor his effort. Shake hands with the opponent's corner coach, as well. Competitions are more than just tests of skill, they are also important social events in which fighters and coaches can meet. It is a chance for you to make good connections with other teams that may one day become important to you.

Excuses Are Pathetic

Winning is great, but your true character shows through in your losses. If you lose, tell your opponent you look forward to fighting again at the next competition. Your victories are built on the losses of your opponents and your losses will build other champions. It's all good. So shake their hand and get to the business of figuring out how to improve.

Also, if you lose, don't make an excuse. Don't say that you haven't been training or you just got over a cold. Don't cite some injury or say you made some mistake on the mat. You didn't lose because you didn't sleep well, your wife or husband just left you, aliens landed on your house last night, etc. You lost because your opponent beat you.

Have you considered that these types of excuses all may be true with your opponent, as well? Why might you assume that the person who just beat you did his best while you didn't? Maybe he has a cold. Maybe he hasn't been training. Most important, who cares? He was better than you just at that moment.

If you think the referee made a bad call, then complain to the tournament organizer. Referees are fallible, and you are as likely to benefit from a bad call as be the victim of one. Referees are doing their best, and you should do the same.

Dissect Your Win

Congratulations—You won! Well done. But now that the celebration is over, take a moment to look closely at each match you win because it is almost always possible to find something that needs work in your game. Most competitors fail to do this, but trust me, it's worth it because it just improves your skill for future matches.

Review any videotape if you have one, and discuss the win with your coach and any other skilled fighters who saw the match. Get their input, and then ask yourself the following questions:

- What was the key thing that led to the victory?
- What specifically could I have done to result in a faster victory?
- Did the opponent score any points against me? And if so, what can I do to stop that in the future?
- Did I execute my game plan? If not, what went wrong?

Sometimes the worst thing that can happen to a competitor is to experience victory too early in his career. The reason for this is that the competitor can become accustomed to the great feeling of victory, and once he loses, it can be very discouraging. So congratulations on your win, but it's over now. There are tougher fights ahead, so learn from your mistakes and get back on the mat.

Dissect Your Loss

Too often people explain a loss by saying, "I should have been more aggressive at the start." Or they might say, "I need to get into better shape." The problem with these types of explanations is that they fail to address the actual events of the match, like:

- Why, specifically, did you not succeed in your takedown or finish attempt?
- What, specifically, did your opponent do to stop your sweep?
- What, specifically, did your opponent do that passed your guard?

There are specific things that your opponent did that caused a specific outcome (his win). You must dissect the match and focus in on those specific areas that can be practiced. Don't dismiss the loss with a blanket statement like "I almost got him with the armbar" or "He was strong."

For each match you lose, closely review any videotape as well as discuss the loss with your coach and other skilled fighters who saw the match. Get their input and then ask yourself the following questions:

- At what key moments in the match did something go wrong (i.e., the opponent scored points, gained a position or executed a successful finishing hold)?
- For each of those moments, what specifically can you do better in the future that would prevent it from happening again? Hint: The answer is never "be stronger" or "try harder." That is not specific enough. Instead, the answer would be something like "have a better sprawl," "keep better posture to avoid an armbar" or "learn a better escape from the triangle." Whatever those answers are, use them to guide your training.
- What did you do well in the match?
- Did you execute your game plan? And if not, what went wrong?

I remember a black-belt superfight I had many years ago in Los Angeles. I had never heard of my Brazilian opponent, but I was told he had an excellent Ezekiel (sleeve-tip choke). This particular choke is unusual because it is applied from within the guard, an area a grappler would normally not choke from because of the danger of being put in an armbar.

I was very familiar with the choke and made a mental note to be careful. When the match began, we both struggled for takedowns, and my opponent ended up in my guard. He immediately jumped forward to apply the Ezekiel, just as I had been warned. I defended the choke, then I swept him and passed his guard, which gave me enough points for the lead. I felt confident that I had seen his best move and could defend against it.

At one point about five minutes into the match, I was on top in side control when the referee decided to restart the match in a standing position because we were too close to the mat's edge. I decided to pull my opponent to my guard and hold him there until time ran out because I felt so secure in winning. But as I did that, the opponent attacked me again with the Ezekiel. This time, he was much more effective, and to my great surprise and dismay, I couldn't escape and had to tap out.

This was a rare occasion in a competition in which I had to tap out, and I was really upset. However, rather than dismiss the experience as simply bad judgment on my part or a good attack on his, I decided to look more closely at what happened. In the end, my off-the-mat homework led me to this conclusion: Because I had successfully defended the opponent's main attack, I became overconfident. The opponent took advantage of my confidence and sense of security to launch the attack again, but this time much more effectively than before.

Of course, my homework also helped me build a better defense against the Ezekiel, but this dynamic has now become a key strategy in my attacks from all positions. During a match, I generally will launch an attack even if I know it will not work, in order to give my opponent an opportunity to defend it and build a false feeling of confidence. The moment that I notice the opponent become complacent, I launch the attack and often catch grapplers completely unaware. This has obviously become an important strategy in my game, but I would never have learned about it if I didn't examine my losses. Honestly, I have far more pearls of wisdom from my competition losses than from my competition victories.

One thing that I hear a lot from people after a loss is that they just don't feel like they do as well in competition as compared to how well they fight at their own schools. This is a common problem, and it can have many causes, which is why its important to dissect this feeling after a loss.

First, the reason may be that you just don't perform or execute your techniques as well in a competition. Or it could be that you don't seem to win. If the issue is the latter—that you just don't win—this may be because you're facing opponents who are better in competition and have a higher bracket than you or your teammates have at your school, and that's out of your control. Remember, there may be 500 people training at schools in your area who are at your rank and weight level. You may be able to beat 490 of them, but the top five or 10 may be at the competition and just may be better than you.

But what if you are losing because you don't execute your techniques as well in competition as you do in school? It's probably because you're nervous and overcautious.

Anyone can get nervous, and when you do, you don't function as well. You are more rigid and just don't seem to "flow." The basic cure for this is to keep competing by getting more experience. Try also not to care about the outcome and just grapple for the pure enjoyment of grappling and improving your game. This will help you relax and fight more normally.

The problem may also be that you are being overcautious. This comes from a concern about losing, which is a concern that most people don't have at their school. If you make a mistake while training in your school, you just start over. Yet this is obviously something that you can't do in a competition. To counter this tendency of extreme caution, you need to be willing to relax and take some chances. Specifically, remember to relax the grip of your hands as you compete. Most people grip way too tightly in competition. This slows down their game and tires their hands. A good coach should remind you to relax your grip frequently if he sees you being too cautious.

It is also important to remember that everybody loses at some point. Every great champion has lost many times along the way as he developed his skill. Remember, it's not about how good you are today but about what you can develop into. Competition with its wins and losses is part of your development into the fighter you will be tomorrow. You are on a path to how good you can be, but you are not there yet.

Also, remember that no matter how many people enter into a division to compete, only one will win. That means there are a lot of fantastic grapplers who finish second, third, fourth, etc. So being at ease with losing is crucial to ensure that you will continue to compete and compete again regardless of the outcome. Remember, losses are the coals that fuel the engine of your spirit so you can train harder, and they contain pearls of wisdom and technique if you only look to find them.

Interview with **Gene LeBell**
Judo Legend

Q: What is the most important part of competition training?
A: Sparring with all different sizes, weights and degrees is the most important, and when I say degrees, I mean with beginners or grapplers who've done it for 20 years.

Q: Is it better to train with a *gi* or without a gi?
A: I definitely believe you should practice with both [a gi and without a gi]. If you're the greatest judo or BJJ person in the world but you are going against an amateur freestyle wrestler, then he might take you down. If you do chokes with a gi, then you'd better learn to do the chokes without a gi. What I mean to say is that you've got to be ambidextrous. You've got to know a little bit about everything.

Q: What are your thoughts on conditioning?
A: Don't go into a competition if you're not ready or if you're not in great condition. A BJJ player that is not in good condition is like a car that runs out of gas—it doesn't work. So if your wind isn't good, somebody is probably going to beat the tar out of you. You not only have to [practice] your grappling on the mat but also have to jump rope, push the irons, run up and down stairs—whatever exercises you happen to want to do. Conditioning is probably 70 percent of your fighting, so you have to be in condition.

Q: Should you fight if you're injured?
A: Criticism be damned, but you have to go into [a competition] at 110 percent. If you have a bad shoulder, arm or knee, then you're at 60 percent or 70 percent.

Q: How did you train for competition?
A: In the afternoon, I did 1,000 push-ups every other day without stopping, and I did 1,000 sit-ups every other day so my wind was good; the muscles were there. I also used to carry and run with a log, switching it from shoulder to shoulder, throwing it on the ground and picking it up by bending my knees. When I say a log, [I'm referring to a piece of wood] maybe 3 feet by 8 inches. But my favorite way of training was to get a motorcycle tire—usually the front of a dirt bike. You put on a pair of gloves and go down a road or around a track or from one end of a football field to the other. You roll the tire, and after 10 feet of rolling, [it falls down.] Then you bend down and pick it up. Start off by bending and picking it up with two hands, then toss it like a discus, sometimes using one palm up and the other palm down. You're throwing it not for the distance but for the workout. In other words, when you twist and throw with one or two hands, everything has to work together; you use your arms, forearms, triceps, biceps, legs, and everything has to work at the same time.

Q: At fight time, what are you thinking?
A: I get on the mat—say its 10 feet by 10 feet or 24 feet by 24 feet—and I divide that into four boxes. [One box] is the kitchen, the other the bedroom, the other the bathroom and the last one is the front room. It's my house. My opponent is coming into my house, and he's not welcome. Now if you go into competition, don't go into it [thinking the opponent's] your buddy. He could be your brother, but you have to have a split personality [at competition time] because the most important thing is having total concentration to win.

Q: Why do some people do so poorly in competition?
A: Some people are gym fighters, and some people are competition fighters. The competition fighters throw caution to the wind and win at all costs. A hundred years from now, nobody will know how you won. Instead, they'll just remember that you did.

Conclusion

Where were you on Sunday, three weeks ago? If you can't answer that immediately, then you were not at a world, national, state, regional or even local tournament. Had you been at a competition, you would remember it immediately because a competition is an exciting experience that will last a lifetime.

If you did show up for a competition, then you already won. Of course, you probably hear that at many competitions. All competitors are usually recognized for their effort and are often told that everyone, regardless of the result, is a winner. Maybe you always thought of that as some "touchy-feely" thing, designed to help kids and losers feel less bad.

Well, let me assure you that every competitor is a winner. Even if you didn't technically win your division, you gained valuable experience that gives you a clear road map of what you need to improve on.

Remember how I said in the beginning of the book that you can't control who wins? Now the question is: What holds people back from competing in a tournament? The answer is the fear of losing and more specifically the fear of having others see you lose. Yet tournament organizers don't give medals for losses; instead, they only give medals for wins. Nothing will hang on your wall to remind you of matches you lost, and nobody will think less of you for losing if that happens.

I remember entering a black-belt team judo tournament as the fifth and final team member alongside four of the Machado brothers. We were each matched up, largest to smallest, against the five members of the other teams, regardless of the weight of the competitors. One of the top teams on the West Coast was present, and their fighters were not only very big but also very skilled.

John Machado stepped out onto the mat and found himself facing nothing short of a giant—a huge judo fighter who must have been 6 feet 7 inches tall and easily outweighed Machado by 100 pounds. To make matters worse, this was a judo and not a BJJ tournament, so this huge judo competitor clearly had an advantage.

Machado stared this guy in the eye, and when the referee called *hajime* (begin), he jumped right into the fray. The opponent used his massive size to nearly throw Machado, but Machado recovered. The two competitors tumbled to the ground, continuing the fight from there. Because Machado was so skilled and so aggressive, he got on the judo fighter's back. After 30 seconds, he choked out this tough judo fighter. I couldn't believe my eyes.

Now John Machado is a warrior, has fought in many matches, and I suppose he may have not won them all. But the only match I remember is this stunning victory over this monster of a fighter. It is ingrained in my memory as an example of courage and skill. For that, Machado is one of my heroes.

You see? People don't remember losses because they just don't care. It is you and your ego who care and not others.

So if all competitors are winners, then does a competition ever produce losers? Who are they? They are the people who could have competed but didn't. I mean the grapplers who train hard and don't compete because they feel like they are not in good enough shape, in the right mood, or whatever. They are losers because they lost an opportunity to improve their game and heighten their bracket.

At the same time, people who compete, don't win and then become bitter about it by making excuses fail to honestly look at what they need to improve on. What a shame to go through the experience of training for competition only to miss the most important part.

So what does this all mean? Losing is a path to winning because, from a loss, you learn what you need to do to win. So maximize all aspects of your training in order to compete. Do your homework. Practice your skills. Set your ego aside and see what you are capable of achieving. In each of us is a champion, and that champion shines through us in different ways and at different times. Use sport competition as a training ground to develop that champion's toughness because it may come in handy when you least expect it.

I'll see you on the mat.

Appendices

Appendix A
Competition Listings

The following is a list of useful Web sites that will help you find a competition no matter your skill level or rank:

- **www.ibjjf.org**
  The International Brazilian Jiu-Jitsu Federation hosts *gi* and no gi world championships. Competition events tend to take place in Brazil or California.

- **www.grapplingtournaments.com**
  This site is the home of the World Grappling Games. It focuses more on submission-grappling tournaments and is mostly concentrated on competitions on the West Coast.

- **www.grapplers.com**
  This Web site is the home of the Grapplers Quest submission-grappling championships as well as others. Events take place on both U.S. coasts.

- **www.nagafighter.com**
  The North American Grappling Association sponsors BJJ and submission-grappling competitions around the country, particularly on the East Coast and in the Midwest.

- **www.usgrappling.us**
  U.S. Grappling posts listings for BJJ and submission-grappling tournaments with special attention to East Coast competitions.

Appendix B
Recommended Off-the-Mat Homework Materials

There are a lot of good materials out there, and I have not seen them all. However, here are some of my recommendations for good off-the-mat DVDs, books, etc. as well as recommendations made by other grapplers.

- *BJJ America/Masterclass Grappling Curriculum* DVDs from www.bjjamerica.com

- *Encyclopedia of Brazilian Jiu-Jitsu*, *The Triangle* or any book by Rigan Machado

- *Championship Techniques*, *Brazilian Jiu-Jitsu Black Belt*, or any book by Jean Jacques Machado

- *Jiu-Jitsu Unleashed*, *Mastering the Rubber Guard* or any book by Eddie Bravo

- *Mastering Armbars and Mastering Chokes* DVDs
  These DVDs by John Will and myself go into great detail about armbars and chokes.
  www.bjjamerica.com

- *Saulo Ribeiro: Brazilian Jiu-Jitsu Revolution* DVD series
  www.blackbeltmag.com/shop

- *Marcelo Garcia: Winning Techniques of Submission Grappling* DVD series
  www.blackbeltmag.com/shop

Web sites for staying up to date on competitions and grappling news:
- www.onthemat.com
- www.sherdog.com
- www.adcombat.com

About the Author

David Meyer began training in Brazilian *jiu-jitsu* in 1992 and is one of the first Americans to attain the level of black belt, receiving his rank in 1997. He is a student of Rigan, Jean Jacques, Carlos, John and Roger Machado. He is one of the most successful American competitors in the sport and is the coach and training partner for numerous mixed-martial arts fighters in Los Angeles and San Francisco, currently training with the Cesar Gracie team in San Francisco.

His many titles include 2007 International Brazilian Jiu-Jitsu Federation Submission Grappling Black Belt Senior 2 World Champion, 2004 gold medalist for the Senior Black Belt division of the Pan-American Brazilian Jiu-Jitsu Championship and winner of the 1998 Korean Air Black Belt Challenge. He was the first American to win a medal at the black-belt level at a BJJ world championship, earning the bronze medal in the Black Belt Open Weight Class division in Brazil in 1998. He has been the winner of numerous "superfights" at regional and national BJJ competitions in both *gi* and no-gi competitions and is well respected as both a competitor and instructor.

Meyer began training in martial arts as a young child in 1968, studying *jujutsu* under *sensei* Jack Seki. He received his first *dan* in 1977. He trained in white lotus kung fu under *sifu* Douglas Wong, and he taught jujutsu at Steven Seagal's Tenshin Dojo from 1984 to 1987. Meyer was head instructor of jujutsu at UCLA in Los Angeles from 1980 to 1985. He received his third dan in jujutsu under Seki and holds a fourth dan under professor Wally Jay.

In 2000, Meyer partnered with John Will to create BJJ America and produce the Masterclass Grappling Curriculum and now the Alpha MMA curriculum. The grappling curriculum is in use in 600 martial arts schools in the United States and abroad. This instructional tool is also the official grappling curriculum of the Chuck Norris Karate Association.

Meyer is also a passionate advocate for animal welfare and has been a vegetarian since 1985. He co-founded Adopt-a-Pet.com, the world's largest nonprofit homeless pet adoption Web site in which people can search through photos of pets that are available for adoption in thousands of shelters across North America.

More from Black Belt Books

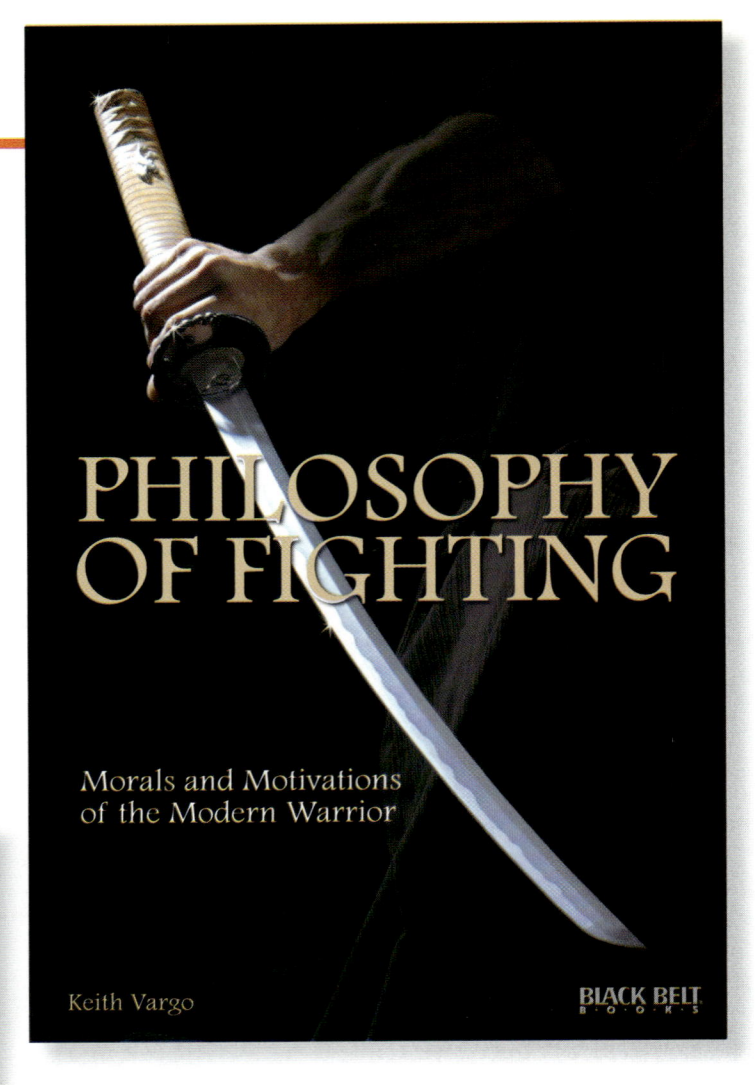

PHILOSOPHY OF FIGHTING
by Keith Vargo

The thoughtful writings of Keith Vargo, the popular author of *Black Belt's* Way of the Warrior columns, are compiled in the *Philosophy of Fighting: Morals and Motivations of the Modern Warrior*. Comprising a decade's worth of discourses, the book entertains and provokes readers by examining the trends, traditions, cultures, fields and thinkers that shape the martial arts with the watchful eye of a psychologist. By exploring philosophical questions, *Philosophy of Fighting* encourages readers to actively consider the key elements that define the modern warrior in a contemporary world. 231 pgs. (ISBN-13: 978-0-89750-174-3)
Book Code 500—Retail $16.95

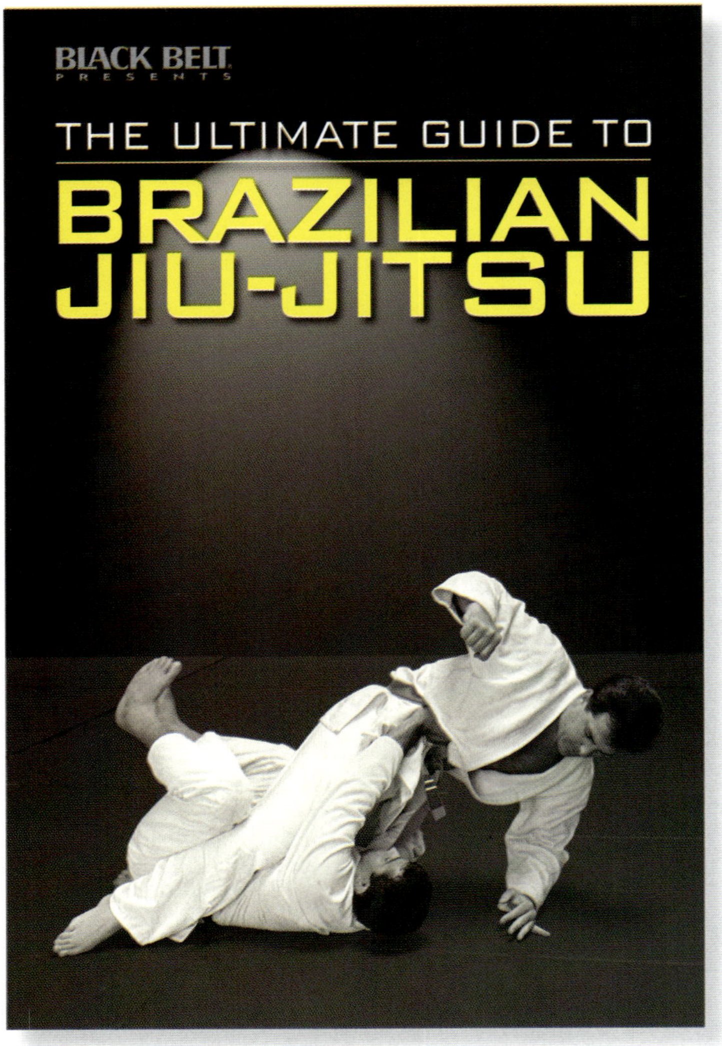

THE ULTIMATE GUIDE TO BRAZILIAN JIU-JITSU
by the Editors of Black Belt

The Ultimate Guide to Brazilian Jiu-Jitsu follows the evolution of this seemingly unstoppable art from an unorthodox interpretation of traditional *jujutsu* to the most dominant position in the grappling world. Spanning two decades of material from the *Black Belt* archives, the book features interviews of Gracie legends, instructions on how to execute the art's brutally efficient techniques and illustrations of iconic BJJ fighters demonstrating essential grappling moves. *The Ultimate Guide to Brazilian Jiu-Jitsu* is the definitive resource on the modern world's most impressive martial art. 191 pgs. (ISBN-13: 978-0-89750-171-2)
Book Code 498—Retail $16.95

To order, call (800) 581-5222 or visit blackbeltmag.com/shop

More from Black Belt Books

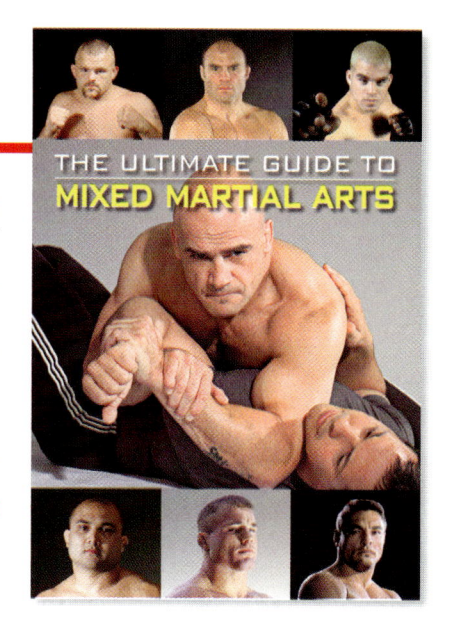

THE ULTIMATE GUIDE TO MIXED MARTIAL ARTS
by the Editors of Black Belt

Only one sport has reinforced elbow smashes to the head, flying knees and liver kicks. From MMA's controversial inception to its mainstream acceptance, from the iconic legacy of Rickson Gracie to the freakish knockout power of Chuck Liddell, from the unstoppable determination of Randy Couture to the emergence of tomorrow's champions, *Black Belt* has covered the sport's genesis and evolution. With *The Ultimate Guide to Mixed Martial Arts*, you will leap into the octagon with Chuck Liddell, experience the artery-crushing chokes of Rickson Gracie, devour Randy Couture's prescription for peak performance, master Dan Henderson's winning training methods and suffer the nasty takedowns of UFC bad-boy Tito Ortiz. A compilation of instructional articles and interviews with the industry's greatest champions, *The Ultimate Guide to Mixed Martial Arts* is the definitive resource on the athletes and techniques of the world's most intense and popular new sport. 216 pgs. (ISBN-13: 978-0-89750-159-0)
Book Code 488—Retail $16.95

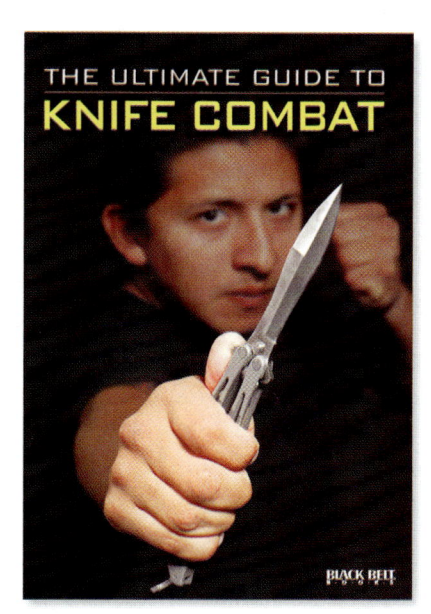

THE ULTIMATE GUIDE TO KNIFE COMBAT
by the Editors of Black Belt

More effective than a fist and more accessible than a gun, the knife is the most pragmatic self-defense tool. *The Ultimate Guide to Knife Combat* celebrates this simple, versatile, sometimes controversial weapon with essays and instructional articles written by the world's foremost experts, including Ernest Emerson, Hank Hayes, Jim Wagner and David E. Steele. *The Ultimate Guide to Knife Combat* presents an international cross section of knife cultures and styles—from the heroic legacy of America's bowie knife to the lethal techniques of the *kukri*-wielding Gurkhas of Nepal—and features essential empty-hand techniques, exercises to improve your fighting skills, and advice on choosing the knife that's right for you. Spanning two decades of material from the *Black Belt* archives, *The Ultimate Guide to Knife Combat* provides everything you need to know about fighting with or against a blade. 312 pgs. (ISBN-13: 978-0-89750-158-3) **Book Code 487—Retail $16.95**

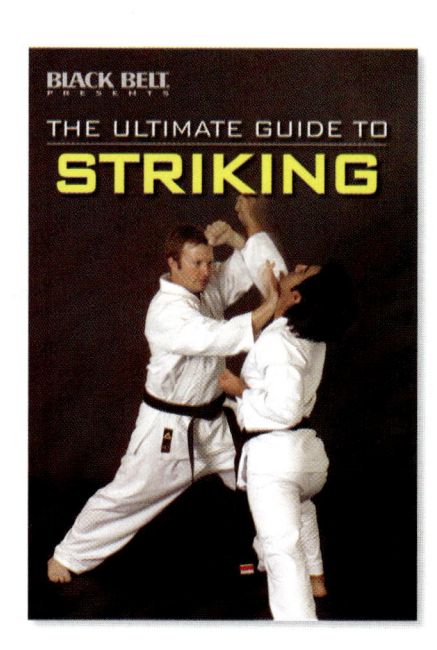

THE ULTIMATE GUIDE TO STRIKING
by the Editors of Black Belt

The Ultimate Guide to Striking examines striking techniques from various martial arts. Topics include *jeet kune do's* most efficient weapons, modern applications of *isshin-ryu* karate, vital-point attacks for women's self-defense, the vicious spinning backfist of *The Ultimate Fighter's* Shonie Carter, the "combat slap," *tang soo do's* lethal elbow strikes, the mysterious art of *mi zong* kung fu, Jeff Speakman's rapid-fire *kenpo* arsenal and more! Through scores of detailed photos and articles printed in *Black Belt* from 1990 to 2005, *The Ultimate Guide to Striking* provides a vast cultural and technical cross section on the topic of striking. This collection is sure to be an enlightening and effective addition to any martial artist's training library. 248 pgs. (ISBN-13: 978-0-89750-154-5)
Book Code 483—Retail $16.95

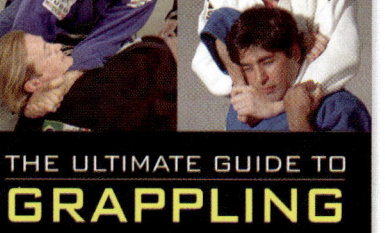

THE ULTIMATE GUIDE TO GRAPPLING
by the Editors of Black Belt

Attention, grapplers! This is the book you've been waiting for. From the arenas of ancient Rome to the mixed-martial arts cages of modern Las Vegas, men have always wrestled for dominance. Ground fighting is the cornerstone of combat, and *The Ultimate Guide to Grappling* pays homage to the art with three decades' worth of instructional essays and interviews collected from the archives of *Black Belt*. With more than 30 articles featuring legends like Mike Swain, John Machado, Gokor Chivichyan, Hayward Nishioka, Renzo Gracie, Bart Vale and B.J. Penn, you'll learn the legacy of Greek *pankration*, reality-based ground techniques for police officers and soldiers, the differences between classical *jujutsu* and submission wrestling, and more! Transform your traditional art into a well-rounded and effective self-defense system today! 232 pgs. (ISBN-13: 978-89750-160-6)
Book Code 489—Retail $16.95

To order, call (800) 581-5222 or visit blackbeltmag.com/shop

More from Black Belt Books

BRUCE LEE'S FIGHTING METHOD: The Complete Edition
by Bruce Lee and M. Uyehara

Bruce Lee's Fighting Method: The Complete Edition brings the iconic four-volume *Fighting Method* series together into one definitive book. Intended as an instructional document to complement Lee's foundational *Tao of Jeet Kune Do*, this restored and enhanced edition of *Fighting Method* breathes new life into hallowed pages with digitally remastered photography and a painstakingly refurbished interior design for improved instructional clarity. This 492-page hard-bound book also includes 900+ digitally enhanced images, newly discovered photographs from Lee's personal files, a new chapter on the Five Ways of Attack penned by famed first-generation student Ted Wong, and an analytical introduction by Shannon Lee that helps readers contextualize the revisions and upgrades implemented for this special presentation of her father's work. 492 pgs. Size 7" x 10". (ISBN-13: 978-0-89750-170-5) **Book Code 494—Retail $34.95**

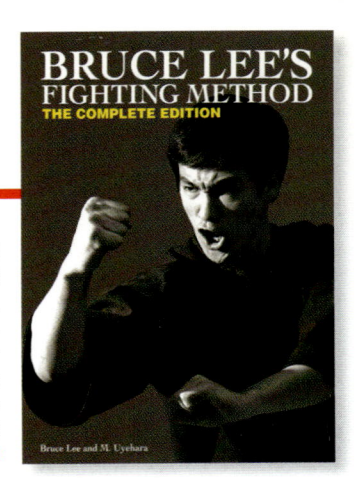

CHINESE GUNG FU (Revised and Updated)
by Bruce Lee

Black Belt Books' new edition of *Chinese Gung Fu: The Philosophical Art of Self-Defense* gives martial arts enthusiasts and collectors exactly what they want: more Bruce Lee. In addition to the master's insightful explanations on *gung fu*, this sleek book features digitally enhanced photography, previously unpublished pictures with Lee's original handwritten notes, a brand-new front and back cover, and introductions by widow Linda Lee Cadwell and daughter Shannon Lee. Fully illustrated. 112 pgs. (ISBN-13: 978-0-89750-112-5)
Book Code 451—Retail $12.95

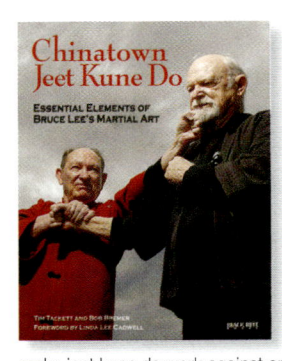

CHINATOWN JEET KUNE DO
by Tim Tackett and Bob Bremer

Chinatown Jeet Kune Do not only lays out the basic structure and principles of Bruce Lee's art but also reveals some of its most effective and least-known tools. Borrowing the best skills and techniques from a variety of arts, including *wing chun* kung fu, fencing and boxing, *jeet kune do* is an eclectic, efficient self-defense system that has revolutionized the martial arts world. Containing detailed photographs and step-by-step instructions on jeet kune do's two basic stances, footwork, striking, kicking, countering and defenses, *Chinatown Jeet Kune Do* shows the reader how to make jeet kune do work against any opponent. Size 8-3/8" x 10-7/8" (ISBN-13: 978-0-89750-163-7) **Book Code 492—Retail $18.95**

THE LEGENDARY BRUCE LEE
by the Editors of Black Belt

A collection of articles detailing Bruce Lee's rise to fame, including Lee's own famous and controversial essay "Liberate Yourself From Classical Karate." 160 pgs. (ISBN-13: 978-0-89750-106-4)
Book Code 446—Retail $10.95

THE BRUCE LEE STORY
by Linda Lee

Here is the complete story of the great martial artist/actor Bruce Lee, told with great personal insight by Linda Lee, including hundreds of photos from Lee's personal albums. 192 pgs. Size: 8-1/4" x 10-1/4" (ISBN-13: 978-0-89750-121-7)
Book Code 460—Retail $19.95

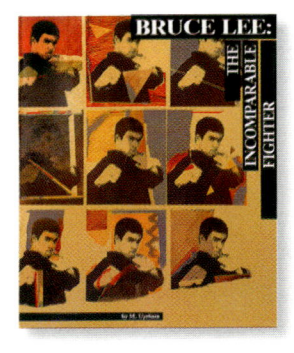

THE INCOMPARABLE FIGHTER
by M. Uyehara

Get to know the true Bruce Lee through the eyes of the author. Pound for pound, he may have been the greatest fighter who ever lived. Read about his good and bad times, his dreams and destiny shattered by his early death. The author, a student of Lee's and one of his best friends, is the co-author of the best-selling *Bruce Lee's Fighting Method* volumes. Fully illustrated.144 pgs. (ISBN-13: 978-0-89750-120-0)
Book Code 461—Retail $19.95

DEAR BRUCE LEE
by Ohara Publications Inc.

Read about how Bruce Lee's life, his art and his untimely death affected and influenced his worldwide legion of fans. Learn about his art *jeet kune do* through his personal replies to letters he received in 1967. Illustrated with photos of Lee. 96 pgs. Size: 8-3/8" x 10-7/8"
(ISBN-13: 978-0-89750-069-2)
Book Code 407—Retail $15.95

TAO OF JEET KUNE DO
by Bruce Lee

This is Bruce Lee's treatise on his martial art, *jeet kune do*. This international best-seller includes the philosophy of jeet kune do, mental and physical training, martial qualities, attack and strategy. 208 pgs. Size: 8-1/2" x 11" (ISBN-13: 978-0-89750-048-7)
Book Code 401—Retail $16.95

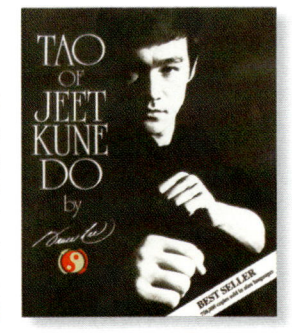

WING CHUN KUNG FU/ JEET KUNE DO: A Comparison, Vol. 1
by William Cheung and Ted Wong

Bruce Lee's original art (*wing chun*) and the art he developed (*jeet kune do*) are compared by Lee's associates. Includes stances and footwork, hand and leg techniques, tactics and self-defense. Fully illustrated. 192 pgs. (ISBN-13: 978-0-89750-124-8)
Book Code 464—Retail $14.95

To order, call (800) 581-5222 or visit blackbeltmag.com/shop